Redesigning Management Education and Research

Redesigning Management Education and Research

Challenging Proposals from European Scholars

Edited by

Stéphanie Dameron

Paris Dauphine University, France

Thomas Durand

CNAM Paris, France

Edward Elgar

Cheltenham, UK • Northampton, MA, USA

Published by
Edward Elgar Publishing Limited
The Lypiatts
15 Lansdown Road
Cheltenham
Glos GL50 2JA
UK

Edward Elgar Publishing, Inc.
William Pratt House
9 Dewey Court
Northampton
Massachusetts 01060
USA

A catalogue record for this book
is available from the British Library

Library of Congress Control Number: 2011931011

MIX
Paper from
responsible sources
FSC
www.fsc.org   FSC® C018575

ISBN 978 0 85793 358 4

Typeset by Servis Filmsetting Ltd, Stockport, Cheshire
Printed and bound by MPG Books Group, UK

Contents

Contributors

Olivier Basso Singleton Institute, Brussels, Belgium

Pierre-Jean Benghozi Research Director CNRS, École Polytechnique, France

Julienne Brabet Professor, Paris Est Créteil University, France

Eric Cornuel Affiliated Professor, HEC and Director General, EFMD Brussels, Belgium

Stéphanie Dameron Professor, Paris Dauphine University, France

Philippe-Pierre Dornier Professor, ESSEC Business School, France

Thomas Durand Professor, CNAM Paris, France

Eric Godelier Professor, École Polytechnique, Paris, France

Armand Hatchuel Professor, Mines Paris Tech, France

Romain Laufer Emeritus Professor, HEC-Paris, France

Alain Charles Martinet Emeritus Professor, Jean Moulin University Lyon 3, France

Peter McKiernan Professor, University of Strathclyde, UK

Bernard de Montmorillon Professor, Paris Dauphine University, France

Jean-Paul Mounier formerly ESCP Europe and HEC MBA, Paris, France

Marielle Audrey Payaud Associate Professor, Jean Moulin University Lyon 3, France

Roland Pérez Emeritus Professor, Montpellier 1 University, France

Dennis Tourish Professor, Royal Holloway, University of London, UK

Preface

The field of management education and research gave birth to an industry, the business of business schools, with fierce international competition and thus competitive strategies on the part of players active in the arena: business schools and their deans, individual professors, journals, accreditation bodies, academic societies and so on.

Yet we believe that some collective strategies are necessary to influence some of the de facto regulation mechanisms that have appeared over the years (for example business school rankings, accreditation processes, the Bologna process within the EU, journal rankings, the race for publications and so on).

In a world that is becoming multipolar, we further believe that the relevant level to discuss these issues has to move from the specificities of national contexts to encompass a broader regional perspective – and for us, as European scholars, this typically means Europe. This is why we offer to engage in strategic conversations with our colleagues throughout the European Union and beyond to raise these issues and generate debates and actions.

This book is a contribution to this endeavour. This is an edited book, with chapters written by a series of management scholars. This project was initially launched under the umbrella of the Société Française de Management (SFM, the French Academy of Management). SFM aims to produce soft law to contribute to shaping the field of management education and research. We call for an initiative of a similar sort in the European context.

Introduction: the story in short

Management education and research crystallise some of the successes, failures and contradictions of our modern societies.

On the one hand, the demand for training in management keeps growing and so do the expectations from stakeholders within and outside organisations to better understand how businesses emerge, grow, evolve and disappear and how these businesses may be run in various contexts. Enrolment at business schools is increasing throughout the world, and more research is conducted and published every year – with an explosion of the literature that makes it extremely difficult for both academics and practitioners to follow all that goes on in the field. This is taking place in a world economy that keeps growing despite some ups and downs, with international trade bound to develop further despite the limitations of the resources of our planet, and with entire regions of the globe reaching the income per capita that they had been dreaming of, hoping for a better life with access to mass consumption, better housing, health, education, travel and so on. In this sense, management education and research at business schools may be viewed as both benefiting from and fuelling the world economy. Business schools aim at providing (a) educated individuals trained to deal with the complexity of the task of leading 'organised collective action' and (b) new insights to improve the practice of management for a variety of forms of organisations in a variety of contexts.

On the other hand, the success of business schools raises many disturbing questions. How could the community of researchers in finance not see the flaws of a subprime situation that their sophisticated models made possible? To what extent is the knowledge produced by management researchers at Western business schools appropriate to the socio-cultural-political context of, say, a small family business in Tunisia or a cooperative in north-east Brazil? What happens to scholarly inquiry if most management researchers seem to take it for granted that the main issue in business is performance of the focal organisation itself, for example treating social or environmental concerns at best as constraints, if not as mere externalities? What should we think of the education delivered at business schools that trained the deficient and greedy top managers who led their companies into dishonesty, scandal and ruin? How come, in the name of private entrepreneurship, that our democratic societies offer so little democracy in the governance of firms? There could be many other such questions. Note that we do not question here the role of management per se. This is a quite different debate, and we firmly believe that organised collective action needs to be managed. Instead, our main point here is to suggest that the development and success of the business of business schools may be questioned despite all the good they may bring to our societies and economies.

We argue that the institutional setting and the dynamics of the rules of the game that regulate the world of management education and research created a 'business school bubble' and may in fact contribute to weakening our current business school system from within. More specifically, we argue that business schools have lost their way while competing in the game of rankings. We further argue that European business schools make a mistake in blindly following their North American cousins. And we send a call to the community of management scholars in Europe (and beyond) in the hope that they will join our effort to influence the institutional setting and the rules of the game of our field in new and more suitable directions.

COMPETITION IN THE BUSINESS SCHOOLS ARENA HAS BOOSTED THE FIELD

There is no doubt that the increasing competition within management education and research in the last two decades has ushered in a more professional approach in both teaching and research. The quality of the service delivered to students and executive education audiences went up (for example newer cases, better follow-up of projects, more structured and better-documented curricula and so on). The question of the quality and relevance of the teaching may be a different matter, as we shall see. At the same time, the volume and intensity of publishing activities exploded. More money went into the system as prices (tuition fees), faculty salaries, donations and research grants went up. In the process, the whole system of management education and research has considerably improved its efficiency. In this sense, we argue that competition boosted the industry of business schools.

One may question the relevance of the invasion of academic institutions by market rationales and competitive behaviour. Yet the fact is that increased demand in management education generated more resources allocated to business schools, and thus competitive strategies from deans to tap the sources of funding as a way to build and maintain reputation, in turn helping attract better faculty, better students and better researchers.

This then fed back positively into reputation and permitted higher tuition fees and access to more funding, and so on. This led to business models for business schools aiming at entering a virtuous self-reinforcing circle: more funding, leading to more research and better education, leading to improved reputation, leading to more funding, and so on.

In a way, most of the business schools in the Western world and to a certain extent in other parts of the world are playing that game – globally, regionally or nationally, according to their ambition, scope and status. This is far from being anecdotal, as it has very strong concrete implications for the way management education and research are now regulated.

REGULATION MECHANISMS THAT HAVE EMERGED IN THE BUSINESS OF BUSINESS SCHOOLS

Business schools are chasing reputation and funding as a way to better serve their constituencies (the students, their families, the alumni, the faculty, the business community they serve, the donors, the government bodies that sponsor their teaching and/or research initiatives, and so on).

A major problem arises when it comes to assessing a business school's reputation. This is where rankings come into the picture. How can a prospective student select a place to which to apply? How can families find out whether to support such choices? How can recruiters make up their minds about the standards of a given institution? How can teachers and researchers decide where to apply for a faculty position? How can public bodies identify the 'best' possible places in which to invest public money on management education and research? How can deans select the partner that best fits their home institution from among the possible candidates in a country they know little about?

As long as the structure of the business of business schools remained national, or limited to the traditional zone of influence of a given country, with its language and culture, such as the countries that once were part of an empire, there was a de facto informal ranking of institutions conveyed by social and business networks within the geographical and cultural zone. Oxbridge was seen as academic excellence in the UK and the Commonwealth. HEC, ESSEC and ESCP Europe were identified as the places to study management in the French-speaking countries. Harvard and Stanford were the Mecca of management for all those who admired the success of the US-based multinational corporations. But when competition becomes more global, when prospective students from emerging economies try to find their way into a Western business school, when studying abroad becomes a standard in Europe, then some support is needed to find the way in: thus the ranking developed at Shanghai University, Della Bradshaw's rankings in the *Financial Times* or the accreditation mechanisms.

Accreditation is a process that signals that certain business schools have been carefully scrutinised by a panel of peers and awarded a certificate. There is no ranking involved. It is a pass/no pass grade, meaning that the certificate is awarded or not. Accreditation is also a way to promote quality improvement in business schools, encouraging them to engage in a series of initiatives and checking their progress, while also periodically reassessing their accreditation status. The accreditation bodies (essentially associations of business schools that choose to offer such services – typically AACSB, AMBA and EFMD) are competing to gain worldwide visibility and legitimacy, doing their best to promote their accreditation certificates and processes as some form of norm.

Rankings are a different breed. Some journalists found a niche with a yearly series of issues that sell well. The business school rankings usually combine a set of criteria, objective or subjective, quantitative or qualitative. Data are collected from the business schools, which have little choice but to respond if they want to appear in the list – and some may be tempted to use whatever means they can to improve their position in the list.

Among the criteria used to rank business schools are the 'research activities' of a place, and thus its 'research outputs'. This leads to yet another form of ranking, the journal rankings. As it turns out, the trend has been that a research publication may be considered as meaningful only if it has undergone the scrutiny of academic peer reviewing. To make it even stricter, the reviewing has to be double-blind. (Note that, in the era of the internet and search engines, blind reviewing may end up being blind only in theory.) Research publication is thus focused exclusively on journals with formal double-blind reviewing. This fits perfectly with the need to speed up and simplify the assessment process, both at business schools that assess the output of their faculty and at places issuing business school rankings (the *Financial Times*, Shanghai University and so on). The idea of journal ranking appeared as a solution. A simple list of the supposedly best journals, the so-called starred journals, does the trick. There is no need to assess the papers published, and thus no need to read their contents. A simple count of the number of papers published in the relevant journals becomes the proxy for academic excellence in research. In turn, this feeds back into the business school ranking mechanisms. It also works for promotion and recruitment panels at business schools. This means externalising the heavy assessment tasks to anonymous reviewers and journal editors – and not even paying for it. This is quick, easy and cheap – at least at face value, because reviewing has a significant hidden cost for the community and the individuals who perform the task. Furthermore, all this free subcontracting is done in the name of science. How could anyone argue against peer reviewing, as this is the basic mechanism widely accepted in science to produce new knowledge via contradiction and debate?

Another element needs to be brought in. The legacy of the Second World War, with the United States emerging as the dominant power in the Western world and the success of American-based multinational corporations, led to the impressive dominance of North American management and thus North American business schools in the second half of the twentieth century. English became the lingua franca of management. More research was conducted in the USA than anywhere else – obviously in English – and hence there was more work published and more journals launched. This mere effect of volume had a logical mechanistic implication: the journals that appeared as leading the field were all American-based. They still are. The reviewing process instituted by the editors of such journals increasingly meant that authors had to play by the rules imposed on them (type of topic addressed, methodology, references selected, nature of the contribution expected and so on, which was not just a question of format, but became a matter of content as well).

As it turned out, after the Gordon-Howell and Pierson[1] reports at the end of the 1950s, the core of management research conducted in North America progressively went for a route towards more rigour, in turn mimicking hard sciences and economics in a quest for scientific legitimacy. This soon meant systematic use of statistics as a way to test hypotheses, in the hope of contributing to theorising, thus de facto widely adopting a positivist epistemic stance. The US academic arena in management is big enough to have kept some degree of diversity. Yet many researchers simply chose to put themselves in a position to publish what was increasingly expected from them, away from clinical studies, books, monographs and, regrettably, intellectual debate and scholarly inquiry.

We now have the ingredients of the cocktail that currently prevails: accreditation, business school rankings, journal rankings, massive dominance of North American research and starred journals, and mainstream US research going primarily for statistical testing of hypotheses as the standard of good science. These are the elements of the regulation mechanisms that have emerged over the last three decades as the drivers of the business of the business schools. These have had and still have a profound impact on the way the world of management education and research operates, and shape the rules of the game. While they have contributed to boosting the field, as pointed out earlier, we argue that some of their implications are in fact quite damaging.

THE ADVERSE SIDE EFFECTS OF THE DE FACTO REGULATION MECHANISMS THAT HAVE EMERGED IN THE FIELD

Under increasing competitive pressures, business school deans had little choice but to adopt the business school ranking lists as a measurement of reputation and success. Deans have seen this race for ranking as the best way both to access more funding and to attract better talent, thus raising reputation – and so on.

What can deans do to have their business schools go up the ranking ladder? Certainly, increasing the quality of the teaching can help, except that, beyond a certain level of resources allocated, the return on the investment, measured as improvement in the ranking, does not seem to be worth it. While it may still have an impact on the output variables, such as salary increase before and after an MBA, the marginal return from additional effort put into teaching may not be as rewarding as what can be achieved in pushing for publication of more starred articles. In other words, increasing the number of papers published in starred journals seems to offer much more leverage.

As a result, most deans have tended to hire young PhDs with high publication potential. Salaries for these high-flyers have gone up as the international market for prolific publishers in management has increased. The assumption was and still is that publications in starred journals impress the media, the business community and thus the recruiters, the prospective students and their families, and so on. Recruiting prolific publishers (or prolific publishers-to-be) has often disturbed the pay structure of the faculty, with more advanced tenured faculty members sometimes receiving less than the expensive youngsters. This may be a cause of tensions, especially when the newcomers behave as mercenaries, negotiating lighter teaching loads to invest more in their research – thus turning away from the primary role of business schools, namely to educate and train students for their future tasks as managers – and then quickly moving away to more prestigious places upon success in their submission process.

In addition, less attention tends to be paid to the performance of the new recruits in the classroom. Except for a few brilliant individuals who are the pride of our profession – those happy few who can be successful both in the classroom and in getting articles accepted in A journals – in many instances these young faculty members prove more at ease in conducting their statistical tests than in running a classroom session. This is particularly so when it comes to executive education audiences, where seasoned practitioners may for a moment be delving deep into the narrow topic of the PhD thesis of a young professor, but soon express their interest for other topics as well. They end up reminding programme leaders of their expectations given the time and money invested.

A BUSINESS SCHOOL BUBBLE

As a result, while their business schools are spending a lot of money to hire and remunerate prolific publishers, executive education associate deans tend to call upon external players to run part or all of their sessions. These external players (consultants, practitioners and so on) may be assimilated as faculty members by means of adjunct professorships or various devices of that sort. But the bottom line is that business schools sell the research of their faculty as a legitimising ingredient of their brand, while putting external non-researchers in front of the paying audiences. The question of how long companies and executives will accept this remains to be answered. We argue that this constitutes a form of bubble in the business of business schools.

Along the way, the pressure put on publishing in starred journals frames the priorities of young faculty members on the tenure track. Writing books, not to mention textbooks, becomes absurd – a waste of time. This simply means that most of the past prominent thinkers of management, Drucker, Ansoff, Mintzberg, Crozier, Taylor or Sloan, would not make it into today's academic competition. The long format of a book to develop one's thinking is no longer recognised. And that is in the name of science. This is more than frightening.

Business schools have lost their way. Something needs to be done about it. Interestingly enough, many retiring business school deans who deliver their last speech as they leave tend to say something of the sort. Yet their successors immediately keep going as before. There seems to be a lock-in situation, rooted in the ranking system. As we believe that no single individual can unlock the system, we argue that awareness raising is needed and, from there, collective strategies and action.

This book is a call for collective strategies to redesign management education and research.

Our call:
Our field has become an industry of its own, with fierce international competition and thus competitive strategies on the part of players active in the

arena: business schools and their deans, individual professors, journals and so on. We believe that certain collective strategies are necessary to influence the de facto regulation mechanisms that have appeared over the years (for example the rankings, the accreditation bodies, the Bologna process, the race for publications and so on).

We further believe that Europe is now the relevant level for Europeans to discuss these issues. This is why we offer to engage in strategic conversations with our colleagues throughout the European Union (and beyond) to raise these issues and generate debates and action.

This Introduction has made a long story short – at times with short cuts or sweeping generalisation. The chapters that follow cover the same story in more detail.

THE BOOK'S STRUCTURE

Our call to redesign management education and research is structured around four parts.

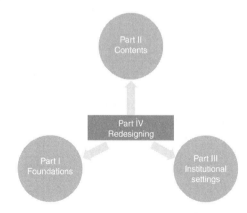

Part I is dedicated to the (re)foundations of management education and research, adopting a historical and comparative perspective. Eric Godelier looks at the history of the complex interplay between social sciences and management. Romain Laufer looks at the history of education in law and management. And Armand Hatchuel makes his point by arguing that management may be viewed as a basic academic field of its own.

Part II addresses the issue of rethinking the contents of management education and research. It begins with an analysis of the specificity of management research as Roland Pérez discusses the extent to which management research is legitimate or not depending on the audiences. Bernard de Montmorillon then explores the contents of what may be investigated and taught, adopting a contingent perspective. Alain Charles Martinet and Marielle Payaud in turn use the specific theme of governance to illustrate how alternative contents, departing from the literature, may be offered on such an important, much debated topic. Their chapter serves as a way to show how concrete proposals for new contents may be made. Peter McKiernan closes this part by discussing the relevance of the new knowledge produced by management research, arguing that Europe may contribute to help the field stay away from too much irrelevance.

Part III deals with the institutions and the regulation mechanisms that are at work in management education and research. Olivier Basso, Philippe-Pierre Dornier and Jean-Paul Mounier discuss the evaluation of business schools and their activities by coming back to the basic role of management education institutions facing their stakeholders. Eric Cornuel presents the EFMD perspective with the EPAS and Equis schemes. Dennis Tourish addresses the evaluation of the contribution of individual faculty members by discussing journal rankings and their effect on academic freedom.

Finally, Part IV offers some direction for future action. Two SFM position papers are presented as an illustration of what a joint effort may produce. This borrows from the work conducted at SFM, the French Academy of Management, to help form a body of soft law.

The first position paper deals with the importance of rehabilitating books and monographs as acceptable and recognised forms of research output. The second position paper discusses the issue of journal rankings. Each of the two position papers analyses the issue and offers a set of concrete recommendations that were collectively debated at SFM.

How do we proceed from there? How do we contribute to redesigning our field, the way our community operates, the governance and evaluation processes, and the institutional setting?

We firmly believe that European business schools can find better ways than the current rules of the game imported from North America. This book is a wake-up call. It is up to us to join forces and act together.

NOTE

1. 'In the late 1950s, business schools as a whole came under close scrutiny from two key academic reports. Both the Gordon-Howell Report and the Pierson Report criticized business schools for including narrow, trade-focused curricula within their programs; for employing poorly trained faculty; attracting academically inferior students; and for implementing simplistic teaching and research methodologies.

During this post-war period, when the U.S. government and economy at large was seeking to advance via an industrial revolution, the pair of reports instigated a sea of change within academia, providing a much-needed wake-up call to many of the nation's oldest, elite business schools. Complacency was no longer an option' (Carnegie Mellon Tepper School of Business, http://tepper.cmu.edu/about-tepper/history/the-b-school-change-agents/the-pierson-report/index.aspx).

PART I

Revisiting the foundations of management education and research

1. Social sciences and management
2. Comparative history of education in law and management
3. Establishing management as a field

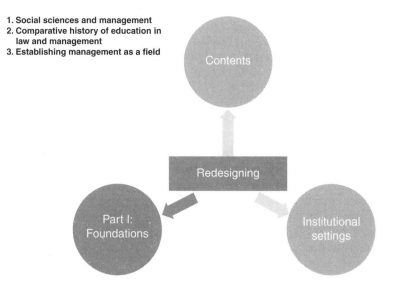

This part is dedicated to the (re)foundations of management education and research, based on a comparative, historical and institutional perspective. In the first chapter, Eric Godelier defines management science through its relationships with social sciences and illustrates these interactions by exploring the tensions between management science and history. In the second chapter, Romain Laufer explores the relationships between law and management. He suggests studying management through an analogy using the notion of jurisprudence. He argues that the process of defining management is intimately associated with the central role played by the judicial process in the resolution of conflicts which may arise in any collective action – especially in the area of business. He then analyses the differences between French and American jurisprudence and the impact on the foundations of management that these differences had within both countries. Part I ends with a chapter that calls for a re-foundation of management as a field. Armand Hatchuel revisits the theme of the identity, rigour and relevance of management research. The author recommends re-establishing management as a new basic science which is – as he puts it – both a 'social' and a 'cognitive' science that studies the conditions, design and legitimacy of 'models of collective action'. In this definition of management research, rigour and relevance are closely intertwined.

While using lenses that are different, the three contributors to Part I follow a common path of establishing the foundations of management education and research, promoting a contingent approach to management. First, they analyse the process of defining management and management science through comparisons with other social sciences. Second, they offer a historical perspective to understand how the management education and research system was shaped. Third, they promote a perspective of management education systems embedded in institutional contexts. All in all, Part I argues that management education and research systems are intimately linked to, and should take better account of, their national and regional contexts.

1. Social sciences and management sciences: convergences or divergences?

Eric Godelier

Regularly in France, management sciences are criticised by several categories of people. Within the discipline, academics from different epistemological traditions debate the question of how scientific they are. They also try to define the best way of doing research in order to be fully recognised by universities and business schools or by other scientific fields of 'pure' sciences, such as physics and mathematics, or social sciences, such as sociology, history and (sometimes) economics. Outside the frontiers of management, academics aim to convince both the public and corporate managers that their science can legitimately speak about corporations and can improve the quality and efficiency of management tools and models. Behind the public discussion, there are various aspects involved. One cornerstone on which many of the debates focused is the complex relationship between management and social sciences. Seen as critical or unhelpful in practice, classical social sciences – for instance political economy, sociology, anthropology or history – may be rejected either by management academics or by practitioners. For them, the orientation of management sciences towards theoretical research or 'useless' knowledge seems suspect. Hence, claiming that, as a new discipline, management sciences have to break with their renowned antecedents, some management academics minimise or reject any methodological or epistemological influence. How and when did this complex relationship with social sciences come about? Is it possible to create what some hold to be a totally new discipline from scratch? This means that, at least theoretically, a new community and its scientific paradigm could be designed through a complete break in the path of social sciences' evolution and progress. These positions will be discussed in this chapter. First, two clarifications have to be made: about the word 'management' and the concept of 'social sciences'.

Very often, the word 'management' is used unclearly, as it has at least three very different meanings. First, 'management' represents all corporations' processes and actors engaged in organised action. In a sense, through the study of its most central and symbolic institution, management sciences can be seen as the science of capitalism. The second meaning is of management as a frame or a way of classifying, describing and analysing social action and processes. Like sociology and history, which have their own approach to social issues and institution dynamics, management sciences provide a useful intellectual model to understand organisations and collective action. The third meaning is more technical. Here, management gathers the technologies and tools used by managers in the design and implementation of action procedures and processes. Even if the three levels are all concerned with the management–social sciences relationship, the chapter will focus mainly on the second meaning. To better understand the roots of management sciences and its relationships with other social sciences, let's specify what we mean by 'social sciences' here.

It is impossible to define 'social sciences' in just a few words. As a start, they could be distinguished from other sciences by their object and by the way they form and apply a particular relationship with reality, i.e. their epistemology and methodology. The object of social sciences is the analysis of individuals embedded in social relations. The aim of social sciences is to understand the nature of these relations (M. Godelier 2007, pp. 26ff.). This means that two linked dimensions have to be looked at: the material and the mental. By mental one must understand the fact that people design not only material things but also representations, norms and values used to shape the society they are living in. This implies several basic assumptions. First, the objects of social sciences are shaped by history. Therefore they are not universal but related only to specific conditions of time and space. This constrains the aim and ways of doing research. Second, 'social sciences' are themselves historically shaped. This means that they originated in a certain place and in certain conditions. Their objects, methods and models are influenced by this apparent process. All of these evolved in time and space. The consequence is that all these elements have to be studied as well as part of the scientific debate. On the one hand, this means that history has created several focused social sciences to explore and explain various aspects of social and human life. On the other hand, the objects studied are so complex that no single discipline is able to describe and comprehend all their dimensions. For instance, historians will never be able to present all of history. This is also true for other social sciences. This conclusion raises the issue of cooperation and sometimes competition between sciences. For instance, the matter of organisation is shared by several social sciences, sociology, anthropology and of course management sciences (Bonnafous-Boucher 2005, p. 15). Finally, even if in the past social sciences tried to produce global theories of the world (Marxism, structuralism, liberalism), these models have been criticised and replaced by more pragmatic approaches and various explanations of social life. This evolution has led to a new equilibrium between fundamental and applied research. It has also expanded the variety of knowledge, methods and models that can be used to describe and analyse society. This deconstruction process has allowed people to explore new directions and subjects, for instance corporations and organisations. But sometimes it goes too far, for instance with radical post-modernism or phenomenology. Here, to the confusion of the reader or the academic, all knowledge and every methodology could be seen as scientific, and that rigorous methodology could be seen as the only way to produce scientific results. This is at the core of tensions amongst social sciences, and particularly management sciences.

Some parts of these definitions suggest ways of understanding why management sciences and classical social sciences have such complex relations. To pursue this, section 1.1 considers the following point: how did management get involved in science, either as a way toward more rigorous practices and models or as a new discipline? This will help to clarify some aspects of the relationship between management and social sciences. This is followed, in section 1.2, by a focus on the relations between history and management sciences as a good example of the kinds of tensions, dead ends and opportunities which could occur. All these elements could contribute to the conclusion that management sciences should be considered as a particular kind of social science.

1.1 THE NATURE OF THE RELATION BETWEEN MANAGEMENT AND SCIENCE: AN OLD ISSUE

A better understanding of these relations requires that we look back to the beginning of management sciences, which we will illustrate by looking at the French case. Three points must be explained. First, management pioneers at an early stage raised the issue of the scientific dimension of management and, indirectly, the nature of relations to be organised with corporations and field managers. Throughout the history of management, approaches have fluctuated between a rejection of conceptualisation and abstract science and the willingness to improve the generalisation of management knowledge thanks to rigorous methodologies and proved theories. Second, the possibilities of dialogue have been influenced either by the institutional developments of management sciences and social sciences or by the socio-economic context in which management has become widespread. Third, the choices made at a certain point in time by management academics, in this case French academics, partly explain the complex relationship with social sciences. In France (but not only there), the importance of science in management moved from a marginal position in the nineteenth century (section 1.1.1), to a rise of rationality and science thanks to Taylor and Fayol (section 1.1.2), and to a recognition of management sciences by French academics (section 1.1.3).

1.1.1   Pre-scientific Management: Designing Human and Technical Solutions through an Education and Social Project[1]

From the beginning of the nineteenth-century industrial revolution, management practitioners and theorists faced the issue of their personal and social identity and legitimacy. In both cases, the problem was to reconcile two antagonistic targets. On the one hand was objective and critical reflection about day-to-day practices to generate universal knowledge and transferable concepts. On the other hand was the satisfaction of managers' requests for tools, models and values useful for efficient action. Each target supposes a specific methodology for knowledge production and legitimation. Each delimits a community of people and a particular set of legitimated values and behaviours. Each one also determines the type of relationship management could have with social sciences and more generally speaking sciences. Nevertheless, the heterogeneity of sources of knowledge (practitioners, consultants, academics) and the wide range of its sub-disciplines limit the possibility of giving a short presentation of the history of management sciences.

The emergence of science in management occurred thanks to a move from an education programme to a scientific project (Hatchuel 2001, p. 8). Starting in the nineteenth century, industrial revolution in France, and more widely in Europe, generated new technical, organisational or social problems. This motivated the first entrepreneurs and managers to design innovative solutions, which nevertheless remained local and concentrated in a plant or a single enterprise. Soon the possibility emerged of establishing general principles and even the first basis of universal management doctrines which could be transferred to other geographical areas, economic sectors or enterprises. At that time, most of the industrial companies were isolated in the countryside. It was not until the second half of the nineteenth century that a speeding up could be observed in the development of an urban industrialised society. As Pollard (1968, pp. 42ff.) described for Great Britain, if the old putting-out system of production had already organised some solutions for producing, financing or managing staff, the size and complexity of capital investments imposed a complete change in management methods. Mine, textile, metallurgy and steel industry leaders had to invent new procedures and practices to improve the efficiency of larger, more complex equipment. They also had to deal with the rigidity of energy sources (steam or hydraulic) which remained difficult to control. Clearly, investment in fixed capital represented a step toward organisational and management innovation. For instance, in the UK, Watt and Arkwright had to explain to their potential clients how to use their machines to best effect. Step by step, they began to suggest reorganisations of production space and enterprise premises, as well as in staff management, finance and marketing policies. These experiences began to be widespread thanks to the movement of workers and engineers between plants and regions (Pollard 1968, p. 199).

In the meanwhile, the idea was also to establish a set of skills and knowledge for future new managers. Nevertheless, in late-nineteenth-century France, education programmes remained very rare. When they existed, they resulted from the willingness of experienced entrepreneurs and industrialists, mainly trained as technicians. They were also set up by engineers who wanted to develop a generalised management doctrine for the use of other managers or trainees.

Since the early nineteenth century, some outlines of management conceptualisation have existed in France, for instance Vital Roux's book in 1800, J.-B. Say in 1828, or J.-G. Courcelle-Seneuil in 1854.[2] After about 1870, the development of management education rapidly became systematic. One aspect was the founding of several business schools. Prior to this period, besides the École Spéciale de Commerce et d'Industrie de Paris created in 1819,[3] few institutions for management learning existed. Where such educational practices existed, they were designed internally by enterprises or organised as part of professional and familial traditions. Company owners and managers often sent their children to their colleagues, suppliers or clients for a training period. Things began to change with the growing number of engineers and the appearance of the first 'administrative' managers.

These new education programmes had two aims: preparation for professional life, and development of a new social category which could be distinguished both from owners and from workers or subordinates (Bouilloud and Lecuyer 1994). In France, the first management courses or books presented examples of innovation implemented in high-performance enterprises or sectors (mines, textiles or the steel industry). Most of the time, the first teachers were former industrialists like C. Dupin. In the late nineteenth century, France, the UK and the United States followed the same kind of evolutionary path (Wren 1994, pp. 83ff.). The first professional or specialised associations were created.[4] Some of them became lobbyists, but all played a central role in the exchange and diffusion of management innovations and management's turn toward science.

1.1.2   The First Steps of Science in French and Western Management

The search for doctrinal and scientific rigour definitely speeded up at the turn of the twentieth century with two leading authors: H. Fayol and F. Taylor. They pursued rationalisation, of office management for the former and of operational plants for the latter. In both cases, they aimed to improve management performance through a new set of methods. Claiming that France had developed only general rules for public management, Fayol set out to design a scientific, or at least more rigorous, theory of private management. At that time, the social figure and expertise of the 'professional' manager were still to be recognised. At the same time, and in a slightly contradictory way, Fayol insisted that the future manager or leader must rely on individual qualities to succeed. Obviously such qualities could not be easily learned. Nevertheless, a breakthrough was made. From then on, reflections on the profession of manager underlined the importance either of managers' technical and social relations abilities or of their personality.[5] By starting this debate, Fayol implicitly raised the questions of management academic legitimacy and the educational content that should be transmitted to future managers. Like Taylor, who taught at Harvard, he considered that only experienced practitioners should be allowed to guide the study of management.[6] Only experience enabled the manager to produce rules and concepts which could be transmitted to other managers, who were engaged in the field, or trainees. The validity of management knowledge or general principles should be evaluated through their practical efficiency. From then on, this ambiguous position deeply influenced relations between management theoretical doctrines and management practices. It separated the communities and ideologies of management academics from those of field practitioners. The arrival of management science in production and plants also complicated the dynamics of management discipline.

Taylor built the legitimacy of his management doctrine on his working experience. He started from technical studies on machine tools but moved rapidly to general concepts which could help to reshape the organisation of plants and enterprises (Hatchuel 1994). This intellectual process had a paradoxical consequence. It produced, on the one hand, practical recommendations and, on the other, an intellectual frame which, by breaking with the field constraints, produced new universal management principles. The problems analysed initially by Taylor were simple and transferable to other practical or educational situations (Taylor 1990). Science is sought for its supposed objectivity and its methodological rigour. Science and rationality were seen as able to bring to an end the class struggle between workers and capitalists. Taylorism became a tool for internal and external debates of management issues, as in the famous trial brought by Louis Brandeis against the rail company Eastern Railroads.[7] The terms used in the trial became well known. Management, its principles and its methods entered social and political debates in the early twentieth century in the United States and very soon across the world.

With Taylor, management moved towards generalisation. Engineers became the symbolic figures of scientific management, and their authority was clearly reinforced (Fridenson 1987, p. 1036). Nevertheless, it is suggested that, beyond this progress, Taylor was at the origin of a muddling up between the sources of legitimacy and inspiration of management. Science, especially in its most classical forms, devises methods and universal doctrines through a form of detachment from reality and local issues. Nevertheless, Taylor insisted on the importance of founding science on real corporations' practices and problems. From then on, his heirs in management – either academics or practitioners – had to cope with this ambiguity.

1.1.3 Science in the French Academy: Between the Practical Efficiency of Concepts and Institutional Recognition

In the history of French management education,[8] it can be noted that there were no management sciences in French universities until the 1950s.[9] Even in the 1960s, management courses were not seen as fully legitimate in France (Chessel and Pavis 2001).

After the Second World War, the backwardness of French management education in universities and more generally in the country was underlined by the productivity missions which visited the United States (Guigueno 1994; see also Barjot 2002). The economic and social context soon changed. The size of corporations started to increase. More and more subsidiaries of US companies were established in France, accelerating the Americanisation of French society (Zeitlin and Herrigel 2004). The demand for trained engineers and managers exploded (Marchand and Thélot 1997). Nevertheless, managers did not want to be assimilated as corporation owners or entrepreneurs (Boltanski 1982; Bouffartigue 2001). They claimed a specific qualification which could legitimate their identity and profession beside the engineers. On the academic side, the solution relied on the vision of management designed as a science of engineering and organised action. Its legitimacy was supposed to be recognised from its use of doctrines validated by practitioners and actual activity (Hatchuel 2001, p. 11). Management sciences defined themselves as the 'science of design and of collective action planning'. Their watchword was 'understand for action'. (See for example Simon 1981.)

In the first stage, the educational response used the technical tools available at that time: operational research, statistics, decision game theory. It also reproduced the corporate functional structure: marketing, accountancy and finance, strategy, staff management and so on. This kind of educational programme was launched in the first *instituts d'administration des entreprises* (IAEs).[10] At the start, the IAEs targeted professionals like physicians, lawyers and engineers who needed complementary skills in management. The advantage of this 'function-oriented' educational programme was that it allowed better communication and exchanges between academics and managers. Nevertheless, it created the possibility of a disciplinary split into sub-domains that centred more and more on themselves.

In the second stage, management sought academic recognition. In the late 1950s, the new objective was to increase the scientific level of management education. The pioneers decided that it should be done through more intellectual and institutional autonomy. Systematic work started to determine the discipline's limits and its specific concepts, methods and objects of research. There were alternative approaches. On the one hand, management sciences had the choice of adopting the concepts and results of older social sciences, with the risk of being seen as an applied science, i.e. a minor discipline, by the dominant criteria of French academic classicism. Nevertheless, this choice of a new crossroads discipline (i.e. a discipline which imports concepts and methodologies from several older and more institutionalized social sciences like sociology, history, political sciences and economics and uses them to analyse management problems, corporation life and organizations) aiming at preparation for practical action had the advantage of staying in contact with enterprises' real management problems. On the other hand, full academic recognition and the gaining of intellectual as well as material autonomy supposed a break with other social sciences. It was seen as a first step toward the design of universal management models and concepts. One strategy was to accentuate mathematisation and abstraction as a point for methodological independence and a fast track toward scientific legitimacy. Paradoxically, this led to a widening of the gap between the academic approach and management practices. It increased managers' criticisms about the uselessness of a science which pretended to be able to understand and reshape day-to-day management. The 1945–74 period undoubtedly saw the development of quantitative methods, which were supposed to appear more scientific. Hence this vision, inspired by the natural sciences, produced a dominant paradigm of what management sciences should be. In particular it contributed to a rejection of older and more critical social sciences like sociology and history.

The third stage of this evolution, full discipline recognition, required the creation of an academic community in universities and educational institutions. The question became particularly crucial at the end of the 1960s. At that time, several sources of tension appeared between different strategies, categories of professor and institutions (Chessel and Pavis 2001). In French business schools, tensions appeared between those educated in the United States, usually young PhDs, and the others. In other places, tensions appeared between practitioners and full professors, frequently trained in economics or law. Lastly, some of the new management professors were well educated thanks to financial support from the FNEGE[11] – mostly in the United States – whereas the others were left behind. These conflicts show the delicate position of management education at the crossroads of three sources of legitimacy: 1) technology and a technical approach oriented toward practice or the mastery of a set of know-how, procedures and tools; 2) training in certain behaviours and values useful for professional life; 3) scientific knowledge based on research and concepts (Pérez 1999). The rapid development of this third dimension took place in the early 1970s.

If the PhD in management was in fact launched in 1968 with the creation of Paris-Dauphine University, it was officially recognised a few years later. Soon, questions arose about the ideal profile of candidates and the contents of the new qualification. The FNEGE supported the idea that empirical data and practical topics should be rewarded, as they were for PhDs in medicine or the engineering sciences (Chessel and Pavis 2001). For its supporters, this was a good strategy to limit the risk of academism and an excessive bias towards theorisation and to maintain a close relationship with business people. Some pushed further by suggesting that future management professors should have been corporate managers prior to their PhD studies. Nevertheless, both propositions appeared to be provocative for numerous academics. In the end, they were abandoned. Finally, in 1975, a specific recruitment process, inspired by the law and economics faculties, was created in the university for management full professors: the *agrégation*. This competitive examination aimed at the outset to combine theory and practice.[12] The direct admission to the status of full professor embedded management sciences into French universities.[13] Despite this obvious progress, the perception of management sciences remained inconsistent.

Outside, they appeared as a new discipline challenging the academic establishment. Some young management professors were accused of leftism by their older colleagues. At the same time they were accused of being CIA representatives or defenders of capitalism because they were engaged in a discipline pursuing the improvement of corporate management. In May 1968 most of the social sciences criticised imperialism and the consumption society (Chessel and Pavis 2001, p. 141). Things changed in the crisis period of the 1970s to 1980s.

One consequence was a re-evaluation of some of the management tools and doctrines used in Western corporations. Classical tools based on rationality and Taylorism faced more and more difficulties associated with being embedded and presented as objective and universal devices able to solve all kinds of problems around the world. For instance, strategic planning, the core of corporate strategy until the 1970s, was criticised for its excessive formalism and quantification (Mintzberg 1994b). By comparison, the Japanese success obliged Western leaders to question their scientific conception of management. The time had come for corporate culture, values and symbols. New Japanese models became widespread around the world (total quality, lean production, just-in-time, Kanban, modularity and value creation) (Ohno 1980). From then on, the new management mood focused on flexibility (Boyer 1986).

In the 1970–80 period, strategic management was reshaped by two major issues: 1) definition of and concentration on core and historical competencies; 2) the outsourcing of less profitable activities. Step by step a new kind of enterprise appeared: the network corporation linking a set of suppliers to a central customer on a long-term basis. The old globalised vertical companies became more decentralised and horizontally oriented organisations, like the Swedish ABB. Coordination or integration of internal components and external enterprises became central in modern management. Logistics, human resources management and accountancy increased their weight in management. The financialisation of strategies got stronger, and top executives or CEOs were put under close scrutiny by shareholders and pension funds (Batsch 2002, p. 82). Risk and rigidity were the new enemies. They were progressively outsourced to smaller companies or to the whole of society (Batsch 2002, pp. 85ff.).

The time had come for the de-Taylorisation of industry, whereas it seems that services were increasingly rationalised and systematically managed. Tourism, restaurants, hotels and distribution created more and more standardised products. In this context, consultants developed their business and became an important vector of diffusion for new management doctrines or methods of rationalisation (benchmarking or re-engineering) (McKenna 2006). Things also changed in the academic field.

The institutionalisation of management went on. Nevertheless, new problems appeared. On the one hand, the period of the 1980s to 1990s was positive thanks to a tremendous increase in the number of students in management studies (Pérez 1999). On the other hand, the economic and business changes reopened the debates on the content and legitimacy of management professors or education institutions. The huge demand for management education decreased the frontiers between classical academic programmes and corporations' or practitioners' expectations. It again raised several questions: should the education be exclusively in class or based on an alternation of courses and in-house training? What balance should there be between theory and practice? What kind of internationalisation of French management education should be adopted? Because French corporations were increasingly embedded in globalisation, the question of international ranking of management diplomas and educational institutions arose. The model of the US MBA was the focus of all the debates. All these questions seemed very like the ones that had been raised since the late nineteenth century. What about research in management?

The crisis led to several drastic changes either in the subjects studied or in the epistemological paradigm used. For a long time, management research focused on technical aspects and rationality, and positivism was the dominant epistemology. Concentrated on tools and functional approaches, management research turned to the issue of 'management processes' and multidepartmental or 'horizontal' problems. Nevertheless, each management sub-discipline made its own progress. In strategic management, human resources management or organisation studies, change was fast through the development of research in project management. New themes were explored like chronocompetition, concurrent engineering, or individual or collective learning.[14] Taylorism was revisited. Other disciplines in management followed different paths.

In marketing, change took two different directions (Pras 1997). On the one hand, research inspired by neoclassical economics improved the knowledge of consumer behaviour. On the other hand, transactional marketing started to focus on the exchange issue, especially on the role of market price. All of these studies were mathematically formalised and normatively oriented.

In finance, besides corporate finance, the importance of market finance rapidly increased. 'Value creation' and corporate financial performance became central objects for researchers. Once again, here they used the hypothesis of neoclassical pure and perfect competition and homo economicus rationality (Goffin 1998).

At the same time, dialogue with practitioners and actual facts pushed academics to question the status of the discipline, which was often presented as a crossroads discipline, and to find new frontiers between concepts and management practice (Hatchuel 2001, pp. 12–13). From then on, management sciences moved in two separate directions. Most of the researchers decided to go deeper into abstraction, which they saw as the only way, and proposed general theories unable to resolve the crisis.

The aim was to transform management sciences into the most scientific part of social sciences, reshaping the old epistemological basis of economics. The objective was to produce universal and ahistorical theories (Déry 1994), ready for practitioners, 'in laboratories'. The search for discipline purity, scientific independence and functional specialisation was a characteristic of this strategy. For its supporters, the ultimate reference was a vision of sciences, for instance in physics (Ronan 1988), most often reduced to what they used to be in the nineteenth century. On the opposite side, a minority of researchers adopted the critical stance to the dominant positivist epistemology. It was inspired by the constructivism previously developed elsewhere in classical social sciences. They tried to find new answers to the question of the situation and status of the social scientist engaged in the research process. Sometimes they suggested using a more sophisticated theory of the researcher–topic relationship. Action research and field studies imported from ethnography started to become widespread in French management sciences (see for instance Berry 1984). In France, but also in other Western countries, researchers did not have to devise ready-made models for managers but organised a dialogue with them which might allow them to understand the influence of their own frame of mind and to build their own representations of the problems they had to solve. Interdisciplinary dialogue was promoted and seen as conducive to understanding the complexity of management problems. This required the use of several social sciences to analyse and cover all the dimensions of management issues. Universal or abstract models were no longer produced, but local regularities were described and transformed step by step into intermediate theories.

If these two scientific strategies were clearly separated until the 1980s, they drew closer in the 1990s, on the issue of scientific management knowledge and the practices of managers in corporations (Cohen 1997).

Science is now well embedded at the core of French management sciences. Nevertheless, relations with classical social sciences and its status amongst them, and more generally with sciences in French educational and research institutions, are still under debate. A good example of the complexity of the issue is the dialogue with history.

1.2   AN EXAMPLE OF THE COMPLEX RELATIONSHIP BETWEEN MANAGEMENT AND A SOCIAL SCIENCE: HISTORY[15]

Twenty years ago, a French management review, the *Revue française de gestion*, published a special issue on 'the roots of enterprise' (Doublet and Fridenson 1998; more recently see Godelier and Seiffert 2008). The conclusion was optimistic. There were good signs in terms of common research, comparative approaches and methodological or epistemological dialogue. Since then, more managers and academics seem to have used history as a frame for corporate understanding, and more historians have focused their work on enterprises and organisations. Nevertheless, even if academic recognition of 'management historians'[16] has clearly improved, the dialogue between these two fields relies mostly on personal initiatives rather than on a conscious and systematic interdisciplinary academic strategy. A growing number of professional historians[17] are focusing their attention on management processes and enterprises, a scientific turn which is relatively new and interesting.

Section 1.2.1 evaluates the influence of the long and specific scientific tradition that has shaped these two academic fields step by step. Each of them has its own origins, its own objectives and its particular historical evolution. Clearly, such a strong matrix could contribute to establishing a durable barrier of misunderstanding and suspicion.

As soon as they start to study the evolution of enterprise, its organisation and management processes throughout history, management researchers and historians face the striking challenge of legitimating their work in two complementary processes. Within their own scientific field, the new object and method have to be officially recognised by their peers. Outside their discipline, objective conditions must be organised in order to allow the dialogue to begin and to progress. This is not an easy task, as shown in section 1.2.2.

1.2.1 Crippling and Ancient Disagreements?

Some disciplines of management sciences[18] are very cautious about the way French business history studies corporations and management practices and tools. From their point of view, this approach limits the possibilities of dialogue and interdisciplinary work. They believe some French business historians overfocus on large corporations and the industries of the first and second industrial revolutions. They have pointed out the lack of research on small and medium-sized companies or on services, the absence of theories, and a methodology relying mostly on monographs. On the other side, historians also have their point of view. More and more management academics are using history without awareness of or education in methodology.[19] They find the theoretical models of management globally weak for several reasons: the poor quality of the facts used for demonstration; a tendency toward too hasty or incautious generalisation and abstraction; and an epistemological position too attached to an outmoded positivism. Sometimes this position is even hidden behind the vague term 'constructivism'. Where do these tensions come from? A quick glance at the past will help us to understand that French historians have only recently started to study business life and corporations. As seen above, the history of the development of management sciences in France is very helpful in analysing the tensions with history.

From the end of the Second World War until the late 1960s, there was some contact between history and management. Some pioneers in economic history started to focus their research on enterprises: Bertrand Gille (1961) and Jean Bouvier ([1961] 1999, 1973) wrote famous monographs on banks,[20] and in his doctoral dissertation Claude Folhen (1955, pp. 230ff.) analysed the textile industry. Apart from them, very little research was done on companies until the 1970s (for more information see Beltran et al. 1995). This early interest in corporations may be explained by the search for an explanation of the development of a particular industrial branch, a region or the dynamics of national macroeconomics (Marmonnier and Thiétart 1988, p. 167). One important exception, Alfred Chandler's *Strategy and Structure: Chapters in the History of Industrial Enterprise* (1962), is well known among French academics in management. However, basically we can state that history was not often chosen as a tool for advancing understanding. Why? Let's examine several explanations.

On the one hand, in the 1960s, economic history was still largely influenced by structuralism and Marxism, both having shaped the way historians constructed economic phenomena. Many researchers have focused on the industrial revolution and technical innovation; others have analysed cycles and economic crises (Vilar 2006) or long series of price fluctuations. The growing influence of the journal *Annales* explains the new interest in business and corporate history. In the 1970s and 1980s, the École des Annales started to focus its analysis on a local scale, including social institutions and enterprises (Bourdé and Martin 1983, pp. 171–226). During that period, the issues which had been raised since the 1960s by the new economic history and Lafayette University (Indiana) arrived in France. This new approach widened the sources of history and deepened research on a limited set of topics. For instance, studies were begun on the influence of railways on American growth (Heffer 2006).

However, the position of French management sciences after the Second World War was still fragile, as seen before. From then onwards, there were constant fluctuations between abstract and empirical approaches. Of course, the possibilities of collaboration between management sciences and history are clearly different within each of the two methodologies: the abstract and the empirical.

On the abstract track, history is seen as an auxiliary discipline to be used by management sciences. Its role is to provide facts that can prove abstract management theories. But, to be accepted, history has to adopt scientific discourse, legitimated questions designed by management sciences for themselves as well as their results. On the empirical track, history and management sciences are equal partners. They first have to harmonise their scientific approaches, developing common methods and shared research issues, and then they need to allow a better integration of both perspectives. This project has made significant progress. Nevertheless, misunderstandings are still frequent and noteworthy, with the reasons most often found in the evolution of each discipline.

First, there is divergence on the object of investigation. It must be remembered that, for a long time, French history had neglected the study of enterprises (Fridenson 1989). Gradually, French historians were asked to analyse the present time (Franck 1993). Logically, historians continue to use the same methodology and to follow their traditional scientific project on enterprises and management. This means understanding and reconstituting the 'truth', the obscure dimensions and complexity of a fact or an event, by revealing hidden history. In doing this, history is clearly embedded in fundamental research. Here, studying enterprises and management supposes a rigorous, critical, methodical use of documents and sources gathered by the historian, led by a permanent spirit of doubt (Franck 1993, p. 86). Applied to management tools and practices, this process inevitably leads to studying their origins, the contexts in which they have appeared, and the outcome of their standardisation or divergences. Clearly, the result is an inquiry about the relativity of management models and practices in time and space and the localness, rather than universality, of their efficiency. Business and corporate history keep alive questions about the efficiency and actual impact of management. This is a clear source of annoyance and irritation for managers and some academics. Why?

From the point of view of management sciences, what is important is the ability to combine, at the same time, science and practice. This is the study of management situations (Girin 1990), which supposes the study of the practical know-how of the members within the enterprise and, more broadly, of the organisation's operations. 'Managers want to be efficient, practical and down-to-earth. From their point of view, history seems an academic exercise proposing very few links with the actions they are supposed to manage' (Doublet and Fridenson 1988). For some people, new management knowledge is often conceived through a sharp break with old practices and theories. This thought process dominates French management, which postulates the universalism of models and theories. Therefore, what cannot be expressed or reduced to a scientific question, preferably mathematically formalised, holds no interest. Managers and academics mainly focus their attention on the present or the future, not on the past. They have for a long time now seen history as a work for noble souls, a useless, but amusing, curiosity except for important commemorations or corporate communication and its short anniversary books. Rare are the managers, such as Roger Martin, former CEO of Saint-Gobain, who have used history as a framework for their strategy (Martin 1992).[21]

Many things seem to make management and history very different: the disagreement over methods, the epistemological framework, scientific projects and aims, and the validation of results. Does this mean that no dialogue is possible? On the contrary, the present intellectual and historical contexts seem to be offering real opportunities for fruitful exchanges.

1.2.2   Preconditions for Dialogue?

Since the 1990s, in one way or another, more and more academics in management have been using history in their research. The next step toward a smoother dialogue is to design a process which combines rigorous methodologies and scientific knowledge and results recognised as legitimate by both disciplines. Before this can happen, there are two categories of conditions to satisfy: an evolution of scientific paradigms and a change in methodological practices.

One might think that the research process could be defined by a fundamental hypothesis: the concept of the enterprise seen as an institution in which members and management practices are designed and embedded in a socio-historical dimension. This assessment seems obvious, but in fact it is not so easy for it to be recognised and implemented. This supposes understanding what separates enterprises from other kinds of social institutions and organisations such as trade unions, the church, the state, the city or the family. It requires the adoption of a specific point of view. There are at least two points of view that are of interest.

The first focuses on a study of enterprises based only on their internal problems, which is the current approach of management sciences. Unfortunately, following this track of thought, many management theories describe enterprises as disembodied, fully rational organisations in which abstract 'actors' design tools and implement them without emotion or mistakes. Such an analytical framework is inspired by a reductionism which presents management phenomena as separate pieces to be recomposed, step by step, as a complete object. The criteria used to separate the parts, and the analytical process are directly inspired by the official structure of the enterprise: hierarchical levels (workers, supervisors, managers) or technical functions (marketing, finance, production and so on). This intellectual position is closely related to positivism. More or less officially, it has been inspired by pure, or vague, neoclassical economics, and through it by the paradigms of rationality and individualism, the methodology which dominates microeconomics. It is puzzling that so few management academics have broken with this paradigm in recent years. Herbert Simon and James March proved, beyond a doubt, the limits and theoretical dead ends attached to this approach.[22] On the one hand, this scientific position seems to allow a dialogue between management academics and managers engaged in day-to-day practices. On the other hand, using these criteria and representations could closely link the evolution of management to people and field practices with other targets and methods of legitimate evaluation. There is a certain paradox in using these scientific methods and, at the same time, formal abstraction, which sees rupture with actual management practices and day-to-day working life as the height of scientific quality. Hence, management theories and methodologies are better if they are artificially formulated in dark rooms, far away from real enterprises. The future of management sciences is supposed to be independent of practice as well as of traditional social sciences (sociology, anthropology and, of course, history). The theoretical hypotheses of the models and their results are rarely compared with empirical facts, nor with historical reality, except when history is used to 'validate' the choices made. Even then, when historical events or facts should logically lead to a questioning or critical analysis of the theories and models, some seem ready to conclude that 'reality is wrong'.[23]

A second point of view is important: to discard the idea of universalism in management. This task is not easy either, for universalism is a widely accepted view. One may find it for instance in books which look back at the history and origins of management, supposedly as old as humanity. For instance, Daniel Wren describes in his famous work how ancient Egyptians used methods of management: 'Management as an activity has always existed to make people's desires manifest through organized effort. Management facilitates the efforts of people in organized groups and arises when people seek to cooperate to achieve goals. People have always participated in organizations, and organizations have always existed to serve the ends of people' (1994, pp. 10–15). Later in the text, he declares that, prior to the industrial revolution, the first organisations were the house, the tribe, the church, the army and the state. Here, notions of organisation and management are presented as universal and timeless elements thanks to the clear demonstration that the issue of organising collective action is as old as the early moments of humanity. Undoubtedly, coordinating people and resources is a social activity which has always enabled hunting, planting and harvesting, organising day-to-day life or structuring social and housing space. Designing practices to save rare resources or lighten human work has also been a constant preoccupation since prehistory, for all societies are 'organised' with rules and logic more or less consciously shared by their members. Nevertheless, these elements do not allow people to come to the conclusion that the rules of collective action observed in past or distant societies are the same as those used either by current or occidental managers or by the doctrines managers have used since the nineteenth century.

The difficulty, with the legitimacy of management sciences at stake, is to demonstrate why and how in one moment of history (the mid-nineteenth century) certain parts of the world (mainly Western Europe and the United States of America) began to think systematically and consciously about the issues of organising. In this project of dialogue, history could be an important ally for management. The aim of this process is to understand step by step how, as a kind of individual and collective action, practices and sciences of management have emerged.[24] Thanks to history, the definition of normative criteria to validate methodologies or scientific results, prior to any actual scientific research or field study, has lost much of its interest. The loosening of this constraint has allowed a better dialogue with history. How can this dialogue be established? It implies some heavy recontextualisation.

Understanding the organisational structure of enterprises, the rules and tools of management and their influence on the coordination of individual behaviour and collective action could be a common scientific goal to work towards. Beyond geographical or historical differences, all of these are designed to articulate the convergence of people toward a common objective. Enterprises – like other forms of organisations – cannot be seen as transparent or as empty shells filled with imported general social rules. The enterprise must be analysed as a specific place for devising rules which make the institutionalisation of the organisation and the working relations of its members possible. Through this process, enterprises contribute to the evolution of macrosocial institutions and to the reproduction of certain rules modelled by the latter. We can therefore conclude that the environment historically and socially validates and embeds organisations and rules originally targeted at the needs of production and coordination. Once historians and management academics have recognised this renewed epistemological paradigm, several practical details will have to be worked out to instil an interdisciplinary dialogue.

A first point of divergence is the importance of methodology in the research mechanism and the role it plays in the recognition process of researchers within their discipline and, more broadly, in the acceptance process of management sciences within the social sciences. For history, methodological expertise is not a prerequisite to be fulfilled before start-ing research. This does not mean, as some management academics seem to think, that history is not interested in methods. On the contrary, there have often been intense debates on methodology which have regularly shaken the discipline (see for instance Veyne 1979 or more recently Noiriel 1997 and Bédarrida 1997). Using a myriad of facts, historians, step by step, construct a scheme. In an inductive process, they combine intui-tion and validation through cross-controls and confrontations between sources, hypotheses and disciplines in order to answer a set of questions. In writing history, historians' elegance relies on their ability to hide them-selves, and the method they have used, behind the narration. Their 'techni-cal' expertise appears in the closeness between the results they present and the social realities they are working on (Braudel 1984, p. 23). Is it possible, then, to have their results scientifically recognised?

This short text does not make it possible to present an exhaustive study of the answers which have been recognised throughout time and space. However, for a long time, the field of history sought objectivity by using positive epistemology. Focusing on objective methods and on subjects from the distant past seemed to guarantee a healthy separation from sub-jective interests and any emotional reactions of the researchers, which in turn protected the objectivity and a scientific historical approach (Noiriel 1997, p. 41). From this position, history could not study current issues and objects or those judged to be subjective, like contemporary history or indi-vidual and social mentalities. Neither could it focus on organisations and enterprises seen as strictly determined by the social environment. Thus, it was better to study a branch, a local market or national economic and social structures. Even if, from time to time, corporate history or current history are once again being criticised, this suspicion has globally been overcome (Godelier 1998). Community recognition by peers has long played a fundamental role in the scientific validation of historical research. The immense size of the field to be studied, the complexity of dependencies between topics, and the multitude of temporalities suppose a continuous dialogue among historians, which allows a coordination and combination of research. This also creates an 'increase in the number of concepts at the historian's disposal and therefore a lengthening list of questions he will be able to apply to his documents' (Veyne 1979, p. 147).

In contrast, in management sciences, methodology plays an important role in the design and validation of the research process. For numerous academics, it is not only a support for knowledge production but also a lever toward institutional and social recognition of their own work and of the entire discipline. One reason for this particular attention is the fact that management sciences struggled for a long time to establish a separate identity from economic methodologies (Lorino 1991). Leading to recognition and epistemological legitimacy, methodology has increasingly been seen as the cornerstone for management research processes. The robust discussions between the supporters of constructivism (Louart and Desreumaux 1997) and qualitative methods and those in favour of quantitative methods are clear proof of this trend. Nevertheless, in both camps, management academics seem to have adopted a vision of the method as a technology to be learned prior to the beginning of the research process. This thought process can also be explained by the epistemological paradigm which dominates management sciences and from which management is seen to have a strong position among the social sciences owing to its being a descriptive and explicative science, but also a predictive one. Management sciences devise a plan to support an action thanks to more or less normative knowledge (Riveline 1991), aiming to improve the efficiency of managers (for instance Mintzberg 1994a, p. 24) in their day-to-day actions. This is not an easy task, because management sciences have to prove their conceptual and operational strengths. Can history be useful for such a programme? The answer depends on the epistemological paradigm used by management academics. It also depends on whether the dialogue is carried on with researchers or management practitioners.

If management sciences try to programme their development by strictly following a certain vision of the history and formalisation of natural sciences, dialogue will be difficult. This means that history should be subordinate to management questions and concepts. More and more management academics are writing papers and doing research presented as history. Unfortunately, most of these attempts are a list of chronologically aligned facts called 'history', based on a very short period of analysis (five to ten years at the most), when the academics involved obviously know little about the rigour and concepts used by professional historians. This often leads to the publication of smallish books with few questions and little analysis (Roche 1986, p. 19). Such a trend could lead to a negative vision of management as an arrogant discipline, attempting to explain, on its own, the multiple dimensions of its subjects, when they are, in fact, a complex combination of techniques, economics and social dimensions. This quick detour into history might seem easy and accessible even to those without training, but it is subject to a boomerang effect. It seems to be the ultimate proof for certain management academics that the field of history lacks conceptual rigour and systematic methodology. However, others in the same scientific field take a different view.

They see history as a discipline which could help management sciences to understand managerial thought and practice. This supposes a historical approach to the discipline to understand how the technical tools, leading managers, educational institutions, and networks used to diffuse doctrines and general know-how have actually emerged. It might also be helpful to rebuild the path followed by management models and study the influences between enterprises, regions and even countries. Here history could be a major influence in management sciences clearly understanding how management models have appeared. It could nourish the scientific discussions in management sciences, bringing more factual critical analysis of their sources (Ronan 1988)[25] and intellectual categories (Midler 1986) as well as a better knowledge of general management practices, thus being a catalyst for the development of the discipline. This scientific dialogue compels historians to be aware of the debates, and their results, within management sciences, but without being blindly submissive to them. This dialogue must consider the possibilities and the constraints of interdisciplinary transmission of concepts and methods (Livian and Louart 1993). This use of history is founded on a strong assumption: that the variety and complexity of management issues impose a multidisciplinary approach. Management practices must be studied from an objective point of view. Exactly as Marcel Mauss (1923–24) describes the ultimate goal for all social sciences, management facts must be analysed as a complete social fact. This project could lead to the reinforcement of management results and theories as soon as they have successfully passed the 'fact examination' of history. Managers are just as concerned by the dialogue between management and history as academics.

For managers, history is very often used to provide success stories or to underline the excellence of corporate methods or the high quality of CEO leadership and charisma. Here history is narrowed to a kind of erudite journalism. More rarely, history is used as a way of rigorously retracing the evolution or dynamics of a management tool or a doctrine.[26] Visiting the past therefore could be a first step toward a diagnosis of management problems and, eventually, a guide for change. This approach is not very far from those used by re-engineering or benchmarking models. Nevertheless, an efficient dialogue between historians and managers supposes that the latter would be ready to allow the former to reveal not only the official paths of management processes, but also management's hesitations and mistakes. Thus, it becomes possible to draw a genealogy of tools, individual or collective representations, and the unconscious logic and behaviour of members. Here history is a lever for unlearning and change, converging toward Donald Schön's conclusions (Argyris 1995). And finally, let us not forget that history is a requirement for specific parts of management, such as corporate culture or human resources management, where the influence of time has to be taken into account.

Clearly management sciences and history share common interests as soon as they are ready to put aside and/or clarify the origins of the methods, paradigms and epistemologies each of them uses. The aim is not to bring the two disciplines completely together, but rather to improve the quality and knowledge of enterprises and organisation in both disciplines. Last, but not least, all these opportunities could prevent managers and management science academics from naïvely believing that rational tools and determination are powerful enough to change reality or the behaviour and reactions of corporate members. If the central objective of management is to realise the full potential of the enterprise (Cohen 1997, pp. 1164, 1170), a return to the past reveals that success and efficiency rely, unsurprisingly, on managers' charisma and leaders' technical expertise, but, more importantly, it shows that their main strength is their ability to create good conditions for cooperation and coordination between corporation members with divergent motivations, means and personal strategies.

1.3   CONCLUSION

To conclude, the difficulty of management sciences in recognising their status as social sciences could be explained by the tensions between two opposite strategies of social and academic recognition. On the one hand is the development of a critical epistemology or a rigorous methodology able to devise a relationship with actual management practices and day-to-day action. Therefore management has to renounce, at least partially, its informal and unconscious posture as the science for enterprise and the progress of capitalism. On the other hand, management sciences could decide to become the scientific legitimation of managerial and corporate social logic and official hierarchy. Claiming the ability to deal with all social actions, they could become *the* science of society once society is conceived as a network of actors and a set of decisions and/or formal organisation processes. For instance, management could be seen by its supporters as more efficient and, gradually, more legitimate as organiser of all political or public management criteria or processes (Gaulejac 2005). The future will tell which strategy could win this race.

NOTES

1. This chapter will focus on the post-Second World War period in France, when the issue of improving the scientific quality of management began to be important. For the previous period see E. Godelier (2004).

2. V. Roux, *De l'influence du gouvernement sur la prospérité du commerce*; J.-B. Say, *Cours complet d'économie politique appliquée*; J.-G. Courcelle-Seneuil, *Manuel des affaires*.

3. The future ESCP Europe business school was established in the rue de la République in Paris. HEC was not set up until 1881. Two educational institutions had existed since the late eighteenth century: the school of Koechlin and Thierry in Mulhouse (1781) and, at approximately the same period, the 'farm-school' of the Duc de La Rochefoucauld-Liancourt (Grelon 1997, p. 30). For more details on the history of French business schools, see the special issue of *Entreprises et histoire*, **14–15**, June 1997.

4. In the USA in 1880, the American Society of Mechanical Engineers was created. In France the Union Sociale des Ingénieurs Catholiques (USIC) was founded in 1905. It replaced the association Abeille organised by the École Centrale Alumnis. There were other networks of engineers, for instance the Civil Engineers Society, created in 1848, or the first engineer alumni associations like the Gad'zarts (École des arts et métiers). I thank A. Grelon for this information.

5. This duality or ambiguity continues to influence the recruitment processes of managers and leaders in modern organisations, as well as the way management is taught in business schools (Chessel and Pavis 2001).

6. For a long time, Taylor refused to teach his scientific principles, arguing that management courses could not be separated from field practice. In the end, he agreed to design and present a course between 1909 and 1914 (Wren 1994, p. 199).

7. Brandeis invented the term 'Taylorism', which was criticised by Taylor himself as too academic (Wren 1994, p. 120).

8. More and more research is available on this topic. See for instance Locke (1989) or Chessel and Pavis (2001).

9. In France, business schools are established outside the universities. More generally, most of the French elite are selected for and educated in specific institutions named *grandes écoles* situated outside the French universities.

10. The first IAE started in 1955 in Aix-en-Provence, launched by Gaston Berger and Pierre Tabatoni. For more details see Batsch (2009).

11. The Fondation nationale pour l'enseignement de la gestion des entreprises (the National Foundation for Corporations' Management Education) was established in 1966 and officially launched in 1968 (Chessel and Pavis 2001, p. 45).

12. From 1969, candidates competing for the economics or law exam had the opportunity to select an option in 'management'. In 2000, in the management examination, the 24-hour 'practical' option or lesson was dropped because of the significant logistical costs that had to be borne by candidates living outside Paris.

13. In 1982, the research public body the CNRS recognised the discipline with the first appointment of a research director in management sciences.

14. Nonaka became a well-known reference at that time.

15. A longer version has been published on BHC On-Line 2008.

16. I define 'management historians' as academics who are educated in management, but also familiar with the field of history.

17. I define 'professional historians' as those educated and trained in the field of history.

18. Especially marketing and finance, but also positivist research from other fields (human resources management and strategic management, for example).

19. This can be seen from the growing number of unsolicited papers which are received by the editors of the French business history review *Entreprises et histoire*.

20. Bertrand Gille (1920–80) founded the corporation section of the French National Archives. Jean Bouvier (1920–87) was one of the most important specialists in bank history in France.

21. Roger Martin (1915–2008) was educated at the École Polytechnique. After the Second World War, he played an important role in the modernisation of the French steel industry. Recruited and promoted in the tube-making company Pont-à-Mousson, he organised an important strategic move from the steel to the glass industry in the late

1960s. He transformed Pont-à-Mousson into Saint-Gobain, which is today one of the leading glass companies in the world.
22. For a complete overview of James March's work in French, see Godelier (2003) or Weil (2000).
23. This is for instance apparent with some supporters of 'agency theories' or of 'transaction cost theories' which are the core of management sciences nowadays. See, in French, Gabrié and Jacquier (1994).
24. Sociology has already started this historical work on the birth of the discipline through the controversies which opposed Émile Durkheim to historians like Denys Fustel de Coulanges (Berthelot 2000).
25. An example is the way French management sciences present bibliographies and footnotes, giving more visibility to recent authors instead of older ones, or to quantity rather than quality with long lists of references which are not always integrated critically by the researcher.
26. See the works of Yannick Lemarchand or Nicolas Berland on the history of amortisation or budget control. On management models, my colleague Jean-Louis Peaucelle has visited Henri Fayol's family archives.

REFERENCES

Argyris, Chris (1995), *Savoir pour agir: Surmonter les obstacles à l'apprentissage organisationnel*, Paris: InterÉditions.
Barjot, D. (ed.) (2002), *Catching up with America: Productivity Missions and the Diffusion of American Economic and Technological Influence after the Second World War*, Paris: Presses de l'Université de Paris-Sorbonne.
Batsch, L. (2002), *Le Capitalisme financier*, Coll. Repères, Paris: La Découverte.
Batsch, L. (ed.) (2009), 'Hommage à Pierre Tabatoni', unpublished paper, Université Paris-Dauphine, March.
Bédarrida, François (ed.) (1997), *L'Histoire et le métier d'historien en France (1945–1995)*, Paris: Éditions de la MSH.
Beltran, Alain, Jean-Pierre Daviet and Michèle Ruffat (1995), 'L'histoire d'entreprise en France: essai bibliographique', *Les Cahiers de l'IHTP*, **30**, June.
Berry, M. (1984), 'Ethnographie des organisations', Séminaire du CRG, École Polytechnique.
Berthelot, Jean-Michel (2000), 'La sociologie: histoire d'une discipline', in Karl Van Meter (ed.), *La Sociologie*, Paris: Larousse, pp. 11–26.
Boltanski, L. (1982), *Les Cadres: La formation d'un groupe social*, Paris: Les éditions de minuit.
Bonnafous-Boucher, Maria (2005), *Anthropologie et gestion*, Paris: Economica.
Bouffartigue, P. (ed.) (2001), *Les Cadres: La grande rupture*, Coll. Recherche, Paris: La découverte.
Bouilloud, J.-P. and B.-P. Lecuyer (eds) (1994), *L'Invention de la gestion: Histoire et pratiques*, Paris: L'Harmattan.
Bourdé, Guy and Hervé Martin (1983), *Les Écoles historiques*, Coll. Points, Paris: Le Seuil.
Bouvier, Jean ([1961] 1999), *Le Crédit Lyonnais de 1863 à 1882*, Paris: Éditions de l'EHESS.
Bouvier, Jean (1973), *Un siècle de banque française*, Paris: Hachette.
Boyer, R. (1986), *La Flexibilité du travail en Europe*, Paris: La Découverte.

Braudel, Fernand (1984), *Écrits sur l'histoire*, Coll. Champs, Paris: Flammarion.

Chandler, Alfred (1962), *Strategy and Structure: Chapters in the History of Industrial Enterprise*, Cambridge, MA: Massachusetts Institute of Technology.

Chessel, M.-E. and F. Pavis (2001), *Le Technocrate, le patron et le professeur: Une histoire de l'enseignement supérieur de gestion*, Coll. Histoire de l'éducation, Paris: Belin.

Cohen, E. (1997), 'Épistémologie de la gestion', in Y. Simon and P. Joffre (eds), *Encyclopédie de gestion*, vol. I, Paris: Economica, pp. 1159–78.

Déry, R. (1994), 'Enjeux et controverses épistémologiques dans le champ des sciences de gestion', in J.-P. Bouilloud and B.-P. Lecuyer (eds), *L'Invention de la gestion: Histoire et pratiques*, Paris: L'Harmattan, pp. 163–89.

Doublet, Jean-Marie and Patrick Fridenson (1988), 'L'histoire et la gestion: un pari', *Revue française de gestion*, **70**, September–October, 1–3.

Doublet, Jean-Marie and Patrick Fridenson (eds) (1998), *Revue française de gestion*, Special issue, **70**, October–November.

Folhen, Claude (1955), 'Une affaire de famille au XIXe siècle: Méquillet-Noblot', PhD thesis, Université Paris 1.

Franck, Robert (ed.) (1993), *Écrire l'histoire du temps présent*, Paris: Éditions du CNRS.

Fridenson, P. (1987), 'Un tourant taylorien de la société française (1904–1918)', *Annales ESC*, **5**, September–October, 1031–60.

Fridenson, Patrick (1989), 'Les organisations, un nouvel objet', *Annales ESC*, **6**, November–December, 1461–77.

Gabrié, Hubert and Jean-Louis Jacquier (1994), *La Théorie moderne de la firme*, Paris: Economica.

Gaulejac, Vincent de (2005), *La Société malade de la gestion: Idéologie gestionnaire, pouvoir managérial et harcèlement social*, Paris: Le Seuil.

Gille, Bertrand (1961), 'La fondation de la Société générale', *Histoire des entreprises*, **8**, November.

Girin, Jacques (1990), 'L'analyse empirique des situations de gestion: éléments de théorie et de méthode', in Alain Charles Martinet (ed.), *Épistémologie et sciences de gestion*, Paris: Economica, pp. 141–82.

Godelier, Eric (1998), 'Le discours politique: source vivante ou source figée?', in *Pierre Bérégovoy: Une volonté de réforme au service de l'économie (1984–1993)*, Paris: Éditions du CHEFF, Ministère de l'économie et des finances, pp. 51–8.

Godelier, Eric (ed.) (2003), *James March: Penser l'organisation*, Paris: Hermès.

Godelier, E. (2004), 'Le changement de l'entreprise vu par les sciences de gestion ou l'introuvable conciliation de la science et de la pratique', *Entreprises et histoire*, **35**, 31–44.

Godelier, E. and M.-D. Seiffert (eds) (2008), 'Histoire et gestion: vingt ans après', *Revue française de gestion*, **188–189**, November–December.

Godelier, Maurice (2007), *Au fondement des sociétés humaines*, Paris: Albin Michel.

Goffin, R. (1998), *Principes de finance moderne*, Paris: Economica.

Grelon, André (1997), 'Écoles de commerce et formations d'ingénieurs jusqu'en 1914', *Entreprises et histoire*, **14–15**, 29–45.

Guigueno, V. (1994), *L'Éclipse de l'atelier: Les missions françaises de productivité aux Etats-Unis dans les années 1950. Mémoire de DEA*, Paris: ENPC/Université Marne-la-Vallée.

Hatchuel, A. (1994), 'Frédéric Taylor: une lecture épistémologique. L'expert, le théoricien, le doctrinaire', in J.-P. Bouilloud and B.-P. Lecuyer (eds), *L'Invention de la gestion: Histoire et pratiques*, Paris: L'Harmattan.

Hatchuel, A. (2001), 'Quels horizons pour les sciences de gestion? Vers une théorie de l'action collective', in A. David, A. Hatchuel and R. Laufer (eds), *Les Nouvelles Fondations des sciences de gestion: Éléments d'épistémologie de la recherche en management*, Paris: Vuibert, Coll. FNEGE.

Heffer, Jean (2006), 'Nouvelle histoire économique', *Encyclopédie Universalis*, Paris, CD Rom.

Livian, Yves-Frédéric and Pierre Louart (1993), 'Le voyage de la culture et de la motivation des sciences sociales à la GRH', in Julienne Brabet (ed.), *Repenser la gestion des ressources humaines*, Paris: Economica, pp. 39–67.

Locke, R. (1989), *Management and Higher Education since 1940: The Influence of America and Japan on West Germany, Great Britain and France*, Cambridge: Cambridge University Press.

Lorino, Philippe (1991), *L'Économiste et le manager*, Paris: Éditions La Découverte.

Louart, Pierre and Alain Desreumaux (eds) (1997), *Constructivisme(s) et sciences de gestion*, Actes du colloque, Lille: Université des Sciences et Technologies de Lille.

Marchand, O. and C. Thélot (1997), *Le Travail en France*, Coll. Essais et recherches, Paris: Nathan.

Marmonnier, Luc and Raymond-Alain Thiétart (1988), 'L'histoire, un outil pour la gestion?', *Revue française de gestion*, **70**, September–October, 162–71.

Martin, Roger (1992), 'Stratégie industrielle: l'éternel retour?', *Entreprises et histoire*, **1**, April, 3.

Mauss, M. (1923–24), 'Essai sur le don: forme et raison de l'échange dans les sociétés archaïques', *L'Année sociologique*, second series, **1**, in M. Mauss, *Sociologie et anthropologie*, Coll. Quadridge, Paris: PUF.

McKenna, C. (2006), *The World's Newest Profession: Management Consulting in the Twentieth Century*, Cambridge: Cambridge University Press.

Midler, Christophe (1986), 'Logique de la mode managériale', *Annales des Mines: Gérer et comprendre*, **3**, June, 74–85.

Mintzberg, Henri (1994a), *Grandeur et décadence de la planification stratégique*, Paris: Dunod.

Mintzberg, H. (1994b), *The Rise and Fall of Strategic Planning*, New York: Free Press.

Noiriel, Gérard (1997), *Sur la 'crise' de l'histoire*, Paris: Belin.

Ohno, T. (1980), *L'Esprit Toyota*, Paris: Masson.

Pérez, R. (1999), Rapport au Ministre de l'éducation nationale, de la recherche et de la technologie sur les disciplines de gestion, Paris.

Pollard, S. (1968), *The Genesis of Modern Management: A Study of the Industrial Revolution in Great Britain*, 2nd edn, Harmondsworth: Penguin.

Pras, B. (1997), 'Qu'est-ce que le marketing?', in Y. Simon and P. Joffre (eds), *Encyclopédie de gestion*, 2nd edn, vol. 3, Paris: Economica, pp. 2753–80.

Riveline, Claude (1991), 'Un point de vue d'ingénieur sur la gestion', *Annales des Mines: Gérer et comprendre*, **25**, December, 50–62.

Roche, Daniel (1986), 'Les historiens aujourd'hui: remarques pour un débat', *Vingtième siècle*, **12**, October–December.

Ronan, C. (1988), *Histoire mondiale des sciences*, Coll. Points, Paris: Le Seuil.

Simon, H.(1981), *The Sciences of the Artificial*, Cambridge, MA: MIT Press.

Taylor, F. (1990), 'Direction des ateliers', in F. Vatin (ed.), *Organisation du travail et économie des entreprises*, Paris: Les Éditions d'organisation, pp. 27–138.

Veyne, Paul (1979), *Comment on écrit l'histoire*, Coll. Points, Paris: Le Seuil.

Vilar, Pierre (2006), 'Histoire économique', *Encyclopédie Universalis*, Paris, CD Rom.

Weil, Thierry (2000), *Initiation à la lecture de James March*, Paris: Presses de l'ENSMP.

Wren, D. (1994), *The Evolution of Management Thought*, 4th edn, New York: John Wiley.

Zeitlin, J. and G. Herrigel (eds) (2004), *Americanization and its Limits: Reworking US Technology and Management in Post-War Europe and Japan*, Oxford: Oxford University Press.

2. Proposition for a comparative history of education in law and management: about the notion of jurisprudence

Romain Laufer

In 1887, Woodrow Wilson, who later became president of the United States, began what is often considered as the first academic article dealing with the science of administration with the following words:

> I suppose that no practical science is ever studied where there is no need to know it. The very fact, therefore, that the eminently practical science of administration is finding its way into college courses in this country would prove that this country needs to know more about administration, were such proof of the fact required to make out a case. (p. 197)

This quotation contains two propositions relative to the history of management education in the United States which are worth noting. On the one hand it dates the beginning of the academic development of the 'eminently practical science of administration' to the end of the nineteenth century. On the other hand it relates this emergence to a need resulting from the state of society at that time.

If the curriculum of universities is the place where one can find the signs of the existence of a practical need for some specific kind of academic knowledge, then we must acknowledge that the need for the study of administration has never stopped being felt since Woodrow Wilson wrote these lines. Business schools have developed all over the world, MBAs have been created which attract an ever growing number of students, doctoral programmes have emerged to provide these schools and students with professors, and high-quality academic journals have proliferated which contain the knowledge developed by doctoral students and their professors.

If this historical development is to be considered as the reflection of the state of society then one should not be surprised if the uncertainties of our times express themselves in the growing number of questions, objections and criticisms addressed to the role played by business schools in this conjecture. These criticisms are addressed both to the relevance of teaching and research developed in the schools and to their potential responsibility for the development of the present global crisis, be it because of the dominant models of management which have come to be developed and promoted with a minimum amount of caveats (such as sophisticated financial instruments, 'mark to market' accounting, and the principle of the maximisation of 'shareholder value', which have often been considered as playing an important role in the development of the present crisis) or because of the way in which they failed to develop adequate ethical standards in an economic world which tended to be ever more dominated by the obsession with monetary gains. This last point has led to an innovation whose symbolic meaning cannot be overstated: a new ritual has recently been introduced in the commencement ceremony of the Harvard MBA: an oath is to be sworn in a way which was, until now, reserved to members of specific professions such as doctors and lawyers.

We would like to show that this event is just another example of the way in which the history of academic teaching and research in management has constantly been connected to the history of academic research and teaching in law. To establish this proposition we shall have to consider the three following questions: 1) the question of the meaning of this connection between law and management as fields of academic study; 2) the question of the existence of a method which allows the establishment and study of this connection with precision; and 3) the question of the way in which such an analysis could allow us to better understand the present state of economic and social uncertainty as it expresses itself in the development of the present global crisis or in the fears associated with the recent development of the notion of major and /or catastrophic risks and with the very general and enduring feeling which has been lingering for so many decades now that the world is becoming ever more complex and uncertain.

To these three questions correspond three arguments:

1. The first of these arguments states that, as law belongs by definition to the realm of social institutions, the fact of considering management from the point of view of its connections with law implies that we propose to study management from an institutional point of view. From that point of view the introduction of a practical field of knowledge in the programmes of universities may be interpreted as corresponding to a shift in the degree of institutionalisation of this very field of knowledge.

2. The second argument states that such an institutional approach to the history of management as an academic discipline can be best developed if one considers the history of the specific branch of the academic teaching of law known as jurisprudence.

3. As for the third argument, it states that one can rely on the work of British anthropologist Mary Douglas to link in a precise manner what appears as a generalised feeling of uncertainty with the notion of institution. The issue of certainty and uncertainty which we met at the very beginning of our analysis (through the way in which the relevance of the teaching and research developed in academia is being questioned) will constitute the centre of our argument.

To develop such an argument within the limits of a chapter would not be possible if it could not be considered on the one hand as the expression of a method for the study of social institutions – a method centred on the notion of a system of legitimacy – which has been developed over many years in many publications to which we are able to refer when necessary (Laufer and Paradeise 1990; Laufer 2009) and on the other hand as the expression of a future programme of research which, by definition, can be stated only in a relatively cursory manner.

The argument will be developed in four sections. Section 2.1 contains a general presentation of a hypothesis linking uncertainty, law and management through the notion of jurisprudence which pertains to the realm of legal institutions. Section 2.2 shows how the increasing need for a common definition of management has manifested itself in academic journals since the 1960s. Section 2.3 shows, relying on a concrete example (an analysis of the preface to *The Functions of the Executive* by Chester Barnard), how it is possible to establish in a precise manner the link between management, the notion of jurisprudence and the development of research and teaching in management. Section 2.4 deals with questions of method, that is, the way in which the notion of a system of legitimacy (such as has been developed over the years in many previous publications) could allow us to link in a precise manner the history of the development of the academic field of management with the history of the transformations in legal norms. Section 2.4 corresponds to a proposition both for the test of our general hypothesis and for the development of a practical programme of research relative to the history of teaching and research in management. To conclude, potential consequences of this analysis for the future of research and teaching in management will then be considered.

2.1 GENERAL PRESENTATION OF THE HYPOTHESIS LINKING UNCERTAINTY, LAW AND MANAGEMENT

To develop our hypothesis we shall proceed in three steps: first we shall consider the way in which Mary Douglas allows us to link in a very precise manner the notions of certainty and uncertainty and the notion of institution; then we shall address the link that can be established between management and jurisprudence; finally we shall show through a concrete historical example (an analysis of the preface of *The Functions of the Executive* by Chester Barnard) how one can establish empirically the link between jurisprudence and the development of research and teaching in management.

2.1.1   Uncertainty and Institutions According to Mary Douglas

In an article entitled 'Dealing with uncertainty' Mary Douglas writes:

> Certainty is not a mood, or a feeling, it is an institution: this is my thesis. Certainty is only possible because doubt is blocked institutionally: most individual decisions about risk are taken under pressure of institutions. If we recognise more uncertainty now, it will be because of things that have happened to the institutional underpinning of our beliefs. And that is what we ought to be studying. (p. 145)

Three propositions are thus stated: 1) There is an intimate relationship between the notions of certainty and uncertainty and the notion of institution. 2) The recognition of the fact that we live in an uncertain world is the result of a historical transformation in the institutional fabric of our world. 3) These two points should lead us to adopt a programme of research centred on the study of the institutional underpinning of our beliefs.

To this general statement she adds the four following comments:

> We need certainty as a basis for settling disputes. It is not for intellectual satisfaction, nor for accuracy of prediction for its own sake, but for political and forensic reasons. (p. 146)

> The real problem is not knowledge but agreement. (p. 146)

> A liberal democracy ... needs authority to back interpretation and control dissent. (p. 146)

> [W]e have definitely entered a period where uncertainty is formally recognized. This very esoteric aspect of our culture might have some theoretical interest

for risk analysis. For the present argument what is important is that it would inevitably have arrived in some form or other in an open democracy. The form it takes with us is mathematical, analytical, the result of pushing to extremes the forensic aspects of certainty, and trying to extend the certainty-seeking practice of science. (p. 147)

From these comments we can derive the three following propositions: 1) The notion of conflict and conflict resolution is central to the definition of institutions proposed by Mary Douglas. 2) If the authority which allows the control of dissent in a democracy can be described as relying on law and science, one is entitled to recognise in it a form of Max Weber's legal-rational type of legitimate authority (as opposed to the charismatic or the traditional types of legitimate authority). 3) In a democracy there is a dynamic mechanism linked to the principle of individual freedom, allowing an explanation of the historical process of institutional transformation, which leads to a situation where arguments drawn from law and science are pushed to their limits, that is, to a point where uncertainty has to be explicitly recognised.

Mary Douglas's definition of institutions provides some justification for the way in which we propose to link the analysis of the institutionalisation of management to a study of the teaching of law. It remains to be explained in what sense the notion of jurisprudence can be instrumental in establishing such a link.

However, before dealing directly with the relationship between management and jurisprudence we must first try to resolve a linguistic puzzle associated with this last notion.

2.1.2   Resolving a Linguistic Puzzle Relative to the Notion of Jurisprudence

The first merit of the notion of jurisprudence is that it reminds us that, if the institutions of all Western democracies rely on a legal system, legal systems differ from country to country: institutions are defined nationally. The word 'jurisprudence' does not have the same meaning in English and in French. From that point of view we could say that our purpose is to study what this difference may teach us about the meaning of 'management', a word, by the way, which originally belonged to the French vocabulary and which has never ceased to circulate between the French and English languages to the point where the French language became unable to recognise it as its own and the French Academy had to decide (in the early 1970s) that it could be admitted into the French language as an Anglicism, as if it had been previously banished. Before we go any further into the exploration of the meanings of the word 'jurisprudence' it is worth noting that we should not be surprised if, in analysing institutions, we have to consider questions of language, for language constitutes in itself one of the major building blocks of the institutions of a society. From that point of view the very fact that, in France, language, like law, has to be defined officially by a set of coherent propositions elaborated by the decisions of an official assembly must be considered as an illustration of one of the major idiosyncratic features of its institutional imagination.

Let us consider now the notion of jurisprudence. In France since 1610, according to a historical dictionary of the French language (Rey 2006), this word has described 'the set of all the jurisdictional decisions which have been taken on a given matter or in a given country, considered as a source of law'. In modern English the first meaning of 'jurisprudence' according to the Oxford dictionary is 'theory or philosophy of law'. This difference seems to contradict the common view relative to the way in which French dogmatism is opposed to British empiricism or American pragmatism: it is those who are supposed to rely the least on theory who give the more theoretical meaning to the notion of jurisprudence, while those who are supposed to be the more dogmatic choose a definition which seems to be made to correspond to the actual practice of the courts.

The paradoxical character of this situation expresses itself in a similar manner when one considers the way in which one traditionally opposes countries dominated by a system of common law, where law is supposed to be gradually elaborated by the way in which courts are led to deal with the cases which are brought in front of them, and countries dominated by a system of civil law, where law is supposed to be defined by a coherent set of normative rules defined a priori, the task of the courts being to submit to these codified rules the diversity of the cases which are brought in front of them.

This paradox becomes even more striking when one considers the difference in the status given to the theory or philosophy of law in the curriculum of legal studies in France and the United States: while American universities have given an important place in the teaching of law schools to jurisprudence (in the Anglo-Saxon meaning of the word) at least since the end of the nineteenth century, French *facultés de droit* have not included philosophy of law in the curriculum until very recently.

What the difference between the teaching of law in France and the United States seems to tell us is that, in the field of law, dogmatism (considering law as a code one is supposed to apply) tends to avoid theory while pragmatism (considering law as an elaboration which results from the resolution of a long sequence of singular cases) seems to imply that due respect be paid to it. This can be understood if we note that in the first case jurisprudence is defined as what is necessary to connect the norms contained in the codes with the infinitely diverse character of reality as it manifests itself through the cases which are submitted to the courts: philosophy of law must keep quiet if it wants to avoid any rivalry with the norms which it is supposed to sustain. It is because the starting point of American law is the infinite complexity and diversity of conflict situations which are brought in front of judges, who lie between an old common law which has been abolished (when the United States declared independence from the British Crown) and the new common law which they are supposed to elaborate, that theory becomes necessary to put some order into what would otherwise appear as the product of purely arbitrary decisions unable to bring to citizens any degree of juridical security: in this case jurisprudence is the theoretical or philosophical effort which law must accomplish to give some degree of meaning to the multiplicity of cases which are submitted to its rulings. It is this meaning of the notion of jurisprudence which we are going to consider in what follows.

2.1.3   Management as Jurisprudence

These considerations relative to the notion of jurisprudence allow us to propose a first intuitive justification of our hypothesis. Management is usually considered as being an essentially pragmatic field of action. That is why many professionals tend to consider managerial theories and, even more, general theories of management with scepticism. Many would be tempted to consider such a project as an ultimate consequence of the type of Cartesian spirit commonly associated with a typically French form of intellectualism that pragmatism is supposed to condemn. Indeed, is management anything else but the radical form of a pragmatic imperative which states that managers must do what they can? They must manage in the sense of muddling through; they must adopt the most appropriate course of action when confronted with the type of singular situations which are the fabric of the world business people have to face in their everyday life. Is it not what is expressed in the teaching of management being dominated by the well-known case method? But if that is so, is it not possible to compare the situation of managers to that of American judges, who, for lack of a formal code defined a priori which they would just have to apply to the cases brought in front of them, have to elaborate for each case the decision best suited to the singular circumstances they must consider? In front of the infinite multiplicity and diversity of individual cases, how could the American common law judges, in the same manner as managers, justify their decisions to anybody, including themselves, if they could not relate them to some rational principles (such as the rationale or 'reason why' that the most pragmatic of managers never hesitate to require from those who are supposed to recommend some course of action). Thus it is precisely because management is pragmatic, because it accepts each case as unique and, if successful, as a potential model for future occurrences, that managers, like American common law judges, need to be able to refer to some system of jurisprudence without which their decisions, which are the expression of their discretionary power, would run the risk of being considered arbitrary. Consequently one can understand why the first books which ever dealt with management proudly wore the name of 'principles', whether they were the 'principles of scientific management' or the 14 principles which constitute the core of Henri Fayol's *Administration industrielle et générale*.

We could say that this vision of systems of law and management which have to be all the more theoretical (in the Cartesian meaning of the term) in that they define themselves as being pragmatic (in the American meaning of the term) can be considered as an occasion of verifying what Alexis de Tocqueville (1840, p. 2) tells us of the relationship which binds America to Descartes: 'America is therefore one of the countries in the world where philosophy is least studied and where the precepts of Descartes are best followed.'

Before examining our hypothesis any further, we must consider why such a proposition has not been stated before. For this purpose we shall follow the lead indicated above by Woodrow Wilson: if a new manner of dealing with a practical field of knowledge such as management appears, it will be because some need for it is being felt. To show the existence of such a need we shall turn our attention towards the debate relative to the definition of the notion of management as it has developed in academia since the 1960s.

2.2   THE INCREASING NEED FOR A COMMON ACADEMIC DEFINITION OF MANAGEMENT

In a seminal article entitled 'The management theory jungle' (1961), Harold Koontz, who was to become president of the Academy of Management (in 1963) and chancellor of the International Academy of Management (until 1975), wrote:

> Although students of management would readily agree that there have been problems of management since the dawn of organised life, most would agree that systematic examination of management, with few exceptions, is the product of the present century and more especially of the last two decades. Moreover, until recent years, almost all those who have attempted to analyse the management process and look for some theoretical underpinnings to help improve research teaching and practice were alert and perceptive practitioners

of the art who reflected on the many years of experiences. Thus, at least in looking at general management as an intellectually based art, the earliest meaningful writings came from such experienced practitioners as Fayol, Mooney, Alvin Brown, Sheldon, Barnard and Urwick.

If we accept the authority of this writer, as seems to have been the case for all those who have had the opportunity to express themselves in the *Academy of Management Journal* since then, we must recognise that a history of the need for a formalisation of the notion of management can be described as the following three stages: the first one stretches from the 'dawn of organised life' until the turn of the twentieth century; the second stage is described in the above quotation as finishing in the early 1940s, since, according to Harold Koontz, most 'systematic examination of management' is supposed to have taken place during the two decades which precede the date of publication of his article in 1961, two decades which constitute the beginning of a third and last stage.

We may note that each of these stages corresponds to a different level of institutionalisation of the notion of management. During the first period management does not exist as an academic field at all; its definition refers to the common meaning of the word in the English language (coping with a problem, muddling through a situation). The second period corresponds to the moment when the need is felt for formal teaching of management; what characterises it is, on the one hand, the foundation of the first business schools (Wharton School of Finance and Commerce in 1881, Tuck School of Business in 1900, Harvard Business School in 1908, and so on) and, on the other hand, the fact that the efforts made to define management as an 'intellectually based art' remained limited to the propositions of 'experienced practitioners'. Finally the third period corresponds to the development of management as a fully fledged academic field of study. This last period is characterised by the development of new academic institutions such as the Academy of Management in 1936, and the proliferation of academic journals such as the *Journal of Marketing* (1936), the *Journal of Finance* (1946), *Management Science* (1954), the *Administrative Science Quarterly* (1956) and the *Academy of Management Journal* (1958).

In an article entitled 'Opportunities ahead for the Academy of Management' in 1960, Joseph W. Towle, the then president of the Academy of Management, could write:

> Today in the midst of our changing American scene, the professor of business administration has finally been recognized on the college campus. His once precarious position among teachers and scholars now appears to be assured. No greater citation of the accomplishment and the value of the business schools can be found than is evidenced by the publication of the Ford and

Carnegie Foundations' reports. Even the criticisms in these reports attest to the importance of the collegiate schools of business.

The transformation of higher education in business proposed by these well-known reports recommended the generalisation of doctoral education for professors in management and the development of research, with an insistence on the need for a greater integration of behavioural sciences as well as for the promotion of the application of quantitative methods and analytic thinking in both teaching and research. However, all these developments were leaving one question untouched: the issue of the very definition of the field of management, which, to use Harold Koontz's words, remained a 'jungle'. It would take too long to consider in detail all the articles which followed Koontz's address to the academic community. We shall content ourselves with singling out two articles.

The first one, 'The management theory jungle revisited', was written by Koontz himself in 1980. What it tells us is that he can only acknowledge the fact that the problem has not been solved but has become more complex: where he had been able to distinguish six 'schools' in his first article, he had now to recognise the presence of 11 different visions of what the field of management is or should be.

The second article, 'The tactics of jungle warfare', was written by Lyndall F. Urwick in the *Academy of Management Journal* in 1963. To give to this very short paper the attention it deserves would require much time and space. We shall content ourselves with the following remarks.

The first remark is that obviously Urwick, who is one of the 'experienced practitioners' whom Koontz was referring to in his article, survived long enough to be able to answer him.

The second remark is that he confirms that there is no consensus on a common definition of management:

'Inky warfare' is both an occupational disease and the favourite hobby of some professors. Through practice they become extremely skilled at the gentle art of verbal infighting. For an outsider who, having been prevented by the demands of a more lethal warfare [a reference to his participation in the Second World War] from proceeding beyond a first degree, is therefore not even a passable academic, to venture into the area of hostilities is therefore a hazardous step. But on the other hand an outside view may be helpful. (Urwick 1963, p. 316)

The third remark is that there is a steady historical trend toward the acceptance of an ever more encompassing definition of the notion of management:

> When the formal study of management was first proposed, rather more than
> half a century ago, and it was first proposed in connection with business under-
> takings [criticism arose from those of different trades] each one saying that
> 'his business is different'.... The man who made boots was quite unable to
> convince himself that he could learn anything from the man who made boats.

This he says has passed, and it is increasingly accepted that management
is equally applicable not only to any business undertaking but to voluntary, government and charitable institutions and indeed to any form of
organized human cooperation for a defined objective.

The fourth remark is related to the way in which Urwick thinks that
it would be possible to produce a consensus on a definition of the field
of management. The method he proposes is borrowed from the formal
process of conflict resolution such as is defined in the institutions of
political life, a process in which the legal system plays a central role:

> The well established distinction between the 'political or legislative, executive
> and judicial' aspect of government can go far to assimilate the views of different
> theorists, if they will once accept it....
>   ... there is therefore an executive function of government, embodied in the
> United States in the Presidency, which deals with action. But, because any indi-
> vidual who deals with action may be oppressive or mistaken in the treatment of
> individuals, there is also a judicial function of government to see that it does not
> happen.
>   Admittedly the judicial function has been very imperfectly developed in
> systems of business government, though some recent legislation is a step in that
> direction. And probably a great deal of the friction in business between manag-
> ers and workers can be traced to the absence of machinery for this purpose.

For our purpose it is particularly interesting to note that the process of
defining management is intimately associated by Urwick with the central
role played by the judicial process in the resolution of conflicts which may
arise in any collective action and especially in the area of business. This is
precisely the point of view which is proposed by our hypothesis.

Before turning to questions of method we would first like to consider
how our hypothesis may be tested on a concrete example.

2.3   CONSIDERING A SPECIFIC EXAMPLE: THE LINK BETWEEN MANAGEMENT THEORY AND JURISPRUDENCE IN THE WORK OF CHESTER BARNARD

If the masterwork of Chester Barnard, *The Functions of the Executive*, is
well known and recognised as one of the most important in the field of

management, it does not seem that the same can be said of the preface which Barnard wrote for it. This is all the more regrettable because of what it tells us of the nature of his project, the difficulties he had to confront in accomplishing it, and the way in which he managed to overcome them.

As we shall see, his project was to establish management as a common language shared by all executives. The major obstacle he had to confront was linked to the ambiguous institutional status of organisations in their relationship with the authority of the state and its laws. As for the solution, it came from his reading of nothing less than two of the major treatises of jurisprudence of the time. Thus this preface allows us to establish the relevance of an approach to the study of management which proposes relying on an analogy with the notion of jurisprudence.

2.3.1　A Language which Allows Executives to Understand One Another

Many times I have noted that executives are able to understand each other with very few words when discussing essential problems of organization, provided the questions are stated without dependence upon the technologies of their respective fields. This is chiefly observable when men of radically different fields discuss such questions. . . . It is not due to any common nomenclature or general study of organization systems.

Until recently there has been little literature that could serve as common understanding. Nothing I knew corresponded either to my experience or to the understanding implicit in the conduct of those organizations. (Barnard [1938] 1968, p. xxvii)

Thus it is by observing executives that Barnard was led to the idea that there exists a common language which allows managers to understand each other and that this language is made possible by the way in which it avoids any reference to the most singular dimensions of the situations they are dealing with ('without dependence upon the technologies of their respective fields').

2.3.2　A Language that No Social Science Has Been Able to Develop

Always it seemed to me, the social scientists [he quotes sociologists, socio-psychologists, economists, political scientists and historians] just reached the edge of the organization as I experienced it and retreated. Rarely did they seem to me to sense the process of coordination and decision that underlies a large part at least of the phenomena they described. More important there was lacking much recognition of formal organization as a most important characteristic of social life and as being a structural dimension of society itself. (Barnard [1938] 1968, xxviii–xxix)

In these words Barnard tells us that management cannot be assimilated into the language of social sciences (as the Ford and Carnegie Foundations would have us believe). Social sciences stop precisely at the point where the language of management takes over.

2.3.3   A Language Not Accounted for Because its Search Has Been Obstructed by the History of Thought Relative to the Origin and Nature of Authority

> The search for the universals of organizations has been obstructed, I suspect, by the long history of thought concerning the nature of the state and of the church. The centre of this thought relates to the origin and nature of authority. Its consequences appear to be legalism that prevents the acceptance of the essential facts of organizations.
>
> No theory of organization that conflicts with the doctrine of the law can be acceptable unless it also explains these doctrines.
>
> The doctrine of states as sources and bases of formal organizations in society – relevant to all corporate organizations, such as those of municipalities, universities, business institutions, armies – is inconsistent with the theory that all states are based upon organizations. But the latter hypothesis cannot be accepted unless it is able to explain both the fact of states and their obvious dominance in some respect over organizations from which they arise. Thus I find myself in an impasse. On the one hand theories which accounted for important aspects of society were unsatisfactory when confronted with the theory of the state. On the other hand, the latter utterly failed, even when spun out of their endless application in judicial decisions to explain the most elemental experience of organized effort. (Barnard [1938] 1968, xxvii)

Issues relative to the theory of the state and of the legal system are the obstacle that one must confront in developing the language of executives. Those who want to venture beyond the 'edge of the organization' must confront the fact that, on the one hand, by the very creative power of their actions executives are participating in the transformation of the institutions of society, but that, on the other hand, the legitimacy of organised action can result only from their submission to the order of the state and its legal system. This allows us to understand why the notion of jurisprudence played such an important role in the elaboration of Barnard's theory of management and in what sense it is possible to give an institutional definition of management as being a quasi-jurisdictional process relative to the conflicts which arise within an organisation: jurisdictional to the extent that it can be considered as a system of conflict resolution, and quasi-jurisdictional to the extent that it remains restricted conventionally within the borders of the organisation and to the extent that the state, having the monopoly of legitimate violence (according to Max Weber), does not have the means to enforce its rulings if they are not accepted: the conflict must then be brought before the courts.

2.3.4 How Barnard Succeeded in Overcoming these Obstacles

Major texts of jurisprudence are quoted by Barnard in relation to the elaboration of his theory:

> It may be of interest if I relate briefly the circumstances which have led me to write this book. The honour of Dr. A. Lawrence Lowell's invitation came at the time when belatedly I was reading Justice Cardozo's Yale Lectures, 'The Nature of the Judicial Process.'
> ... The confusion resulting from these considerations [the impasse quoted above] was first partly overcome by the chance reading of Ehrlich's *Fundamental Principles of the Sociology of Law*. (Barnard [1938] 1968, xxvii)

We may note that Barnard underlines the fact that it is by chance that he came across these texts which allowed him to escape the impasse in which he found himself. The fact that this preface does not seem to have attracted much attention, that the more theoretical dimension of Barnard's work has brought him constant criticism from most of his colleagues, and finally that one of his major disciples, Herbert Simon, has not referred to the notion of jurisprudence in his own work (apart from the relatively indirect fact that rational justification under the regime of bounded rationality is said to be procedural and not substantial) seems to tell us that there must have been good reasons for avoiding giving an explicit status to the link between management and jurisprudence in the Anglo-Saxon meaning of the term. We shall argue that this is due to the fact that the recognition of the institutional nature of management is linked to the explicit recognition of a situation where the existence of uncertainty can no longer be rejected. The way in which Barnard's preface has been ignored could be considered an illustration of the energy with which, according to Mary Douglas, society defends its institutions against the very idea of uncertainty: 'The most fundamental idea which upholds the possibility of society, more fundamental even than the idea of God, is the idea that there can be certain knowledge. And this turns out to be extraordinarily robust, passionately defended by law and taboo in ancient and modern civilizations' (2001, p. 154). It is because we have 'definitely entered a period when uncertainty is formally recognized' that an institutional approach to the notion of management is becoming possible.

2.4   QUESTIONS OF METHOD: THE NOTION OF A SYSTEM OF LEGITIMACY AND THE STUDY OF THE 'INSTITUTIONAL UNDERPINNING OF OUR BELIEFS'

Following the recommendation of Mary Douglas, we propose to centre our study on the 'institutional underpinning of our beliefs', which we shall operationalise thanks to the notions of the legal-rational system of legitimacy, the history of the legal-rational system of legitimacy, and the crisis of the legal-rational system of legitimacy as they have been developed in many texts over several decades.

All modern Western democracies are characterised by the separation between two sectors: the private sector and the public sector. What distinguishes the French and the American systems is that they are two extreme instances of the legal-rational system of legitimacy: in the first, the state and public administration are dominant, and in the second civil society and private enterprise prevail. This is why we should concentrate our attention respectively on the history of the legal norms governing the public sector in France and on the history of the legal norms governing the private sector in the United States.

However, for the sake of brevity we shall content ourselves with the way in which the history of French institutions may be derived from the history of the legal norm defining the public sector, knowing that a similar and convergent analysis can be made for the history of the legitimacy of the private sector in the United States.

2.4.1   The History of the French Public Sector

In France, in order to guarantee the separation of powers (especially between the judicial and the executive branches) a special body of judges had to be established to monitor the public sector. Thus, courts have to decide explicitly what should or should not fall under either of the two jurisdictions. They do so by defining what is known as the 'criterion of administrative law'. The evolution of this criterion corresponds to the history of the legitimacy of decisions and actions within the public sector. According to all textbooks on the topic, this history develops in three stages, separated by two transitional periods.

The first stage (from 1800 to 1880/1900) corresponds to the reign of the public power criterion: all activities carried out by civil servants are considered to fall within the domain of public law. In a garrison state, it is the origin of power, that is, the status of the actor, which determines the legitimacy of an action.

The second stage (from 1880/1900 to 1945/60) corresponds to the primacy of the public service criterion: anything done to render a public service falls within the domain of public law. In the welfare state, it is the finality or outcome of power, that is, the function fulfilled by the actor, which determines the legitimacy of an action. At this stage the development of a legal control over the exercise of the discretionary power of administrative action confronted judges with a dilemma: they had to control the finality of action of the administration without judging it from a purely pragmatic point of view. To do this the State Council relied on a theory of decisions which assumes that it is possible to separate the facts on which a decision is based from the decision itself: it was decided that judges could refer in their judgements to the facts involved in the decision considered but had to leave to the administration the determination of the *qualification des faits*, that is, the issue of determining whether the consequences derived from these facts were correctly evaluated. We may note that this astute construction relies on a set of epistemological presuppositions which are characteristic of Auguste Comte positivism: the possibility of separating judgements of fact from judgements of value and the belief that judgements of fact are objective enough to provide a judge with well-defined legal criteria for judgements.

The third stage (from 1945/60 to the present) corresponds to what is known as the crisis of the criterion of administrative law, that is, the confusion concerning the limit between the public and private sectors. Inasmuch as this limit constitutes an essential dimension of the system of shared symbols required by the system of conflict resolution, it indicates a crisis of the system of legitimacy. It has become impossible, today, to justify an action either on the basis of its origin (first stage) or on the basis of its finality (second stage). There remains the possibility of arguing that henceforth actions will have to be justified (legitimised) by the methods used. Management, which belongs to the realm of methods of action, emerges as an essential and official component of social institutions. The role of these methods is to allow public actors to give an appropriate answer to the objections raised against their actions. Inefficiency is one of the major reproaches addressed to public administration. Against the reproach of inefficiency, arguments can be derived from the use of the methods of management, as these methods characterise private actors whose first objective it is to optimise the use of resources.

We may note that the two historical turning points we have just defined (1880/1900 and 1945/60) correspond to the ones which we have encountered above in the description of the history of the development of management that we have been able to derive from the writings of Harold Koontz and Lyndall Urwick. As for Barnard, his work may be considered as the inauguration of the third period, a period when uncertainty has to be taken into account to some extent. It is this uncertainty which expresses itself in the way Barnard tells us that he had to consider directly the 'impasse' which results from a direct confrontation between law and management, the solution to this impasse coming from the reading of treatises of jurisprudence.

It could be argued that, if the development of academic teaching and research in management remained very limited in France until the 1960s, it was because until then the social legitimacy of actions could be established by a legal system dominated by the public sector and the system of administrative and financial rules which governed it. It was only when the crisis of the criterion of administrative law occurred that methods of actions coming from the private sector, that is, management, had to be given a status in the dominant system of social legitimisation. Indeed, management appeared to invade the realm of public law itself, as is shown by the way in which the State Council introduced as legal criteria radically pragmatic notions such as 'the theory of the balance sheet' and 'the theory of manifest error' in its doctrine (Arrêt Ville Nouvelle Est, 1971 in Long et al., 2009).

2.4.2   Management, Law and Jurisprudence: A Programme for Future Research

However plausible the arguments in favour of an institutional approach to the study of the history of academic teaching and research in management developed so far could be, the proof of the validity of the proposed approach requires that it be subjected to a precise empirical test. Such is the meaning of the programme of research now described. We shall first state the hypothesis we want to test; secondly we shall briefly specify the method which should allow us to test empirically our hypothesis; finally we shall give two examples of potential application of this approach.

The hypothesis
The history of higher education in management is intimately linked to the history of higher education in law and more precisely the history of the teaching of jurisprudence in the Anglo-Saxon meaning of the term (that is, the theory or philosophy of law).

The method
To demonstrate this point we can rely 1) on the existence of a corpus of analysis relative to the history of 'the institutional underpinning of our beliefs', thanks to a conceptual framework built around the notion of a

system of legitimacy, 2) on the existence of a very abundant and precise corpus of existing research relative to the history of curricula offered by university departments of law and management, devoting particular attention to the lectures on jurisprudence offered by law schools, and last but not least, 3) on the analysis of the large number of texts of great intellectual standing which constitute the corpus of the academic literature dealing with jurisprudence in the Anglo-Saxon meaning of the term.

First test: description of the parallel history of academic teaching of law and management in the United States

The history of American law has been described by Bernard Schwartz as a process of constant adaptation of legal institutions to the requirement of the development of the nation. He shows how

> English law transformed itself to respond to the characteristics of a new nation having the size of a continent before adapting itself to the demands of the wild capitalism of the 'gilded age', then to the concerns of the beginning of the Welfare State. This history ends up today with the law being affected by this institutional crisis that one may observe in American society as a whole. (Schwartz 1974, p. 12)

The first crisis, which corresponds to the shift from 'the period of elaboration' to 'the period of reconstruction and the gilded age' is characterised by the revolution in the teaching of law introduced by Christopher Columbus Langdell at Harvard Law School when he replaced the study of textbooks by the case method. This comparison will be all the more meaningful if one understands how the constitution of a formal set of case books corresponds to the formal organisation of the field of law with each branch of the field being provided with a specific set of cases (such as 'contract', 'tort' and so on) which are given as illustrations of the principles that are supposed to govern their resolutions. From that point of view it is worth noting that case studies were considered less an exercise in the free interpretation of different situations than a dogmatic pedagogic method through which future law graduates would recognise the presence of the principles the case studies were supposed to illustrate. The foundation of Harvard Business School in 1908 and the way in which it relied on the case method for its teaching exemplify the link we are trying to establish between the history of the teaching of law and that of management.

The link between jurisprudence and the development of academic research in management is exemplified by the role played by scientific management in the decisions of one of the major figures of American law of that time, Justice Louis Brandeis. The relationship between his jurisprudential writings and the work of Frederick W. Taylor can be perfectly documented.

The second crisis corresponds to the shift from the period of reconstruction and the gilded age to the crisis which characterises the present state of the law. It can be followed first through the work of Barnard and the way in which it is linked to the sociological or realist school of jurisprudence as they are represented in the works of Cardozo or Ehrlich. A more detailed analysis of the way in which the teaching and research in law and management have evolved since then could be established through consideration of the development of schools of jurisprudence such as 'law and society', 'law and economics', 'critical legal studies' and 'law and literature'.

This evolution corresponds at the pedagogical level with a new approach to the treatment of case studies. The traditional dogmatic approach is replaced by a 'clinical approach' which consists in letting everyone develop freely the multiplicity of interpretations and argumentations which are liable to be provoked by the case under consideration.

The goal of the proposed study is to establish to what extent these developments do actually find their equivalent in the evolution of academic research and teaching in management as they can be observed through the proliferation of academic journals and through the reports of the Ford and Carnegie Foundations, which demonstrate the efforts made to reach a high level of scientific respectability.

From that point of view it is worth noting that the Nobel prize in economics has been awarded to researchers who can be considered specialists in management, such as Herbert Simon in 1978, and professors of finance such as Franco Modigliani in 1985, and Robert C. Merton and Myron Scholes in 1997, as well as to behavioural economists such as Kahneman and Tversky whose research could very well be considered to establish a link between economic rationality and marketing, for marketing could be said to deal with the economic consequences of the irrationality which characterises human behaviour to the extent that it depends on opinions, that is, subjective evaluations of alternatives.

Second test: comparative analysis of the history of academic departments of management in the USA, France and Great Britain
To test our hypothesis which states that there is a constant relationship between the teaching of jurisprudence in law schools and the development of graduate studies in management in universities we cannot be satisfied with having tested it on a single country, however meaningful it may be. This is why it is important for our purpose to develop a comparative analysis of the development of management in academia in several Western countries. As these histories show strong contrasts, it would be more meaningful for the validity of our hypothesis if it allowed an explanation of these differences.

In France, management did not develop as a fully legitimate field of graduate studies until what we have called the third period. Before that, higher education in management developed outside universities in special institutions (which were the beginnings of what is known as the system of *grandes écoles*), as for all other technical fields of study. Management topics were taught by professionals, a situation which recalls the position of American law schools before Christopher Columbus Langdell imposed the idea that law should be taught by professors working full time for the university. The status of schools of commerce remained inferior to that of other technical schools such as engineering schools until the end of the 1960s when the state imported the teaching methods of American business schools by means of the Fondation Nationale pour l'Enseignement de la Gestion des Entreprises (FNEGE). It is worth noting that this programme was promoted at the political level by the same person who had created the École Nationale d'Administration (ENA), which played such an important role in the administration of French public (and private) organisations: Michel Debré.

The case of Great Britain may surprise whoever thinks of Anglo-Saxon countries, countries of common law, as being similar in terms of legal history and culture. One must acknowledge that British pragmatism did not express itself in the development of business higher education along the lines of the American model. Not only did its development begin, as in France, during the third period, but it could be argued that it reached full recognition later than in France, for it was a long time before it could penetrate the two famous British elite academic institutions, Oxford and Cambridge. Only quite recently have these institutions recognised the institutional importance of management degrees in giving access to the most prestigious positions in industry, commerce and finance, and it was not until 1996 that this recognition resulted in the inauguration of the Judge Institute of Management by the Queen at Cambridge and the opening of the Saïd School of Business at Oxford.

The objective of the empirical inquiry is to show that this evolution parallels the history of the training of members of the British legal profession. What characterises the history of legal education is the way in which legal education remained dependent on a traditional system of apprenticeship where the Inns of Court played a major role. Similarly for a very long time it was considered that being educated in the classics would be the best academic training one could get before learning the practice of business directly on the job.

The analysis of the British case should lend support to our hypothesis, as it shows that the history of jurisprudence as a topic taught in universities did not follow at all the same pattern as that of the United States.

It was only in the 1960s and 1970s that the field of legal education gained some visibility with authors such as Hart and Ronald Dworkin.

2.5   CONCLUSION

We have shown that it is possible to link the history of academic teaching and research in management with that of law. More precisely we have shown that this link can be studied by following the course of the notion of jurisprudence in the Anglo-Saxon meaning of the word, that is, theory or philosophy of law. Lastly we have proposed that it is thus possible to develop a comparative analysis of the history of higher education in management in Western countries. The most important consequence of this comparison between the teaching of law and the teaching of management is that it could lead to the recognition of jurisprudence as a legitimate field of research and teaching in management.

Having found a principle which allows us to understand the historical development of our field should logically result in a diagnosis of our present situation and in a prognosis as to its future. However, we should not ignore that the proposed approach confronts us with at least three paradoxes:

1.   Management is a pragmatic field of knowledge, or a 'practical science' as Woodrow Wilson characterised it. We propose consideration of the possibility and importance of developing an approach which, as is supposed by the notion of jurisprudence, is theoretical and/or philosophical in nature.
2.   The present time is characterised by a process of globalisation, and management education is dominated by the development of a global market for degrees, professors and students, but we propose consideration of an approach which, being based on comparative legal histories, is intimately linked with a notion of the nation state that seems to have lost its former importance.
3.   Finally management is dominated by the notion of projects and innovation, and we propose an approach which, being based on history, seems to be desperately, and depressingly, backward looking.

In the face of such contradictions two attitudes are possible. The first one consists in rejecting altogether all this reasoning as pertaining to intellectual endeavours which are essentially foreign to common sense and thus to what should be studied and taught in management. The other one consists in considering these contradictions as being nothing else but symptoms of the confusion which characterises the situation of crisis that management has been confronting lately, a situation which corresponds to the fact that 'we have definitely entered a period where uncertainty is formally recognized'. If this second attitude seems to be somewhat more difficult to adopt it could be because of what Mary Douglas tried to teach us about the way in which 'the idea that there can be certain knowledge' is fundamental to the very existence of society. However, signs exist that we are finally reaching a point where the notion of uncertainty has to be faced in its more radical meaning, as is shown by the following quotation from an article written by Edmund Phelps (2009), Nobel prize winner in economics in 2006, director of the Center for Capitalism and Society, Columbia University:

> But why did big stockholders not move to stop over-leveraging before it reached dangerous levels? Why did legislators not demand regulatory intervention? The answer, I believe, is that they had no sense of the existing Knightian uncertainty. So they had no sense of the possibility of a huge break in housing prices. . . . Some had the instinct to buy insurance but did not see the uncertainty of the insurer's solvency.

One may wonder why all these economic actors ignored the Knightian notion of uncertainty. It was in no way secret or devoid of any academic recognition. Frank H. Knight was one of the founders of the famous Chicago school of economics. His book *Risk, Uncertainty and Profit*, derived from his thesis, has never ceased publication since 1921. None other than George Stigler (who was awarded the Nobel prize in 1982) provided a preface to its 1951 edition.

Once again we may turn to Mary Douglas for an explanation. In her book *Risk Acceptability According to the Social Sciences* she states:

> Sometimes the curiosity of scholars fastens steadily upon certain formulations and problems, to the neglect of others. . . . We may expect some random patches of inattention because of the impossibility of attending to everything at once. But regularly scheduled obliviousness is more intriguing. Persistent shortsightedness, selectivity, and tolerated contradiction are usually not so much signs of perceptual weakness as signs of attention to protect certain values and their accompanying institutional form. . . . Gaps and contradictions in a system of thought are a good guide to the institutional fabric which supports it and to which it gives life. (1986, pp. 2–3)

That this text was written in the context of the analysis of the reception of the book she wrote with Aaron Wildavsky, *Risk and Culture* (1983), is consistent with the interpretation of Phelps's remark as denoting a radical shift in the institutions of capitalism, a shift which bears a direct relationship to the major financial crisis which started in 2008.

It is impossible in a conclusion to comment on this point more precisely. We shall just note briefly how Edmund Phelps's argument implies that pure theory, jurisprudence and history be taken into account.

Pure theory is what is required to distinguish the commonly used notion of uncertainty (especially in the managerial literature developed so far), which corresponds to a situation characterised by some quantifiable probabilistic model, from Knightian uncertainty, which corresponds to the situation where essential dimensions of the model under consideration cannot be quantified at all.

Jurisprudence is required as far as the issue of the question of knowing 'why . . . legislators [did] not demand regulatory intervention' is central to the reconstruction of a viable financial market.

That history also is involved can be shown indirectly by the fact that we know that one of the major actors in the regulation of the system, Ben Bernanke, has been chosen, at least in part, on the basis of the research he led on the financial determinants of the 1929 crisis.

Consequently our last comment will be devoted to the following question: in the event we agree that it would be meaningful to develop the notion of jurisprudence as an integral part of management education, can we define its content and methods in such a way that it is possible to develop it as a rigorous domain of research?

To this question it is possible to offer two types of answer: the first one consists in showing that such a field is already being developed spontaneously in management education and research; the second one consists in wondering whether it would be possible to propose an integrated conceptual approach to these developments that would emulate the consistency of those developed in legal jurisprudence.

From the first point of view we may note the following three points:

1. The growing importance of neo-institutionalism in contemporary management research as well as in social sciences (an importance sanctified more than once by the Nobel Academy through the recognition of the work of Douglass North, Ronald Coase and more recently Oliver Williamson and Elinor Ostrom) is in keeping with the proposition that management should be considered from an institutional point of view.

2. If we consider the most recent trends of research developed in legal jurisprudence, such as law and economics, law and society, law and rhetoric, and law and literature, we may note that it would not be altogether difficult to subsume large chunks of managerial research into corresponding categories.

3. If certain knowledge has to be based on scientific reason, as is

supposed in a world dominated by the Weberian legal-rational type of authority, the emergence of rhetoric as an acceptable paradigm in law (Perelman), economics (McCloskey), sociology (through the study of narrativity) and epistemology (Stephen Toulmin) can be considered as corresponding to a situation of crisis to the extent that the value of any statement can be considered to depend on its ability to persuade. Here again, as with the notion of uncertainty, the link with the notion of crisis cannot be made rigorously as long as one refuses to consider the ultimate consequence of the role of rhetoric from a rigorous intellectual viewpoint, which can only be done when one confronts the notion of sophism, a notion which has accompanied the development of philosophy since the time of Plato and Aristotle.

It is precisely by taking sophism seriously, showing that it allows us to link in a rigorous fashion philosophy on the one hand, through the role sophism plays in the history of philosophy from Plato and Aristotle to John Dewey and Karl Popper, and management on the other hand, through the fact of analysing marketing as a modern (bureaucratic) form of sophism, that it has been possible to develop over more than 30 years of research, teachings and publications a conceptual framework based on the notions of a system of legitimacy, the history of systems of legitimacy, and a crisis of legitimacy, which could be proposed as an example of the type of approaches that could participate in the constitution of the field of managerial jurisprudence.

Whether this approach is worth pursuing is up to the reader to judge. But if our hypothesis is correct there is a need for the development of approaches adapted to 'a period where uncertainty is formally recognized'.

It is to be feared, given the essentially empirical and pragmatic orientation of managerial research and teaching, that the approach proposed will appear somewhat repellent to many. This is why we shall conclude by two arguments, one theoretical and the other purely pragmatic.

Our ultimate theoretical argument consists in stating that the notion of jurisprudence offers a unique means by which to witness the universality of the pragmatic importance of theoretical thinking. This point was made by Oliver Wendell Holmes (1899, p. 420) when he wrote: 'but although practical men generally prefer to leave their major premise inarticulate yet even for practical purposes theory is the most important thing in the end'. To measure the value of this statement it is necessary to recall that Justice Holmes is one of the major figures of the history of American law and, at the same time, a member of the Metaphysical Club, where he could meet William James, one of the founding fathers of American pragmatism.

As for the ultimate pragmatic argument, it will consist simply in noting the fact that the notions of crisis and catastrophic risks have become an integral part of the environment with which managers are confronted. Managers have to face uncertainty in the radical meaning of the word, and the contradictions and paradoxes which go with it. It would be relatively easy to show that most fields of research and teaching dealing with this dimension of management (crisis management, management of environmental risks, corporate social responsibility, regulation and lobbying, institutional communication and so on) did find useful resources in approaches that could be qualified as belonging to the realm of jurisprudence.

A meaningful starting point could be a careful reading of the text of the oath Harvard Business School felt it necessary to institutionalise in 2009:

> As a manager, my purpose is to serve the greater good by bringing people and resources together to create value that no single individual can build alone. Therefore I will seek a course that enhances the value my enterprise can create for society over the long term. I recognize my decisions can have far-reaching consequences that affect the well-being of individuals inside and outside my enterprise, today and in the future. As I reconcile the interests of different constituencies, I will face difficult choices.
>
> Therefore, I promise:
> - I will act with utmost integrity and pursue my work in an ethical manner.
> - I will safeguard the interests of my shareholders, co-workers, customers, and the society in which we operate.
> - I will manage my enterprise in good faith, guarding against decisions and behaviour that advance my own narrow ambitions but harm the enterprise and the societies it serves.
> - I will understand and uphold, both in letter and in spirit, the laws and contracts governing my own conduct and that of my enterprise.
> - I will take responsibility for my actions, and I will represent the performance and risks of my enterprise accurately and honestly.
> - I will develop both myself and other managers under my supervision so that the profession continues to grow and contribute to the well-being of society.
> - I will strive to create sustainable economic, social, and environmental prosperity worldwide.
> - I will be accountable to my peers and they will be accountable to me for living by this oath.
>
> This oath I make freely, and upon my honor.

REFERENCES

Barnard, Chester ([1938] 1968), *The Functions of the Executive*, 30th anniversary edition, Cambridge, MA: Harvard University Press.

Douglas, Mary (1986), *Risk Acceptability According to the Social Sciences*, London: Routledge.

Douglas, Mary (2001), 'Dealing with uncertainty', *Ethical Perspectives*, **8** (3), 145–55.

Douglas, Mary and Aaron Wildavsky (1983), *Risk and Culture: An Essay on the Selection of Technical and Environmental Dangers*, Berkeley, CA: University of California Press.

Holmes, Oliver Wendell (1899), 'The theory of legal interpretation', *Harvard Law Review*, **12**, 417–20.

Knight, Frank H. (1921), *Risk, Uncertainty and Profit*, Chicago: University of Chicago Press.

Koontz, Harold (1961), 'The management theory jungle', *Journal of the Academy of Management*, **4** (3), December, 174–88.

Koontz, Harold (1980), 'The management theory jungle revisited', *Academy of Management Review*, **5** (2), April, 175–88.

Laufer, Romain (2009), 'New rhetoric's empire: pragmatism, dogmatism and sophism', *Philosophy and Rhetoric*, **42** (4), 326–48.

Laufer, Romain and Catherine Paradeise (1990), *Marketing Democracy: Public Opinion and Media Formation in Democratic Societies*, New Brunswick, NJ: Transaction Publishers.

Long, Marceau, Prosper Weil, Guy Braibant, Pierre Devolvé and Bruno Genevois (2009), *Les grands arrêts de la jurisprudence administrative*, Paris: Dalloz, pp. 581–93.

Phelps, Edmund (2009), 'Uncertainty bedevils the best system', *Financial Times*, 15 April.

Rey, Alain (ed.) (2006), *Le Dictionnaire historique de la langue française*, Paris: Le Robert.

Schwartz, Bernard (1974), *The Law in America: A History*, New York: McGraw-Hill.

Tocqueville, Alexis de (1840), *Democracy in America*, vol. 2, New York: J. and H.G. Langley.

Towle, Joseph W. (1960), 'Opportunities ahead for the Academy of Management', *Journal of the Academy of Management*, **3** (3), December, 147–54.

Urwick, Lyndall F. (1963), 'The tactics of jungle warfare', *Academy of Management Journal*, **6** (4), December, 316–29.

Wilson, W. (1887), 'The study of administration', *Political Science Quarterly*, **2** (2), June, 197–222.

3. Management as a basic academic field: foundation, roots and identity[1]

Armand Hatchuel

3.1 INTRODUCTION: SOLVING THE 'TRANSLATION PROBLEM' IN MANAGEMENT RESEARCH: A EUROPEAN APPROACH

The management literature has documented a wide range of criticism about the orientation and relevance of standard management research (Starkey and Madan 2001; Shapiro et al. 2007). It has also advocated an enhancement and enrichment of the methods and epistemology of the field (Nodoushani 2000; Hatchuel 2001, 2005; Huff and Huff 2001; Starkey and Madan 2001; Weick 2001; Van de Ven 2006). The US Academy of Management has also repeatedly encouraged similar evolutions of the field (Huff 2000; Cummings 2007). Thus, there is now a widely recognised debate about the future of management research, and the academic conversation should, therefore, explore and discuss alternative currents in management research. Among several possible ways, special attention should be given to some European approaches where neither the post-war turn towards quantitative factor performance-based statistical analysis, nor the view of management as an applied social science, has encompassed the whole field.

In this chapter we overview one of these currents that has been labelled a 'foundationalist' perspective in management research (FPM) (David et al. 2001; Hatchuel and David 2007). The word 'foundationalist' comes from a collaborative book published in 2001 entitled *Les nouvelles fondations des management sciences* [The new foundations of management science][2] (David et al. 2001). If FPM had its roots in the French academic context, its development had deep connections with other European trends in management. It has been nurtured by long cooperation with Swedish researchers (Adler et al. 2004), and it has benefited from exchanges with UK and US critical literature (Huff and Huff 2001; Pettigrew 1997, 2001; Starkey and Madan 2001; Starkey et al. 2004; Shani et al. 2007). But, for the sake of simplicity and brevity, we will not describe all these approaches in this chapter. We shall focus on the distinctive assumptions of FPM which were elaborated during at least two decades of epistemological debate by a group of French academics. Before presenting an outline of the chapter, let us summarise the main propositions of FPM which will be further developed in the body of this chapter.

3.1.1 Management Research as a New Basic Science

One of the core ideas of FPM is that management research should be defined as a new basic science, a science which is both a 'social' and a 'cognitive' science and which studies the conditions, design and legitimacy of 'models of collective action' in old and modern societies. In this approach 'collective action' is not considered as an obvious notion or as a straightforward empirical phenomenon. It is perceived as the central enigma for research, the phenomenon that has to be modelled in order to be understood (Hatchuel 2005). Within FPM, there is no closed repertoire of 'rationalities' or 'organisational forms'; any rationality or organisational form is built on explicit (or implicit) models of collective action. And the invention of new models of action expands our view of rationality and organisation. What political science invented for the action of states or cities can now be done by management science for any type of collective action, provided it includes reflexivity (or self-cognition) as an integral component of 'action'. Such understanding of management corresponds to the epistemological turn towards 'action' which occurred during the twentieth century in several disciplines (Hatchuel 2005).

3.1.2 Rigour in Management Research Results from the Appropriate Combination of Different Types of Interactions between the Researcher and the Object

A key epistemological statement of FPM is that, depending on how 'collective action' is defined, research requires different cognitive conditions of investigation and different modes of interaction between the researcher and the field of study. Hence, rigour in management research cannot be defined per se, and there can be no unique sign of rigour. Rigour needs the combination and integration of a variety of research methods tailored to the model of action under study. This explains why researchers who developed FPM have explored the scientific opportunities offered by collaborative research with partners (Hatchuel 2001; Adler et al. 2004; David and Hatchuel 2007; Hatchuel and David 2007). They also defined new design principles for research-oriented partnerships. These principles depart fundamentally from standard action research (David and Hatchuel

2007) and have been used in a large number of organisations. They offer a fruitful and consistent solution to the 'translation problem in management research' (Shapiro et al. 2007).

3.1.3 Relevance as a Constitutive Issue in Management Research

Like all models of collective action, research has its stakeholders, not least the research community itself. But when research needs the contribution of those who are under study, the latter will have their own views about relevant research issues and methods. The views of these stakeholders are both a subject of investigation and a guiding force for research. Thus, relevance enables research and becomes interdependent with rigour. And the challenge for management research is to design research protocols where rigour supports relevance and relevance is a condition of rigour.

Finally, FPM is based on the idea that the limitations of standard management research have a common and neglected cause: the lack of a solid definition of the scientific identity of the field. Clearly, a professional field can flourish without such a definition, but an academic field that has no clear theoretical unity will face a major risk: specific signs of rigour could be confused with the definition of the science and interpreted as signs of relevance. If such an identity and unity are clarified, the issues of rigour and relevance will be neither confused nor perceived as incommensurable criteria. They will form a dynamic and open challenge for the expansion of responsible and actionable management knowledge in modern societies.

Are these propositions a valuable and consistent contribution for the enhancement of management research? In this chapter, we suggest that FPM may solve the widely discussed 'relevance gap' and 'translation problem' in management research. But, above all, it may settle the foundations of management science as a distinctive basic science and not as an applied one (Hatchuel 2001, 2005).

We turn now to an outline of the chapter. In section 3.2, we give indications of the French management research context and describe the epistemological debates that gave birth to FPM. In section 3.3, we present the main assumptions of FPM about the identity, rigour and relevance of management research. In section 3.4, we discuss two important findings allowed by FPM: a theory of management techniques as a critical view of classic organisation theory and a model of collective innovative design as a critical view of standard R&D and project management.

3.2 THE FRENCH ACADEMIC CONTEXT IN MANAGEMENT: TRADITIONS AND EPISTEMOLOGICAL DEBATES

The influence of French research in the management literature is a matter of paradox. The most quoted authors are not management authors but ... critical philosophers like Foucault, Lyotard or Derrida! To understand this surprising situation, some historical background about French management traditions and debates is necessary. However, in this chapter we cannot offer a complete and detached account of a history where we have been personally involved. We will only indicate a few facts and bibliographical landmarks that explain the progressive maturation and originality of French management research.

In the middle of the nineteenth century, France was clearly a country where management issues and research could flourish. The early development of *grandes écoles* in engineering and business ('commerce') produced a new elite of professionals who had to cope with the new organisational and administrative needs of emerging industries and trades. Even if most of these elites were not academics, some of them became conscious that the traditional knowledge coming from political economy, laws of commerce and craft-based work was not appropriate to the new business world. The prominent figure of Henri Fayol is typical of these new elites. After an outstanding career as an engineer, scientist and top manager, he formulated his well-known 'administrative principles' during the same years that witnessed the formation of Taylor's 'scientific management' in America. These new principles were not seen as mere practical wisdom, and Fayol presided over the birth of a new 'administrative science'.

3.2.1 A Dual Tradition in Management Research

However, circa 1920, the academic hosting of such a new doctrine was difficult. French universities were classically divided into faculties (law, medicine, economics, humanities and mathematics). Was 'administrative science' a subfield of political economy or law? A new philosophy of action? Some sort of human engineering?[3] Before the Second World War, the epistemological debate opened by the new management doctrines had few opportunities and places to appear. The Fayolian doctrine became the subject of lectures in the *grandes écoles de commerce* (the 'Taylor system' was taught in engineering schools), but it had no place in the standard tradition of scholarly knowledge, and was hardly seen as a first form of a new science.

During the 1950s and 1960s, French universities engaged in several reforms. Management as a special topic was introduced in the faculties of law, but only as business information for lawyers. Some pioneering universities created special institutes for administrative studies (which gave birth to the present network of *instituts d'administration des enterprises*). However, it was only after the May 1968 changes that management became an autonomous discipline in a few pioneering universities offering academic careers in the field. These innovators had to develop their new curricula almost from a blank sheet. Therefore a special foundation was created (Fondation nationale pour l'enseignement de la gestion, FNEGE) which helped the best students to apply for a PhD in American universities. These students formed a new generation of professors who tended to adopt mainstream syllabi from the United States. Such teaching and research approaches also had an important advantage: they were feasible without close cooperation or direct contact with practitioners.

Most of these developments were undertaken independently from existing and older management curricula in the *grandes écoles*. The latter had a long legacy in management, but they had developed the field in a specific and autonomous way. They had to respond to their own needs, which were to maintain high professional training by continuously and critically developing management methods and thinking. To achieve such a demanding goal, they relied on large and active networks of former students, who were often top managers. The main criterion for relevant management knowledge was the ability to train and convince a professional elite who had been intensively trained in mathematics, literature and philosophy. Some of the *grandes écoles* in engineering and commerce more or less approached management science as an alternative to standard economics, which had little direct value for real managerial situations. They also adopted the new 'action perspective' advocated by early models of operations research, and they taught general management issues as a vehicle for increased reflection about the role of managers and experts in organisations. This perspective favoured a critical view of the newborn mainstream management thinking. Standard research appeared to be too universalistic, too scholastic and without actionable value for future managers. This critical perspective explains the constitution of two different traditions in management research and the creation of a long epistemological debate in the French context.

3.2.2   The New Management Landscape: An Epistemological Debate

In the middle of the 1980s, the French landscape of management research began to evolve. Important renewal trends came from teams and networks that launched new exchanges and cooperation between management universities and the *grandes écoles*. Not surprisingly, one of the favoured areas of investigation and debate was the controversial epistemology and methodology of management science. *Grandes écoles* teams had to clarify the academic value of their focus on relevant and actionable knowledge. University teams had to show the benefits of existing academic research in management. Both had to discuss the scientific domain and content of management research. The National Foundation for Management Education (FNEGE) played a major role by supporting annual workshops on epistemological issues where doctoral students and lecturers could meet a variety of senior researchers and discuss such 'hard' issues. Several collaborative books came out of these encounters (Martinet 1988; David et al. 2001; Thiétart 2006; Martinet et al. 2007). They still have no direct equivalents in the international literature. However, most of them have not yet been translated. These books discuss different broad perspectives for management science. They address questions such as: What is the object of management research? What is a managerial situation? Is management science a social science? An engineering science? What is involved in testing a management theory? In spite of conflicting positions, most authors shared the idea that management science was a young discipline and that there were various 'good ways' to do research in management. Accepted internal diversity was also a condition of the institutional unity of the field. It contributed to its academic legitimacy in relation to older-established disciplines like economics and sociology. Moreover, the link between research and practice was progressively perceived not as a subject of academic conflict but as a feasibility issue: not all management teams had the reputation and networks to facilitate the development of research partnerships.

3.2.3 The Origins of FPM: A Critical View of Mainstream Research and Applied Social Science

The birth date of FPM can be precisely established: March 1998. A group of researchers from three institutions[4] had planned a workshop to discuss unifying concepts in management science. The goal was to synthesise the epistemological work that had been done by several teams in France. A participation of 20 to 25 'specialists' in the subject was expected. But rapidly the organisers were overwhelmed by hundreds of academics wanting to attend the workshop. Finally more than 250 people attended, drawn from almost all the management teams in the country. This was a clear sign of the importance of the renewal efforts that were anticipated by a majority of academics. Eight presentations given at the workshop were later published in a book (David et al. 2001),[5] which experienced significant success[6] and is widely referenced by management students and researchers. It is not possible to summarise all the material of the book, and we shall briefly survey the major critical arguments shared by the book editors in favour of new foundations for management research. The first argument is the criticism of mainstream research; the second argument is a partial rejection of the 'applied social science' model.

Departing from mainstream research: long-term inconclusiveness and the management effect

Mainstream research usually seeks to establish a statistically significant relationship (usually correlation analysis) between certain organisational 'factors' and certain areas of organisational 'performance'. Both constructs are indicators or descriptors designed to allow for the testing of the assumed relationship. This empirical data comes from a sample of organisations (or parts of organisations) which is supposed to 'represent' a wider population of organisations. Data is provided by respondents to questionnaires who give their perceptions on certain organisational factors and performance or transmit more quantitative data (standard accounting measures, sales, profits, costs and so on). This type of study has two types of limitations for management research.

The first limitation is the statistical weaknesses of such studies, which are well known: weak control of the quality of the responses; biased samples due to non-respondents; weak tests of statistical significance; and so on. But such frequent criticisms have nothing to do with the debate about the nature of management science. Statistical validity is an issue that is common to all scientific fields that have to establish quantitative correlations.

The second limitation is inconclusiveness and the 'management effect'. The crucial problem of this type of study is how the knowledge produced (weak or not) fits with the project of management research. Without a clear and rich definition of such a project, these types of studies run the risk of generating no cumulative knowledge and what can be labelled long-term 'inconclusiveness'. Such inconclusiveness presents two symptoms.

The first symptom is when statistical analysis leads to endless controversies about the definition of the factors and performance. The lack of consistency of the constructs creates equivocal interpretations of results, which brings the discussion back to the definition of the constructs and so forth. This analytical trap reminds us that statistical analysis cannot create the theoretical notions and objects which guide knowledge production.

The second symptom of inconclusiveness emerges with the proliferation of studies offering contrasting or conflicting results. Some studies show the positive influence of A on B, and some others show a negative influence.

This type of result is usually interpreted as a lack of maturity of the subject or as a bias in the design of the studies. Yet finding contradictory relations has no meaning per se; its interpretation depends on the theoretical model of the phenomena.

Neglecting the management effect   Indeed, in any statistical study, some influencing factors may have been neglected. Yet the problem becomes crucial if these 'hidden factors' are precisely management itself, that is, the scientific object of the field. Let us take the example of a drug, D, which is tested for illness, I. Let us imagine a statistical study asking doctors to describe the effect of D on patients suffering from I; and results observed on two samples, S1 and S2, of patients show contradictory results. The first interpretation could be that the impact of the drug is controversial. But there is also the possibility that for some reason the doctors do not 'manage' the treatment as expected: some of them do not prescribe D when it is needed, and they prescribe it when it is useless. This would mean that the drug studies missed controlling for 'a management effect', that is, the model of action that describes the doctor behaviour and explains contradictory relationships between selected factors. This is the major risk of any factor performance analysis, as factors do not act by themselves; it is the management process that shapes 'action'.

Now, inconclusiveness cannot be seen in one study. It is a symptom that appears in the long run when multiple examples of similar studies have been published and have nurtured the conversation of an academic community. Mainstream management research has now been active for several decades, and some academic issues have been studied over at least 20 years. This is a sufficient period of time to test if the inconclusiveness syndrome has occurred or not. Obviously such study requires a detailed survey of chapters by experts in the field. This is not an easy task to undertake. Fortunately, *Academy of Management Review* editors (Kilduff 2007) have asked leading scholars in the fields of 'organisational trust theory' (Schoorman et al. 2007) and 'upper echelon theory' (Hambrick 2007) to summarise the progress in their fields during the last two decades. Even if the survey may be biased by the involvement of the authors in the field, both chapters fairly recognise, from our point of view, an impressive level of inconclusiveness. It would take too long to discuss both chapters appropriately; thus, we suggest only that readers check this point for themselves.

Therefore, from a scientific point of view, factor performance statistical analysis should be limited to studies in mature management fields, that is, when factors and performance have a clear actionable meaning for both practitioners and academics. In such contexts, it can be assumed that the 'management effect' is under control, that is, factors and performance are linked to a well-documented and diffused model of action in the studied organisations. A famous work in the literature, the Sussex studies directed by Joan Woodward (1965), can illustrate the fruitfulness of well-designed statistical studies. It showed that the relationship between span of control and batch size was non-linear (a U-shape). This was a direct contribution to management theory, as both span of control and batch size were well-known actionable variables for the studied organisations. The study actually captured a deep managerial phenomenon, that is, how different action logics tend to combine batch size and span of control in a surprising way. Yet Woodward's studies came after two decades of managerial work on industrial organisation which established span of control and batch size as clear design variables for a production plant. The large diffusion of standard models of industrial organisation had transformed plants into 'natural experiments' for industrial management, and the statistical study clearly revealed the non-linearity of the relationship and paved the way for a contingent theory of production systems.

Yet all this leads to a paradox about standard management research. On one hand, statistical analysis should be restricted to the mature phases of a management era (David and Hatchuel 2007) when both researchers and practitioners have stabilised managerial concepts and practice, and when impact and effects can be clearly surveyed and discussed. On the other hand, this observation strongly contrasts with the dominant and systematic use of statistical analysis. To solve the paradox one has to admit that statistical analysis is not used because it fits well with management theory or because it is fruitful (and thus relevant), but is used as a conventional sign of rigour in research even if its application often invalidates the scientific requirements of statistical analysis.

Departing from the 'applied social science' model: paradigm wars and critical distance

If the use of statistical analysis is limited to late validation tests in the more mature areas of management research, we need alternative methods for exploration and discovery in management research (David and Hatchuel 2007). Qualitative and participatory research (or action research) has been widely discussed in the literature. It benefits from growing recognition in mainstream journals of the richness and reliability of the empirical material it provides. Yet, from the point of view of management research, these methods are often associated with a social science background which also conveys 'paradigm wars' and a systematic view of 'critical distance'. Such landmarks of social science should be critically discussed in management.

Paradigm wars   Since its first days, social science has been divided into rival fields: economics, sociology, anthropology, social psychology and so on. This disciplinary division affects methodology and strongly shapes the research object. Economics is based on market studies and individual utility models of choice; sociology stresses groups, powers and institutions; anthropology stresses mythology, rituals and parental structures, and it includes all human groups and activities in its study. These paradigmatic traditions are part of the social science legacy (Burrell and Morgan 2003); however, they have no clear scientific value for management research. Management research should learn from other social sciences, yet it should not define its own object through the lenses of the traditional social science division. Let us illustrate this idea. Is 'hierarchy' a social fact? Yes. Is it an economic instrument? Yes. These questions would receive the same answers if they were asked about 'sales', 'nations' or any notion that shapes modern life. The distinction between social and economic phenomena is impossible to 'observe'; it is built into the tradition that institutionalised different disciplines.

Critical distance   Another trend in social studies (excepting economics) is their traditional critical position which defines social science as a counter-culture against capitalist domination or liberalism. This tradition can be seen as a legitimate point of view and a sign of healthy engagement. Yet this line of thought tends to see management science as the culture of capitalism or as the lingua franca of liberalism. It also leads to the rejection of any partnership with corporations because it would endanger the freedom of thought and the critical dimension of research. Yet both positions are misleading and based on wrong assumptions. Management science has no scientific reason to praise everything done by corporations or the claims of neoclassical economists. Nor is it forced to accept classical market theory or the standard view of shareholders seen as the owners of firms (Segrestin and Hatchuel 2008). And this argument holds for the same reason that allows a specialist of gender studies to criticise feminist movements, or a specialist of Christian movements not to be a Christian.

The same logic can be applied to research partnerships with corporations. Not every type of partnership will allow the critical investigation required by academic work. However, the experience of several teams proves that *some* partnerships with companies are possible and will benefit the advancement of knowledge (Hatchuel and David 2007).

Which new foundations for management research?
In the long run, the epistemological debate clarified the complexity of the 'translation problem' in management and gave birth to a constructive

process. Let us summarise the main propositions that defined the basis conditions for an enhancement of the field:

- The mainstream model of management research was incomplete, as it had no unified management theory, that is, no basic assumptions that ground an academic field. We, therefore, have to define the academic identity of management research.
- Mainstream management research misused statistical analysis, which became a sign of rigour in itself, instead of a population-based control process that should be applied *ex post*, that is, when a dominant management theory (or management language) is *in use* across organisations and is clearly identified both by researchers and by practitioners.[7]
- Management research needed alternative methods that could help to advance management theory and to interpret it not at a population level but at the appropriate level where the 'management effect' could be understood: when and where models of action can be made visible.
- Social science (including social psychology) offered interesting and rich investigation methodologies (qualitative and participative research), but its scientific traditions tended to conceal the scientific identity of management science or to restrict the fruitfulness of collaborative research to interpretative and critical processes such as in classic action research. Again, a clarification of the identity of management research was necessary to redefine and adapt the logic and purpose of collaborative research methods (Hatchuel and David 2007).

These requirements paved the way towards the main propositions of FPM.

3.3 THE MAIN PROPOSITIONS OF FPM: IDENTITY, RIGOUR AND RELEVANCE

Since Poincaré (1905) and more recently Foucault (1966), modern epistemology has told us that academic research needs a consistent fit between three elements: a) the identification of a field, that is, the definition of theoretical 'objects' which indicate the central enigma or new *episteme* (Foucault 1966) for research that comes out of the limitations of established knowledge; b) a series of investigation methods which warrant rigour; c) a series of relevance principles that give value and meaning to the association of the two previous elements. For example, volcanology is the study of the origin and activity of volcanoes. Rigour in volcanology is based on multidisciplinary methods of investigation (physical and chemical measures, qualitative observations, simulation models, history, geography and so on). Moreover, predicting the behaviour of volcanoes can save lives, and such a relevance principle has strongly affected the field and the type of rigour that is expected and actively researched (methods to announce eruptions, typologies of eruptions and so on). This epistemological framework helps to underline the features which distinguish FPM from mainstream management research and from traditional social sciences.

3.3.1 The Identity of Management Research: A New Type of Basic Science

As seen in the previous section, one of the departure points of FPM is that traditional management research is 'lost before translation' (Shapiro et al. 2007): it has neglected to clarify its specific object and has no unified construct for 'management theory'. It is therefore trapped by a narrow view of rigour per se. Now, defining an identity for management science also requires situating its differences with economics, sociology or engineering, even if it has strong interfaces with these fields. Traditionally, management is defined as the study of the activity of certain professionals who are called managers. In addition, management research should produce the knowledge that is useful for managers. The circularity and historical bias of such a definition is obvious. However, it gives interesting hints. Management appeared when a new type of collective action (a new social role) claimed some kind of reflexivity, legitimacy and competence which could not be completely explained through traditional knowledge and established roles. Paul Veyne (2005) suggests that Roman emperors were the first managers, as they could define their position neither by legitimate designation rules nor by traditional forms of sovereignty. The obvious Roman origin of most management words (administration, delegation, coordination and so on) is a strong sign in favour of such a general interpretation. Therefore the more a model of collective action differs from previous rituals, traditions and unconscious or imposed behaviour, the more it will define itself as a reflexive process and as a managed action. This does not mean that management needs complete freedom or total reflexivity. It says only that management is the type of reflexivity that makes some type of freedom visible, and transforms it into an object of study and a space for design in order to generate some recognisable and acceptable collective action. Finally, the notion of 'reflexive practice' introduced by Schon (1994) can be seen as a synonym of 'management' when the reflexive process involves more than one practitioner, that is, other colleagues or clients. This highly abstract definition of management is surprisingly powerful as an interpretative and unifying tool. Contrasting this definition, let us ask: what is the object studied by economics and by sociology?

Economics defines itself as the study of a type of collective action (labelled 'markets') which results from the individual pursuit of self-interest. Clearly, this definition recognises only a special class of self-management where reflexivity is limited to selfish action. Sociology has a broader object, and it usually rejects standard economics by assuming that human behaviour is determined by 'social' relations (groups, powers, ranks, interdependencies and so on). Yet, if one assumes that social relations can be reflexively understood, then social relations are also special types of collective action where models of relations are the management issue. Therefore, saying that management is applied economics or applied sociology is yielding to metonymy, that is, confusing the whole (reflexive collective action) with some of its parts (markets, social relations). In spite of classic academic divisions, there is no reason to restrict reflexive management practice to such special types of collective action as self-interest or social relations. Moreover, social relations and self-interest are obviously interdependent. Thus, the history of social sciences as well as pure scientific logic leads to a definition of management science as a more basic science, which studies the conditions and emergence of reflexive collective action in old and modern societies.

Within such a perspective, what is management research? It cannot be defined as an empirical study of 'organisations', 'strategies' or 'control processes' as if these notions were natural and invariant phenomena offered for observation. Instead, management research investigates and designs (or invents) 'models of collective action' which we use to shape, make visible and reflexively design what we label 'organisations', 'strategies' or control processes. Therefore, the first contribution of FPM is the identification and elaboration of a theoretical category, 'models of collective action', which encompasses the standard contrast between, on the one side, agency as individual cognition and rationality and, on the other side, institutions as hierarchies, norms and communities. It has been suggested (Hatchuel 2005) that this was a misleading contrast owing to the lack of a thorough 'epistemology of action'. 'Collective action' is precisely the phenomenon that produces simultaneously individual cognition (knowledge operators) and institutions (social relations), and management science should be viewed as the science of their dynamic and open interdependency.

Practically, such theoretical assumptions pinpoint two common traps in the research language. Some concepts tend to describe cognitive phenomena without any associated social relations: such as rationality, trust or expertise. Or they present the opposite bias and describe social relations without any cognitive ground: such as networks, hierarchies or command. Let us take the example of 'command' (in its usual sense of 'conduct' or 'govern'). 'Command' is usually defined as a universal type of social relation without any reference to the cognitive capacities of actors, as if commanding an artist was the same thing as commanding a soldier. Such misleading language creates persistent equivocal problems for research. What is the theoretical alternative? Let us see 'command' as one broad attribute of a model of collective action; we can now investigate the types of collective action where we can recognise some sort of 'command'. This will give us the list of the 'known' (or made visible) models where cognitive capacities and social relations shape a form of command and will offer a rigorous departure for any research about 'command'. In addition, management research can go beyond these known models and try to invent new forms of collective action where command presents new features (soft command, democratic command and so on). Finally, 'command' should be seen not as a universal and invariant category, but with the same logic that we use with artefacts like 'chairs'. The creative chair that a talented designer creates is not an occurrence of the universal idea of chair! Nor it is a pragmatic effect of the concept of chair! It is a manifestation of the expandability of the very concept of 'chair' (Hatchuel 2001) through a collective design process. Thus management research should consider models of action neither as universals nor as empirical realities, but as constitutional and revisable models that allow for collective action and make it visible or 'true'.

3.3.2 Rigour as the Combination of Different Levels of Interaction between Researchers and their Objects

Now that we have suggested a distinct identity for management science, it is easier to discuss research methods that are consistent with it. The question is simple: how should we 'observe', 'test' or 'discover' those unusual classes of phenomena that we call 'models of collective action'? As a matter of paradox, this unifying definition of management science retrieves a large variety of research methods and clarifies the controversial issue of 'actionable' management knowledge. A key statement of FPM is that studying 'models of collective action' requires different cognitive conditions of investigation and different types of interaction between the researcher and the phenomena under study.

Let us take some examples. Observing well-known and ready-made accounting data requires a different method from observing stimulated perceptions (that is, responses to a questionnaire) about, say, 'autonomy at work'. Both methods will also be different from the one needed to study the capacity of an organisation to innovate. Why do we need different methods in each case? A different model of collective action is discussed in each case, and any research method has to be consistent with its selected object.

- Accounting is an old model of collective action that has been enduringly designed, shared and learned. The rules of accounting are stabilised by shared cognitive systems and by enforcing social relations (law, professions, duties and so on). Thus, accounting is a 'naturalised' phenomenon in modern societies. Accounting researchers can assume that they *already* have sufficient knowledge to observe what's happening. In addition, a factor performance statistical analysis may become fruitful, because these stabilised rules create the cognitive and relational stability of the factors and of the performance which warrants statistical analysis.
- In the case of stimulated perceptions (or declarations) obtained by a questionnaire, this assumption becomes less acceptable, and researchers should in principle study how the questionnaire is understood and completed or even teach respondents how to do it. This means collaborating with the observed people!
- In the third case (studying capacities to innovate) it would be wrong to believe that researchers have enough previous knowledge to define the type of model of collective action that could generate innovation capacity. Therefore, deep interaction with the field becomes a crucial research method.

Thus, from the study of stabilised 'rules' to the study of 'capacities to innovate', a more intense interaction between observer and observed is required. In any science, the more research attempts to increase its knowledge about some phenomena, the more it needs to intensify its interactions with such phenomena. In many cases, deeper knowledge comes from the transformation, or even destruction, of the object under study. Hence, rigour in management research cannot be defined per se, and there can be no unique sign of 'rigour'. Rigour needs the combination and integration of a variety of research methods tailored to the nature and history of the models of collective action under study.

Moreover, rigour is also a good guide for creating actionable knowledge. If no interaction between researcher and those researched is needed, this should mean that the language of research is *already* shared by practitioners, and results transfer should be easy. Now, if good research requires deep interaction, then the interaction process itself becomes a vehicle for the design of actionable knowledge. Thus it becomes easy to predict that 'translation problems' between research and practice will necessarily arise when research is designed without any interaction with the field and yet there are ambitions to treat issues that, as rigour demands, should be studied through an interaction process!

This explains why FPM has largely explored the scientific opportunities offered by collaborative research with partners (organisations and practitioners) and attempted to define design principles for research-oriented partnerships. Hatchuel and David (2007) have discussed at length these principles, which from their perspective depart considerably from standard action research and offer a powerful solution to the 'translation problem in management research' (Shapiro et al. 2007).

3.3.3 Relevance as a Constitutive Issue of Management Research

In the literature 'relevance' is defined (Starkey and Madan 2001; Schapiro et al. 2007) as the capacity of academic knowledge to have valuable impact outside the academy. This seems a different issue from rigour. Yet we have suggested in the preceding paragraph that rigour may need interactions which introduce those researched as a potential stakeholder of the research process. Moreover, following modern epistemology (Poincaré 1905), the 'good' theory is not the theory which reaches perfect truth (a criterion which is often impossible to test as such) but the theory which has more 'advantages' (elegance, tractability, completeness and so on). Thus, 'relevance' is a constitutive issue of research, as there is always a stakeholder, be it the researcher or the research community itself. Now, if there is no other stakeholder than the academy, relevance may be confused with the easiest, lowest-cost, most tractable form of rigour! But, whenever practitioners or any other stakeholders intervene in the research process, relevance and rigour become different yet interdependent notions (not necessarily contradictory); and this opens a wide range of combinations of rigour and relevance that will foster the production of knowledge in diverse, yet meaningful, directions.

In many cases, rigour in management research directly requires the careful introduction of observed people into the research process. Relevance principles will necessarily reflect the identity of these new stakeholders. For example, cancer research has to take into account the quality of life of the patients. This does not harm the rigour of the research. It only orients the production of knowledge. At the same time, it enables the research process if a consistent partnership is found between researchers and those researched. Therefore, management research has no other choice than to explore the potential of such combinations. Moreover, in management science, 'relevance' itself can be an issue of investigation, as it may correspond to implicit models of collective action. And management research can influence the design of the relevance principles that are used by research stakeholders. In a similar manner, accounting changed the view of fair trade.

Finally, linking the identity of management research to rigour and relevance principles overcomes most pitfalls of the field and leads to a basic science where the research process and the object under study can be consistently analysed with the same theory!

3.4   CONCLUDING DISCUSSION: ABOUT SOME FINDINGS OF NEW MANAGEMENT RESEARCH

FPM claims a new approach for management science and management research. Yet what are the research findings produced by such principles? It is not possible to summarise in this chapter all the literature produced by researchers who share these views. However, we will briefly mention two contributions that illustrate how FPM can produce theoretical, critical and practical findings: 1) a theory of management techniques as a criticism of classic organisation theory; 2) a theory of collective design as a critique of standard R&D and project management.

3.4.1   A Theory of Management Instruments versus Classic Organisation Theory

The idea of 'organisational control' seems universal. This is, however, a false universal. As early as the Middle Ages and during the Renaissance, the inventive renewal of the accounting system showed that commercial activity could not be organised with traditional forms of control.[8] Neither family ties nor feudal hierarchies generated the knowledge and social relations that could allow trade expansion without an explosion of matters in dispute. Accounting systems and rules produced a new model of collective action founded on the cognitive model of 'account' and 'balance', as well as the elaboration of account books and their special jurisdictions. On the other side, they supported the social relation that defined a legitimate 'economic debt'. This model of action has been active for five centuries. However, it already embodies an artificial and non-traditional conception of organisational theory and control. The development of accounting meant it was no longer a question of positions in lineages, prerogatives and rank but of a set of 'management techniques'[9] which determined, independent of common social networks, the validity and justice of a particular kind of collective action.[10] These new management techniques enabled new forms of organised trades and businesses.

The accounting system is only one particular form of 'managerial technique', and it was followed by several other rationalisations of management (Hatchuel and Molet 1986; Hatchuel and Weil 1995; Moisdon 1997). Therefore, management history should follow the history of managerial techniques (corporate law, production planning, knowledge management, TQM). Within FPM assumptions, this category is easier to describe with controlled theoretical generality. Management techniques are embodied and stabilised rationalisations (or models) of collective action, and they possess the paradoxical nature of being used in two ways: 1) as normative rules generating conformity and stabilised action; or 2) as creative models which invent new views or allow for new voices, thus generating new 'organisational realities' (Berry 1983; Hatchuel and Molet 1986; Moisdon 1997). Therefore, the theory of management techniques redefines the concept of 'organisation' (Hatchuel and Weil 1995), and one could hardly recognise an organisation without identifying the management instruments which enable it to be put into action. Thus, organisations can be more accurately defined as collective processes resulting from the historical accumulation and generation of management techniques (Hatchuel and Weil 1995). Their boundaries, unity and governance are observable only if there is a stabilised and recognised management technique associated with these attributes.

The same type of reasoning can be applied to 'rationality': there is no observable rationality without a management technique, be it the simplest, such as using stable names for the designation of things. The history of management instruments is therefore a specific marker for the history and genealogy of organisation and rationality (Townley 2005). It is only recently that sociologists and political scientists (Lascoumes and Le Galès 2005) have become aware of the importance of management instruments as analysers of social change and stability, thus recognising a theory born in management research years before.

3.4.2 A Theory of Innovative Design versus Standard R&D and Project Management

Projects have come to occupy increasing space in contemporary companies and management debate (Midler and Lundin 1999). Yet which model of collective action is implicit in innovative projects? Which managerial technique should embody such models? Recent research (Hatchuel et al. 2006; Le Masson et al. 2010) has critically discussed classic distinctions between linear and turbulent models of R&D, as well as standard project management. All fail to capture the type of collective action that has been 'invented' by innovative firms which do not necessarily model their actions in a rigorous way. In such discovery situations (Hatchuel and David 2007), the role of research is to develop a theoretical model of such creative collective action. Using recent design theory, it has been shown (Hatchuel et al. 2006) that, to cope with highly innovative ideas, managers activate unclear yet suggestive concepts and promote provisional work divisions; these actions generate unknown and emergent, yet expected, realities, and these new 'constructed truths' are used to redefine initial concepts and work organisation. This model of collective action based on the simultaneous revision of concepts and work division cannot be compared to the classic flexibility or adaptive planning described in the literature. In such contexts, strategy is better understood as innovative design (Hatchuel et al. 2010). Such a model of collective action is a highly disturbing process for standard management models, and its diffusion may signal a long-term transformation of contemporary firms, of which we are probably seeing just the beginnings. Beyond a better understanding of innovative firms, such new models of collective action may also trigger the development of new managerial techniques and consequently new organisational settings. This is an appropriate area for new management research.

3.5   CONCLUDING REMARKS

In this chapter I have attempted to show that some European currents, such as FPM, have reached enough scientific maturity to offer consistent solutions to the 'translation problem' in all its dimensions. Yet FPM goes beyond such a goal and develops a systematic foundation of management science that clarifies the identity, rigour and relevance of management research.

A key assertion of FPM is that management research studies and generates models of collective action. It fills a hitherto unoccupied place in academia. It cannot be reduced to economics, sociology or psychology, at least to the extent that the identity of each of these disciplines depends on a particular and restrictive model of collective action (the rational subject, the collective as subject, and the subject as an autonomous entity). FPM also establishes that management research is deeply dependent on the history of management. Rigour needs designed connections with contemporary firms and organisations (including not-for-profit ones); these connections enrich the relevance principles of research and will create research incentives in favour of the exploration and expansion of new models of collective action.

Thus, well-founded management research can be seen as a central process of societies where no dogmatic ideology or encompassing power can inhibit reflexivity and shape the future.

NOTES

1. With the permission of the editorial team of the *Management Decision* journal, this chapter is an adapted version of: A. Hatchuel, 'A foundational perspective on management research: a European trend and experience', *Management Decision*, **47** (9), 2009, pp.1458–76.
2. Foundationalism is also a research current in epistemology and theory of knowledge, but there is no direct influence of this movement on the formation of FPM.
3. The same questions were raised for the rival doctrine of Frederick Taylor (by Wren), but the 'principles of scientific management' were closer to engineering doctrines and were introduced early in engineering schools.
4. Armand Hatchuel (École des Mines), Albert David (University of Dauphine) and Romain Laufer (HEC).
5. In addition to the editors, three authors contributed to the book: Jacques Girin (École Polytechnique), Alain Charles Martinet (University of Lyon) and Bernard Roy (University of Dauphine).
6. A second edition of the book was published in 2008.
7. This does not mean that statistical analysis and data mining cannot generate surprising results. The problem appears when these results are interpreted in management terms. For instance, if a survey shows that some firms are very innovative yet with very low R&D expenditures, the managerial interpretation of this fact depends on the degree of homogeneity of the R&D definition, organisation and cost measurement among the firms. Now, if this degree is high, it clearly means that a similar codification of R&D has already been done in all these firms, and this is precisely what we call a stabilised and uniform 'in use' model of action. This also means that some R&D management model has been diffused and standardised and is also well understood by the researchers.
8. The simplest of commercial 'accounts' can be traced back into the mists of time.
9. An expression generally equivalent to 'management tools', 'managerial techniques' and 'management methods'.
10. One can always slant accounts in one's favour, even mask them, but one must nonetheless produce accounts.

REFERENCES

Adler, N., A.B. (Rami) Shani and A. Styhre (eds) (2004), *Collaborative Research in Organizations*, London: Sage.
Berry, M. (1983), *Une technologie invisible* [An invisible technology], Paris: École Polytechnique Publications.
Burrell, G. and G. Morgan (2003), *Sociological Paradigms and Organizational Analysis*, Oxford: Heinemann.

Cummings, T.G. (2007), 'Presidential address: quest for an engaged academy', *Academy of Management Review*, **32** (2), 355–61.

David, A. and A. Hatchuel (2007), 'From actionable knowledge to universal theory in management research', in R. Shani, S. Mohrman, W. Passmore, B. Stymne and N. Adler (eds), *Handbook of Collaborative Management Research*, Thousand Oaks, CA: Sage.

David, A., A. Hatchuel and R. Laufer (eds) (2001), *Les nouvelles fondations des management sciences* [The new foundations of management science], Paris: Vuibert/FNEGE.

Foucault, M. (1966), *Les mots et les choses* [The order of things], Paris: Gallimard/NRF.

Hambrick, D.C. (2007), 'Upper echelons theory: an update', *Academy of Management Review*, **32** (2), 334–44.

Hatchuel, A. (2001), 'The two pillars of new management research', *British Journal of Management*, **12** (Special Issue), 33–9.

Hatchuel, A. (2005), 'Towards an epistemology of collective action: management research as a responsible and actionable discipline', *European Management Review*, **2**, 36–47.

Hatchuel A. and H. Molet (1986), 'Rational modelling in understanding and aiding human decision making', *European Journal of Operations Research*, **24**, 178–86.

Hatchuel, A. and B. Weil (1995), *Experts in Organizations*, Berlin and New York: Walter de Gruyter.

Hatchuel, A. and A. David (2007), 'Collaborating for management research: from action research to intervention research in management', in R. Shani, S. Mohrman, W. Passmore, B. Stymne and N. Adler (eds), *Handbook of Collaborative Management Research*, Thousand Oaks, CA: Sage.

Hatchuel, A., P. Le Masson and B. Weil (2006), 'Building innovation capabilities: the development of design-oriented organizations', in J. Hage and M. Meeus (eds), *Science, Innovation and Institutional Change: A Research Handbook*, Oxford: Oxford University Press.

Hatchuel, A., K. Starkey, S. Tempest and P. Le Masson (2010), 'Strategy as innovative design: an emerging perspective', *Advances in Strategic Management*, **27**, 3–28.

Huff, A.S. (2000), 'Presidential address: changes in organizational knowledge production', *Academy of Management Review*, **25**, 288–93.

Huff, A.S. and J.O. Huff (2001), 'Re-focusing the business school agenda', *British Journal of Management*, **12** (Special Issue), S49–S54.

Kilduff, M. (2007), 'Celebrating thirty years of theory publishing in *AMR*: award-winning articles from the first two decades revisited', *Academy of Management Review*, **32** (2), 332–4.

Lascoumes, P. and P. Le Galès (2005), *Gouverner par les instruments* [Governing through instruments], Paris: Presses de l'École des Sciences Politiques.

Le Masson, P., B. Weil and A. Hatchuel (2010), *The Strategic Management of Innovation and Design*, Cambridge: Cambridge University Press.

Martinet, A.C. (ed.) (1988), *Épistémologie des Sciences de Management* [Epistemology of management sciences], Paris: Economica.

Martinet, A.C., F. Alvarez, G. Colombo and P. Corbel (2007), *Sciences du management: Epistémique, pragmatique et éthique* [Management science: epistemology, pragmatics and ethics], Paris: Vuibert/FNEGE.

Midler, C. and R. Lundin (1999), *Projects as Arenas for Policy and Learning*, Norwell, MA: Kluwer.

Moisdon, J.C. (ed.) (1997), *Du mode d'existence des outils de management* [On the mode of existence of management instruments], Paris: Seliarslan.

Nodoushani, O. (2000), 'Epistemological foundations of management theory and research methodology', *Human Systems Management*, **19** (1), 71–80.

Pettigrew, A.M. (1997), 'The double hurdles of management research', in T. Clarke (ed.), *Advancement in Organizational Behaviour: Essays in Honour of D.S. Pugh*, London: Dartmouth Press, pp. 276–96.

Pettigrew, A.M. (2001), 'Management research after modernism', *British Journal of Management*, **12** (Special Issue), S61–S70.

Poincaré, H. (1905), *Science and Hypothesis*, New York: Walter Scott Publishing.

Schon, D. (1994), *The Reflective Practitioner: How Professionals Think in Action*, Aldershot: Arena Books.

Schoorman, D.F., R.C. Mayer and J.H. Davis (2007), 'An integrative model for organizational trust: past, present and future', *Academy of Management Review*, **32** (2), 344–55.

Segrestin, B. and A. Hatchuel (2008), 'The shortcomings of the corporate standard: towards new enterprise frameworks', *International Review of Applied Economics*, **22** (4), July, 429–45.

Shani, R., S. Mohrman, W. Passmore, B. Stymne and N. Adler (2007), *Handbook of Collaborative Management Research*, Thousand Oaks, CA: Sage.

Shapiro, D.L., L.B. Kirkman and H.G. Courtney (2007), 'From the editors: perceived causes and solutions of the translation problem in management research', *Academy of Management Journal*, **50** (2), 243–9.

Starkey, K. and P. Madan (2001), 'Bridging the relevance gap: aligning stakeholders in the future of management research', *British Journal of Management*, **12** (Special Issue), S3–S26.

Starkey, K., A. Hatchuel and S. Tempest (2004), 'Rethinking the business school', *Journal of Management Studies*, **41** (8), 1521–31.

Thiétart, R.-A. (ed.) (2006), *Méthodes de recherche en management*, Paris: Dunod.

Townley, B. (2005), 'Rationalité dans la théorie des organisations', in A. Hatchuel, K. Starkey, E. Pezet and O. Lenay (eds), *Gouvernement, organisation et gestion: L'Héritage de Michel Foucault*, Québec: Presses de L'Université Laval.

Van de Ven, A.H. (2006), 'Knowledge for theory and practice', *Academy of Management Review*, **31**, 802–21.

Veyne, P. (2005), *L'Empire greco-romain* [The Graeco-Roman empire], Paris: Seuil.

Weick, K.E. (2001), 'Gapping the relevance bridge: fashions meet fundamentals in management research', *British Journal of Management*, **12** (Special Issue), S71–S75.

Woodward, Joan (1965), *Industrial Organization: Theory and Practice*, Oxford: Oxford University Press.

PART II

Redesigning the contents of management education and research

4. The legitimacy of management education and research
5. Functional silos versus cross-functional views
6. Governance, strategic management and freedom
7. Relevance of new knowledge produced in management

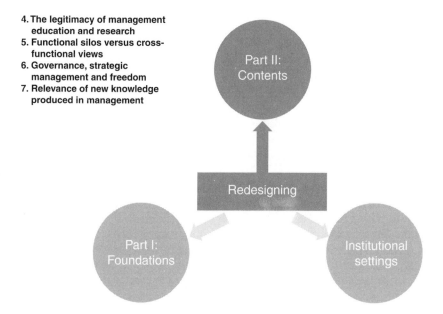

Part II is dedicated to the redesign of the contents of management education and research, adopting a contingent perspective. It begins with a presentation of three main criticisms made about management research, that is, ideological, praxeological and epistemological. Roland Pérez analyses how management scholars may answer these critics. In doing so he shows how and why management research should be regarded as specific and explores some avenues for the improvement of management research and education. Bernard de Montmorillon then studies what managers do within organisations and how their missions have evolved dramatically over the past 20 years. He discusses the issue of transferring knowledge to students through management education in different countries. He advocates that business schools develop the ability to inspire creative, collective and responsible actions. Alain Charles Martinet and Marielle Payaud in turn use the specific theme of governance to illustrate how alternative contents, departing from the literature, may be offered on such an important, much debated topic. Their chapter serves as a way to show how concrete proposals for new contents may be made. Finally Peter McKiernan closes Part II by discussing the relevance of knowledge produced by management research, arguing that Europe may contribute to helping the field stay away from too much irrelevance.

4. To what extent is management research legitimate?[1]

Roland Pérez

This chapter presents some thoughts on the legitimacy of management research. That legitimacy has been and continues to be challenged by several types of actor and circles of opinion, especially since the discipline's entry into the field of institutionally recognised knowledge.[2]

As it is better to know the charges before pleading a case, we will first run through the different criticisms concerning the legitimacy of management sciences, and then discuss each in turn. We shall end by considering a range of additional issues that are important for the field of management.

4.1 THE THREE USUAL ARGUMENTS AGAINST THE LEGITIMACY OF MANAGEMENT SCIENCE

The criticisms directed at management research are as old as the discipline itself. When, in the interests of lucidity, and with a touch of masochism, we take the trouble to examine them, these criticisms are seen to be based on three main arguments, conveyed by separate actors, in specific contexts (societies and periods):

- Ideological criticisms: management is a compromised science (associated with capitalism).
- Praxeological criticisms: management is an art, and thus illusory as a science.
- Epistemological criticisms: management is a pseudo- ('soft') science.

4.1.1 A Compromised Science?

'How can you be a trade unionist and teach management?' This question was put to a young colleague in the 1970s by the head of his department in

81

a French university. At the time, management techniques were considered as mere instruments invented by capitalism to gain a stronger hold on society. Historically, this conception is not untrue, as shown in historical research on these issues (Braudel 1979, for example, speaks of 'instruments of trade' in referring to accounting and the bill of exchange). Consequently, teaching and research related to these management techniques could be seen as a guilty compromise.

These prejudices were so rooted in the minds of people at the time that we remember a draft resolution presented at a national conference held by the newly elected French government in May 1981 to define a new research policy, recommending 'elimination of so-called management sciences, a compromised pseudo-science that serves the purpose of big capital'. Fortunately, like so many other suggestions that came out of this conference, this proposal never became reality. Two centuries after the famous declaration during the French Revolution 'The republic has no need of wise men', a declaration that 'The left has no need of managers' might have been apt.

Of course, mentalities have changed since then, largely because some of those who despised managerial approaches have had to exercise political, administrative and even managerial responsibilities. Being a 'good manager' of an organisation – whether commercial or non-commercial, private or public – no longer carries its former pejorative undertones, and may even be claimed as a positive quality.

Nonetheless, reticences remain in contemporary France, and beyond the political divides they are rooted in stronger ideological and cultural inertias: civil service functions often remain more prestigious (Bourdieu 1989) than the world of production and therefore the world of management. From the distinctions drawn by leading politicians between a 'market economy' and a 'market society', to the pamphlet on a 'society sick with management' (Gaulejac 2005), the managerial stance still tends to have negative connotations.

4.1.2   A Useless Science?

This time the criticism comes from very different circles: not from people outside the management universe who criticise without really knowing what management is about, but from insiders who know about management and practise it daily. They ask management academics questions such as: 'What gives you the legitimacy to talk about management when you are not, and never have been, a manager?' The implicit reasoning underlying such a question is straightforward:

1. Management is more of an art than a science.
2. Like all arts, it is based on qualities that may be innate (for the 'gifted') or acquired through contact with experienced practitioners (learning).
3. 'The alchemy of competence' in management (in the typology developed by Durand 1998) depends more on skills and behaviour than on knowledge in the strictest sense.
4. Management knowledge is often 'tacit' (as defined by Polanyi 1964) rather than explicit, which makes acquiring it through working with practitioners more desirable than learning it through academic channels.
5. Management teaching must therefore reduce the emphasis on academic knowledge to the minimum required for understanding the economic and legal business environment and using the essential techniques (accounting, information systems and so on). This should thus leave plenty of room for real-life situations (placements, case studies, business games and so on).
6. The best teachers of management are practitioners themselves (general managers, executives and consultants). Who else can share that sort of experience?
7. As for management research, 'What are you talking about?'

4.1.3   A Pseudo-science?

This third category of criticisms emanates from yet other circles: they are not ideological criticisms or mockery by 'doers', but an epistemological challenge by other scientists from the 'hard' sciences, particularly the physical and engineering sciences. Scientists or engineers, brought up on mathematical reasoning and the laws of physics and chemistry, are often uncomfortable with questions of management, which they find somewhat irrational and insufficiently rigorous in many aspects; hence comes the occasional nickname of 'soft sciences' (also applied to other disciplines in the field of social sciences).

There is a strong temptation to 'harden' these disciplines by applying conceptual frameworks and 'problem-solving'-type research protocols drawn from the 'exact' sciences, as a requirement to earn official scientific legitimacy. While this also applies to many disciplines in the social sciences – for instance, Auguste Comte's 'social physics' – it was particularly noticeable in management, with the emergence of the management consultant, a specialist in production management, scientific organisation of work, operational research and so on, as symbolised by Taylor and Taylorism.

Management research then attempted to take on the characteristics of research in the hard sciences, generally adopting a positivist stance founded on substantive rationality (à la Simon 1973) combined with a hypothetico-deductive approach and methodologies emphasising mathematical modelling and empirical studies based on statistical tests and econometric processes.

4.2 THE PATH TO LEGITIMATION: A DISCIPLINE OF OUR TIME

From the three strands of criticism presented above, we might expect management researchers, caught in the crossfire between ideological criticism ('You're serving the purposes of capitalism'), praxeological criticism ('What have you ever managed that means you can talk about management?') and epistemological criticism ('Where are your theorems, your laws, your proofs?'), to be tempted to give up and choose a less stressful fate appropriate to their character or mood at the time. Fortunately, most management researchers have taken up the triple challenge, opening up the path to legitimation of management as a science, that is, a collection of knowledge that is identifiable, can be held simultaneously, may be contestable (à la Popper 1974) and when appropriate may be transferable and taught.

Their efforts to defend the field of management had to address the critical points referred to above:

- The response to the ideological criticism was an effort to 'secularise' management sciences, to avoid accusations that it was being 'sold' to anyone.
- The response to the praxeological criticism was an acknowledgement of management sciences as 'knowledge for action'.
- The response to the epistemological criticism was a reaffirmed integration of management sciences into the field of social sciences.

4.2.1 'Secularisation' of Management Sciences

The position of managers as faithful assistants to their bosses (family owners and/or shareholders), creating the instruments of their own domination, has changed on two levels: 1) the pool of actors has broadened: from the general manager to stakeholders; 2) the territory covered has broadened: from businesses to organisations in general.

A broader pool of actors
The traditional schema of a business is centred on the entrepreneur, who accepts the residual business risk, while the rights and responsibilities of

other stakeholders (clients, suppliers, employees, lenders and so on) are defined by contractual relationships binding them to the entrepreneur as an individual or entity.

This simplistic vision has had its day, and little by little a more complex conception of the business has taken over, with specific configurations incorporating the various stakeholders in direct relationships with the firm (those mentioned above) or concerned by its activities (affected by the externalities generated).

This has led management research to move away from exclusive submission to the general manager's viewpoint (whether or not the manager is the owner of the business) and take several other angles into consideration, starting with relations between two figures no longer embodied in the same person: the owner and the manager (the governance issue). Once the first step in this direction had been taken (by Berle and Means 1932), others followed, and increasing attention was paid to 'stakeholders' (for example, Freeman 1984).

This brief overview should not give the impression that all these changes happened smoothly. On the contrary, they met with considerable resistance, often insidious, sometimes passionate and vocal. Today, these objections appear outdated, and the view that management research can take an interest in all aspects and all actors concerned in the life of the business is very broadly – although not yet totally – accepted.

A broader territory

The second area in which management has extended its scope is the territory it covers. Initially, the main entity under consideration was the business (firm, enterprise), and more particularly the private enterprise, whether a sole trader, family business or joint stock company.

Here too, change came about in stages. At first, other forms of business were studied, with the focus on the specificity of their management (cooperatives, state-owned companies and so on); we were still in a business context, but subordination to the legal form of the business no longer applied.

Subsequently, other organisations began to be subjects of investigations into 'management systems' (Tabatoni and Jarniou 1975) in fields increasingly removed from the world of commercial production (for example, the health and social, educational, and cultural sectors), forming 'new boundaries' for management disciplines. Even fields related to powers of the state, such as defence and justice, were no exception, to such an extent that the term 'managerialism' was used to describe management's propensity gradually to invade the whole of life in society, a propensity which is not without risk.

4.2.2   Recognition of Management as 'Knowledge for Action'

While the double extension of management to take in additional actors and fields undeniably paved the way for the 'secularisation' of the new discipline, essentially in response to the ideological criticism, the situation is less clear-cut regarding the praxeological criticism that emanated from managers themselves. Management may indeed be an art rather than a science, but it must be learned mainly for and through practice, in contact with practitioners ('those who are actively involved'), without too much concern for academic research ('those who simply observe').

An appropriate response to this can be found by broadening the debate to other 'knowledge for action' (Argyris 1993; Barbier 1996; Avenier and Schmitt 2007) identified in various areas of human activity: architecture, engineering, education, health and so on.

Let us take an example from medicine, which often serves as a benchmark for management, through its organisation, its age and the legitimacy of its integration into society. No one would dispute that medicine is an eminently professional discipline: that is its very *raison d'être*. Consequently, a doctor's training should place considerable emphasis on hands-on learning with experienced practitioners. In this respect, the French university/hospital reform of 1948, which made significant in-hospital training periods a compulsory part of medical studies, was an important step (in fact it is surprising it did not happen earlier). And yet hospital training periods, even longer and more intensive ones than currently required, would not be enough to make a doctor: a medical student needs to acquire substantial fundamental knowledge.

The same could be said of the training for architects, engineers, lawyers and others. Less stringent requirements apply for management-related jobs, except for the 'number crunchers' (accountants and auditors), whose training is similar to that of the professions listed above. For 'general' management training, however (the MBA being the gold standard), the emphasis is once again on 'practical' situations considered 'close to reality' (business games, case studies and so on), to the detriment of teaching considered too 'academic'. Management education has no (or few) entry requirements in terms of fundamental knowledge.

However, this situation does not prove the illegitimacy of research that takes management acts and situations as its subject. Practitioners are not the only people entitled to talk about managerial activities. It would not make sense to ban literature teachers who are not writers or poets, music teachers who are not composers or performers, politic science teachers who are not politicians, and perhaps – taking this logic to its absurd conclusion – criminology teachers who are not serial killers! Just as it is possible to be a literary critic, musicologist, political specialist or criminologist without being respectively a writer or poet, musician or composer, politician, or criminal, it must be possible to carry out management research (be a 'managementologist') without necessarily having had operational responsibilities in managing a business or an organisation. Nonetheless, the question remains of the credibility of investigating and teaching management without being a practitioner. We will return to this point later.

4.2.3 Recognition of Management Sciences as Part of the Social Sciences

This section aims to respond to the 'hard' sciences' epistemological criticism of management disciplines, which they consider to be lacking in rigour and sufficiently stable paradigms, research protocols and validation of results. This criticism is not unrelated to the previous criticism. The reason MBA-type management courses do not require prior possession of extensive, structured fundamental knowledge (unlike the situation in medicine, for example) is precisely because these management disciplines are not 'scientific' enough, and hence the – sometimes ridiculous – attempts to make them adopt the conceptions and research methods used in the hard sciences (the 'Canada Dry' theory that management research is only a pale imitation of the real thing).

We believe that management research would, on the contrary, gain in legitimacy by avoiding such mimicry and being willingly viewed as part of the social sciences, to which it clearly belongs by virtue of the territory it studies, that is, human organisations with defined purposes.

The specificities of social sciences are well known:

- The most sensitive, which radically differentiates them from other sectors of science, is incontestably the assertion sometimes called the 'Lévi-Strauss theory' that, 'when the observer is of the same nature as the phenomenon observed, he is part of the field of observation' (Lévi-Strauss 1950, author's translation).
- Also specific to the social sciences is the interference between the facts and their representation, which are often closely linked, sometimes taking the form of 'self-fulfilling prophecies' (Orléan 1999). In matters of society, predictions sometimes help to construct reality.
- We add another characteristic, congruent with the others, namely the intricate interferences between the production process and the 'products' in activities relating to social sciences. The processes of research generate 'induced effects' (including externalities and internalities) that are often significant, and sometimes as important as the research outputs themselves (Pérez 2005).

Affiliation with the social sciences is not therefore an easy way out of the third criticism, because it subjects management research to constraints of various kinds: teleological (what is the purpose?), ontological and epistemological (how does one relate to the world and the object of analysis?), methodological (what protocol should be used?) and ethical (how can manipulation be avoided?). It is thus understandable that many colleagues, particularly young researchers, prefer the reassuring path of traditional hypothetico-deductive approaches.

4.3   CURRENT ASSESSMENT: 'GOOD, BUT COULD DO BETTER . . .'. WHAT NEXT?

Questions of 'legitimacy' are not trivial. Terms such as 'legitimacy' and 'illegitimacy' are sometimes used as weapons in social groups engaged in 'strategies to acquire, repair or maintain legitimacy' (Suchman 1995; Rollet 2000). An assessment of management research's long quest for legitimacy in the context of contemporary science could be expressed as: 'good, but could do better . . .'.

4.3.1   Some Positive Trends

The last few decades have seen significant development in management research, driven by society's demand for more management education, and therefore more teachers, and by international competition that makes scientific reputation the chief criterion for accreditation of academic institutions.

In a country like France, this growth can be seen in the number of doctoral theses presented in management, and the number of publications in the academic journals of the field.

Qualitative changes can also be observed:

1. genuinely new research themes: modernisation of existing function-centred themes (marketing, human resources management and so on), development of new themes (such as corporate governance, social responsibility and sustainable development) and the emergence of a critical stream of research (such as critical management studies);
2. diversification of the territory, and particularly a move into the new areas of public, non-commercial or non-profit organisations;
3. diversification of research methods, in which the quantitative and qualitative cohabit and are sometimes combined, in commendable efforts at 'triangulation' (Yin 2003).

4.3.2 Some Persistent Difficulties

These positive developments could be enough to satisfy a scientific community content with increases in its student numbers and qualifications, and the resources – particularly in terms of teaching positions – that come with them (although not always immediately). Such advantages can even arouse envy from neighbouring disciplines.

But the difficulties that persist are clear. We shall list them as seen from France:

1. The management science community is divided into various networks of institutions (universities and state-owned, consular, and private institutions), different specialities and their respective associations, different positions and paradigms, and so on. Diversity is a virtue, but fragmentation is not. Such extensive lack of unity is a failing, because it harms the transparency of the field.
2. The old prejudices discussed earlier, thought to have disappeared, sometimes re-emerge in the persistence of ideological hostility, in employers' efforts to keep control over many management courses (via the network of chambers of commerce and in-house training) or in the recurring attempts to establish a 'truly scientific' (that is, mathematical) approach.
3. Paradoxically, the very popularity of management may be a worry, as use of management tools can lead to surprising or even unacceptable generalisations, which supply ammunition for criticism of 'managerialism' (Gaulejac 2005).
4. Finally, there is cause for concern over the excessive academicism which appears to be a characteristic of much management research, in its various fields and specialities. Under pressure from current norms of scientific output and its translation into publications, many research projects are increasingly disconnected from practical management situations, or refer to them only through a minimal empirical study (lightweight surveys, use of a pre-existing database, and so on). As a result, a large number of researchers have no 'real' expertise in their own area, thus feeding the criticism over legitimacy raised by professionals.

4.3.3 Avenues for Improvement

The difficulties identified above are serious but not overwhelming. Once again we will simply sketch out some avenues. To do so, we return to the three-sided 'management systems' (Tabatoni and Jarniou 1975), which in our opinion remain relevant and could be applied to management of the scientific field itself:

1. purpose system: to redefine the purposes of management research – its aim is to produce 'knowledge for action' that can be used by all stakeholders in organisations;
2. organisation system: to improve the rules for management and governance of the field, via self-organisation of the scientific community and better redefinition of the regulation principles between the state and the market;
3. leadership and participation system: to improve dialogue inside the scientific community, between management networks and specialities; to build genuine dialogue, free of arrogance or complexes, both with neighbouring disciplines and with users of management research, as well as with the international – particularly European – scientific communities; and, finally, to participate in the public debates on the questions that are relevant to our times.

In the social sciences in general, and the knowledge of action in particular, 'Man', as the ancient philosophers say, 'must remain the measure of all things'.

NOTES

1. A first version of this chapter was published French, in 2008, as a contribution to the book *Stratégies et pouvoirs: Mélanges en l'honneur du Professeur Alain Charles Martinet*, edited by M. Marchesnay and M.A. Payaud (Vuibert, Paris, pp. 51–61). The author thanks his colleagues from the research team at ERFI Montpellier (Michel Marchesnay and others) and from the French Academy of Management, SFM (including Michel Berry, Bernard Colasse, Eric Godelier and Thomas Durand), for their comments on the first draft of this chapter.
2. While management practices are as old as humanity (cf. Sumerian tablets) and management teaching in specialist schools dates from the nineteenth century, its institutional recognition in France is conventionally dated to the late 1960s, when a national foundation for business management education (FNEGE) was founded, followed by the Paris Dauphine University with a dedicated academic department (management sciences) and thereby doctoral degrees and a specialist body of university professors.

BIBLIOGRAPHY

Argyris, C. (1993), *Knowledge for Action*, San Francisco: Jossey-Bass.
Avenier, M.-J. and C. Schmitt (eds) (2007), *La Construction de savoirs pour l'action*, Paris: L'Harmattan.

Barbier, J.-M. (1996), *Savoirs théoriques et savoirs d'action*, Paris: Presses Universitaires de France.

Benghozi, P.-J., R. Pérez and Y. Pesqueux (2008), 'Politique et managérialisme', *La Tribune*, 16 January.

Berle, A. and G. Means (1932), *The Modern Corporation and Private Property*, New York: Transaction.

Berry, M., J.-C. Moisdon and C. Riveline (1983), *Qu'est-ce que la recherche en gestion?*, Paris: CGS-CRG.

Berthelot, J.-M. (1990), *L'Intelligence du social*, Paris: Presses Universitaires de France.

Bourdieu, P. (1989), *La Noblesse d'état*, Paris: Éditions de Minuit.

Bourdieu, P. (2001), *Science de la science et réflexivité*, Paris: Liber.

Braudel, F. (1979), *Civilisation matérielle, économie et capitalisme*, Paris: A. Colin.

Chanlat, J.-F. (1998), *Sciences sociales et management*, Québec: Presses de L'Université Laval.

David, A., A. Hatchuel and R. Laufer (eds) (2000), *Les Nouvelles Fondations des sciences de gestion*, Paris: Vuibert.

Dubois, P.-L. and Y. Dupuy (eds) (2007), *Connaissance et management*, Paris: Economica.

Durand, T. (1998), 'The alchemy of competence', in G. Hamel, C.K. Prahalad, H. Thomas and D. O'Neal (eds), *Strategic Flexibility: Managing in a Turbulent Environment*, Chichester: John Wiley & Sons.

Ferrary, M. and Y. Pesqueux (2006), *Management de la connaissance*, Paris: Economica.

Freeman, R.E. (1984), *Strategic Management: A Stakeholder Approach*, Marshfield, MA: Pitman.

Garel, G. and E. Godelier (eds) (2004), *Enseigner le management*, Paris: Hermès.

Gaulejac, V. de (2005), *La Société malade de la gestion*, Paris: Seuil.

Girin, J. (1983), 'Les situations de gestion', in M. Berry (ed.), *Le Rôle des outils de gestion dans l'évolution des systèmes sociaux complexes*, Paris: Centre de Recherche en Gestion, École Polytechnique.

Godelier, M. (2007), *Au fondement des sociétés humaines: Ce que nous apprend l'anthropologie*, Paris: Albin Michel.

Latour, B. (2001), *Le Métier de chercheur: Regard d'un anthropologue*, Paris: Éditions INRA.

Le Moigne, J.-L. (2007), 'Transformer l'expérience humaine en science avec conscience', in A.C. Martinet (ed.), *Sciences du management*, Paris: Vuibert, pp. 31–49.

Lévi-Strauss, C. (1950), 'Introduction à l'œuvre de Marcel Mauss', in M. Mauss, *Sociologie et anthropologie*, Paris: Presses Universitaires de France.

Lorino, P. (2007), 'Un défi pour les sciences de gestion: le tournant paradigmatique du modèle de la décision au modèle de l'activité collective', in A.C. Martinet (ed.), *Sciences du management*, Paris: Vuibert, pp. 69–83.

Marchesnay, M. (2004), 'L'Économie et la gestion sont-elles des sciences?', *Économie rurale*, **283**, September, 72–7.

Marchesnay, M. and M.A. Payaud (eds) (2008), *Stratégies et pouvoirs: Mélanges en l'honneur du Professeur Alain Charles Martinet*, Paris: Vuibert.

Martinet, A.C. (ed.) (1990), *Épistémologies et sciences de gestion*, Paris: Economica.

Martinet, A.C. (ed.) (2007), *Sciences du management: Épistémique, pragmatique et éthique*, Paris: Vuibert.

Orléan, A. (1999), *Le Pouvoir de la finance*, Paris: Odile Jacob.

Percerou, R. (ed.) (1982), *Pour une politique de la formation en gestion*, Special Issue of *Enseignement et Gestion* (Cahiers de la FNEGE), Paris.

Pérez, R. (2004), 'Le choc des paradigmes en sciences de gestion', in E. Godelier and G. Garel (eds), *Enseigner le management*, Paris: Hermès, pp. 138–46.

Pérez, R. (2005), 'Jalons pour un nouveau paradigme en management', in C. Fourcade, G. Paché and R. Pérez (eds), *La Stratégie dans tous ses états: Mélanges en l'honneur du Professeur Michel Marchesnay*, Colombelles: EMS, pp. 73–88.

Plane, J.-M. (2000), *Méthodes de recherche-intervention en management*, Paris: L'Harmattan.

Polanyi, M. (1964), *Personal Knowledge*, New York: Harper & Row.

Popper, K. (1974), *La Logique de la découverte scientifique* (French trans.), Paris: Payot.

Réseau des IAE (2002), *Sciences de gestion et pratiques managériales*, Paris: Economica.

Rollet, A. (2000), *Le Couple produit/territoire: Régulation ago-antagoniste entre projet individuel et projet collectif*, Antony: Cemagref.

Savall, H. and V. Zardet (2004), *Recherches en sciences de gestion: Approche quali-métrique*, Paris: Economica.

Simon, H. (1973), *Administrative Behavior*, New York: Free Press.

Stengers, I. (1997), *Sciences et pouvoirs*, Paris: La Découverte.

Suchman, M.C. (1995), 'Managing legitimacy: strategic and institutional approaches', *Academy of Management Review*, **20** (3), 571–610.

Tabatoni, P. and P. Jarniou (1975), *Les Systèmes de gestion*, Paris: Presses Universitaires de France.

Yin, R.K. (2003), *Case Study Research: Design and Method*, New York: Sage.

5. Redesigning business management education: functional silos versus cross-functional views – a historical and social perspective

Bernard de Montmorillon

Few business concepts have as complex an evolution, as diverse a profile and as problematic a current status as management itself – factors that in turn call for a redesign of management education. When Chester Barnard published his landmark book *Functions of the Executive* in 1938, he drew from his own long and rich career experience. Formerly president of the New Jersey Bell Telephone Company, Barnard was also a public administrator (Barabel 2002). As the book's title indicates, he focuses on those who make business organisations function, make decisions and steer the enterprise, identified henceforth as 'managers' in this chapter. The business enterprise under discussion here is any form of 'collective productive project': a 'project' because enterprise, from the Old French *entreprendre*, literally means a bold undertaking; 'collective' because the organisation depends on people cooperating with one another; and 'productive' because it creates commercial goods or services for others. Barnard's dual skills converge in the importance he ascribes to two conditions of a business enterprise's survival: effectiveness and efficiency. 'Effectiveness' follows the classic definition: a firm's ability to achieve stated goals. In contrast, Barnard defined organisational efficiency as the degree to which an organisation is able to satisfy the expectations or motives of its individuals (employees or members), rather than referring to production cost savings, as we do today. His approach was taken up and expanded upon 20 years later by March and Simon (1958) in their equally important book *Organizations*.

These insights furthered understanding of the manager's dual mission as it developed in response to the increasing complexity of industrial corporations and firms. The first part of this chapter will show the evolution of the accepted meaning of management, first through the logic behind the creation of business schools, and then through the impact of growth and internationalisation in the latter half of the twentieth century. Business schools met a need for trained individuals, capable of making good practical decisions in several domains that engineering schools and universities did not cover. However, over time, a cross-functional or even 'transdisciplinary' dimension became vital; the manager was no longer a service functionary, but also a factor in fostering the crucial cohesion evoked by Barnard, March and Simon.

Even as this accepted meaning of 'management' and 'manager' became established, a profound questioning of it emerged. On one hand, the spread of international business strategies upset social cohesion in regional locations, to the point of calling into question the collective legitimacy of management. On the other hand, developed economies passed the industrial stage and entered a new 'post-modern' phase based on services, which required that managers have new operational competencies. These are the two facets of management that concern everyone involved with business schools – academics, researchers, historians, managers and others; they are also the facets of business education that call for redesign, given the challenges now levelled at both the cross-functional and the classic functional aspects of management.

Our investigation here articulates three concomitant factors: the need to steer corporations, proposed theories of management, and the educational responses offered by teaching institutions. This approach draws on the work of the French philosopher Michel Foucault: in *Histoire de la sexualité* [History of sexuality] (1976) he distinguished between instances of discursive production, power production and knowledge production 'that often [promulgate] errors or systematic misunderstandings' and that seek to 'make history of these instances and their transformations'. His insight is fertile, given that it is impossible to separate discourse, power and knowledge. Using a historical perspective, we aim to unite the theorisation of management (discourse), its professional expression (power) and the teaching of it (knowledge). Obviously, transposing the field of sexuality on to that of management is simply a means of thinking things through carefully! Our investigation will examine the origins of the dominant model and its evolutions before and after the founding of business schools. Next, we will review the conditions that brought this model into question, with a survey of diverse paths in Germany, France and Japan. Finally, we will discuss the rise of the service economy and its radical alteration of the social and managerial components of industrial production.

This chapter does not pretend to provide a comprehensive answer; it simply proposes an analytical framework and sketches some perspectives that business schools should think about, which it in no way recommends: most assuredly, homogenisation of courses and programmes must be avoided at all costs.

5.1   THE EMERGENCE AND CRYSTALLISATION OF THE DOMINANT MANAGERIAL MODEL

For a long time, the art of steering collective projects was primarily a military or religious concern, if one leaves aside political constructs. The earliest known military theory is Sun Tzu's *Art of War*, composed some 25 centuries ago. Xenophon's *Anabasis*, written at about the same time, could be considered a military treatise, and influenced Alexander the Great and, much later, Mao Zedong. The first writing in Western Christianity that defined monastic life as a corporation is the Rule of St Benedict, codified sometime shortly after the founding of the Montecassino monastery in 529. It spelled out the obligations of both abbatial authority and the responsibilities of monks to the community. These ancient military and religious writings' effects were felt rather late in terms of managerial thinking, when they were rediscovered and exploited at the end of the twentieth century. While military thinking has nourished business strategy education for reasons we will revisit, the organisational literature remains unsupported by documents that describe the administration of important monastic orders, such as the Benedictines, Cistercians, Franciscans or Knights of Malta. Doubtless, the reason for this curious gap lies in the fact that industrial corporations – mostly industrial factories – hardly needed an administrative strategy and were primarily concerned with technical and functional organisational systems. For a long time, they were efficiently managed using principles from Taylorism – updated by Toyotism – where a company's organisers remain separate from the workers and lower-level executives who carry out its objectives. Only recently has it become necessary to encourage cooperation and buy-in of employees or members of service organisations, since their active contribution determines service quality. Today, service activities imply a dynamic and positive partnership with the client, necessitating what Friedrich Hayek (1945) termed 'active cooperation'.

5.1.1   Functional Management of Factories

For the most part, business schools emerged at the end of the nineteenth century. Their missions and, more generally, their promoters' and the business world's concept of the enterprise and its operation converged significantly. Our non-exhaustive overview will discuss the first 'embedding' of management activities in these schools.

The genesis of business schools

In Europe, the organisation of higher education changed significantly at the end of the eighteenth and the beginning of the nineteenth century. The French experience provides a meaningful, although particular, example, marked as it was by the Enlightenment and the French Revolution. In 1716, the French administration, seeking coordinated development of ground transportation, created an engineering corps for bridges and roads known as Ponts et Chaussées. In 1747, it went on to create a specific programme within Ponts et Chaussées to educate civil engineers. These efforts aimed to provide France with high-level civil servants and scientists capable of guiding the country's technical development. Further initiatives included a college for mining and other extractive technologies, the École des Mines (founded in 1783), and a multidisciplinary school, the École Polytechnique, established through the National Convention[1] in 1794 and 1795. The École Polytechnique was explicitly conceived to provide primary education in mathematics, physics, chemistry and engineering to students who would later enter the other schools cited here – it offered a kind of 'pre-specialisation' training. In 1793, the Convention also dissolved the French universities, which had originated in the Middle Ages and previously provided higher education in major cities (Paris, Toulouse, Montpellier and so on). In 1806, the French emperor, Napoleon, reorganised and merged the universities into the University of France. He placed education under secular state control, centralising the curriculum and academic standards of the entire nation for the next 200 years.

The French university system, singular and imperial (and later royal or republican), was organised regionally into five main faculties: law, medicine, science, letters and theology. The faculties' mission has always been to train the lawyers, doctors, scientists, humanists and theologians France needed to ensure justice, improve citizens' health, continue university-level education and guide moral development. Mirroring this tradition, Napoleon's administration confirmed or organised specialist colleges, assigning them the mission of training officers, public servants and scientists needed by the state's services. The École Spéciale Militaire trained officers for the French army; the École Normale Supérieure schooled teachers; and the École des Mines and the École des Ponts et Chaussées educated future public servants and engineers. The École Polytechnique served as a preparatory school for the applied sciences – mathematics, physics, chemistry and so on – so its graduates could enter the state's specialised public service and military schools. The same line of thinking created a special college for communications, the École de Télégraphie, which later became the École de Télécommunications. The groundwork was set: the nation needed elite professionals to serve the state, its public officials and its military and legal missions. These missions required ever greater levels of technical competency, based on a mastery of scientific progress.

But virtually no managers were trained in any of these schools, simply because there were no 'organisations' to manage. On one side were farmers, artisans and retailers; on the other, public administrators and military officers. However, from this somewhat simplified but fertile schema sprang the forerunners of business schools – and their emergence is significant in terms of both their mission and the need they answered.

We shall look briefly at two more French examples, since France is where the first business schools were conceived, albeit outside the rigid university system described above. In 1819, a group of professionals created a college for business and industry in Paris, the École Spéciale de Commerce et d'Industrie (known as ESCP Europe today), one of the first of its kind. One of the school's champions was Vital Roux, whose experience is very significant to our review: in 1787, he helped create the first insurance company in France, the Compagnie Royale d'Assurance, and participated in designing the French Commercial Code a few years later. As early as 1800, he believed it was necessary to train 'traders', that is, wholesalers and merchants, and declared, 'Commerce will be an essential science for study . . . fortunes that have too long been intrigue's spoils will become work's reward . . . institutions that can educate traders will become more necessary' (Wikipedia 2010).

An industrial arts college, the École Centrale des Arts et Manufactures, was created ten years later in 1829, and its history presents two interesting traits. The school aims to encourage 'the development of practical applications for recent discoveries to help French industry enter the industrial age'.[2] One of its most committed and generous promoters, Alphonse Lavallée, wanted the school to train 'doctors for factories'. Civil engineers received training to implement scientific innovations for factories, now recognised for the first time as worthy of such attention. A new type of school for a new kind of leader was established, alongside the universities educating officers and public servants for legal and military missions and the special colleges educating professionals for the state's civil service. The new school encouraged mastery of trading, retailing, financial services and internal factory dynamics (doctors!). The 'manager' appeared with the growth of factories and traders, as manufactured products became a mainstay of national and international commerce. In this context, the 'manager' ensured an essentially operational, functional role – like a military officer or public official – serving an owner, trader, ship owner or industrialist, much as fellow members of other schools served the state.

The need to ensure this technical education for factory administrators spread in Europe and the United States in the second half of the nineteenth century. Obviously, it existed in all industrialised countries, but the trend's French roots and evolutionary context must be emphasised. The Paris Chamber of Commerce and Industry acquired ESCP in 1869. Another higher-learning institution, the École des Hautes Études Commerciales (HEC), was established in Paris in 1881, the same year that saw the creation of the Wharton School at the University of Pennsylvania in the United States. This business school trend spread at the end of the nineteenth century, with the Handelshochschule in Leipzig, the University of Chicago Graduate School of Business and the University of California at Berkeley's College of Commerce, all founded in 1898, preceded in 1889 by the Business School of the University of Manchester, Great Britain's first school of this type.

Functional missions

The business schools' programmes flowed directly from the logic that spurred their creation, organising themselves rather uniformly around the central topics – manufacturing, commerce, finance, security, accounting and administration – identified and systematised by Henri Fayol in his landmark 1916 work *Administration industrielle et générale* [Industrial and general management]. He ascribed five main missions to the administrator (today's manager): forecasting, organisation, coordination, control and command. In doing so, Fayol contributed enormously to shaping the model of industrial and commercial factories that would predominate until the end of the 1970s – the functional organisation. This model dominated for several reasons related to the historical genesis of specialised business schools, which were needed to teach 'advanced' techniques for running factories. Aligned with the massive capitalist industrialisation of Western economies during the nineteenth and twentieth centuries, the industrial factory became the primary mode of productive organisation.

The industrial and functional managerial model drawn from the factory spread during the post-war years. At the same time, it acquired a new, cross-functional aspect, owing to the social dynamics generated by the vast human conglomerates that factories had become.

5.1.2   Cross-functional Management of Organisations

Management teaching (knowledge) underwent a transformation with the emergence and consolidation of a cross-functional perspective, which, like systems frameworks, progressively spread via the dual impact of the factory's evolution (power) and its conceptualisation (discourse). We will use this same 'Foucauldian' reading in an attempt to describe this dynamic.

As early as 1938, in *Functions of the Executive*, Barnard insisted on the need for efficiency, meaning the ability to keep all employees engaged and motivated. The conceptual underpinnings of this notion were established in the 1930s, a particularly fertile time for intellectual thinking about businesses. We will discuss three important contributions from this decade.

Emergent conceptions from the 1930s

In 1932, Adolf Berle and Gardiner Means argued that a separation of ownership and control between shareholders and management – between owners and directors – was a hallmark of large publicly traded US corporations. This new conception of the firm postulated a managerial model where a salaried director, rather than the entrepreneur-owner, exercises decision-making power. Furthermore, such a director acts even more independently of the owner(s) as the number of shareholders (generally uninterested in the day-to-day affairs of the company) increases. Their revelation of this dichotomy was very influential: it fed John Kenneth Galbraith's thinking (1967) and his critique of the 'technostructure',[3] and reappeared in arguments about agency theory, that is, how the principal owner-shareholder can effectively control his agent-director-employee.

The second major contribution of the 1930s comes from Edward Chamberlin (1933) and his theory of monopolistic competition. Chamberlin analysed the pricing power firms achieved in competitive situations, gained from product differentiation. Attracting customers became a managerial task articulated with the search for lower production costs. Marketing is the direct descendant of this highly influential perspective.

The third influential contribution came from Ronald Coase's (1937) article about the 'nature of the firm', where he argues that internal coordination costs can be more efficient than the market because there are always specific market costs – the 'transaction costs' central to Oliver Williamson's analysis 50 years later. Thus, a new managerial logic emerged conceptually before the Second World War: the need to coordinate relationships between the principal actors in a firm. These key actors are no longer just the factory's or business's workers and salespeople, but also investors who provide capital, customers for its goods and services, partners who contribute to the manufacturing process, and also – very specifically – those in charge of coordination.

These emergent conceptions aligned with the changes that marked firms during the post-war years. We cannot provide a complete account here, but will simply identify the changes that most directly affected management, and therefore business education. Before describing them, we must make one observation: the tremendous growth of the post-war years reinforced the functional aspects of management and its teaching in several domains. Marketing renewed, enlarged and transformed the classic field of sales training. Similarly, finance emphasised the ever more sophisticated financial resources needed for a firm's development. Finally, we note the relatively late development – at least in Europe – of personnel management and human resources policies. In Europe, such activity centred on labour relations; in the United States, the focus was on organisational behaviour. By the end of the 1970s, the managerial model had not fundamentally changed from its earlier form. Managers still managed 'factories' that offered needed products to consumers while paying workers and employees enough to become consumers themselves; this is the well-known 'Fordian' model of control that proceeded initially – we cannot emphasise it enough – from entrepreneurial control. However, as soon as this first period ended, firms underwent significant transformations, heralded by the conceptual contributions noted above, and leading to a profound change in management theory and practice.

The evolution of companies after 1950

Large companies underwent marked structural transformations in the second half of the twentieth century. First, most became groups of companies. In Great Britain and the United States, such groups took the form of holding companies or conglomerates of relatively unrelated and often independent businesses. In Europe, especially Germany and France, subsidiaries in related industries formed around a large, central company that coordinated activities for all its member enterprises. As early as 1962, Claude Champaud demonstrated what he termed the 'power of concentration' of large, publicly traded companies. Many firms increase in size by restructuring into groups around a central parent company: some maintain an independent industrial activity, and others specialise in the holding company's activities. National interests often play a large role in their choice of activity (Montmorillon 1986). The requirements of running these vast groups necessarily led to a greater range of guidance, control, consolidation and financing tools. This was particularly true as the trend toward mergers and acquisitions demanded more complex capital-markets-based (rather than firm-based) financing. Private and institutional shareholders grew more distant from company directors and managers, becoming 'objects' to manage through dividend distribution policies, management-friendly board appointments, and special attention to certain shareholder groups (employees, leading institutional investors, those capable of protecting against takeover risk, and so forth), before the trend changed direction and shareholders started seeking – at least apparently – more control.

The second transformation, especially in the 1980s, saw groups becoming networks, under the influence of Williamson's (1985) representation of the firm, as drawn from Coase. Networks for franchising, subcontracting and leasing multiplied; business strategies quickly took up the question of internalisation versus externalisation for production as well as for administration and operations, all with astonishing commonalities. Usage of new terms spread: the 'firm as the nexus of contracts', the 'extended enterprise' and even the 'virtual enterprise'. Just as with the group enterprise, the network enterprise raised specific and hard questions about coordination; their resolution required the emergence – and therefore the education – of managers with the capacity to master this new cross-functional dynamic.

A third, obvious trend accentuated the need for cross-functional managerial ability: internationalisation. We do not need to provide a full chronicle here; the macroeconomic markers for internationalisation are well known. They include: ever higher global annual growth in international trade compared to internal GDP, with a few years excepted; accelerated growth in foreign direct investment between developed economies and then towards emerging markets; the first instances of global trade regulation through successive rounds of GATT; and enlargement of the World Trade Organization's field of action. These changes followed firms' business strategies, from the largest to the smallest companies, all competing in a global marketplace. Once again, a need arose for appropriate guidance at the highest executive levels, as well as at operational ones.

This triple and general structural evolution of managerial practices – seen equally in American, European and Japanese companies – produced a trio of linked effects: profound change in management as a necessary organising 'power', and revitalised 'knowledge' in the dissemination of management practices, supported by an appropriate 'discourse'. Unsurprisingly, several conceptual currents spread at the same time, concepts that would mark management circles and strongly affect organisational issues. Once again, we will use Foucault's framework to address economic transformations in the world of production, theoretical discussions describing those changes, and concomitant management education practices.

The dominant managerial model

March and Simon published *Organizations* in 1958, which marked if not the advent then at least the diffusion of a new concept of the firm – the enterprise organisation. Henceforth the productive project would take on a collective aspect. In this model, the enterprise appears to rest on a coalition of various stakeholders – employees and shareholders, as well as suppliers, customers, economic partners and local governments, consumer groups, unions and non-profits. Their contributions must be sufficiently remunerated to continue. Management must take charge of defining the enterprise's productive purpose and must ensure the coalition's continuity to achieve it, beyond efficiently managing each of its essential functions. This requires that managers be trained for a completely new field of action. A few years later, March joined with Richard Cyert to propose *A Behavioral Theory of the Firm* (1963), which characterised the recurring behaviours that mark a firm's economic decisions.

At the same time, another theoretical current took shape, with roots in the seventeenth-century work of Pascal and Leibnitz. In 1968, Ludwig von Bertalanffy published a summary of his work on general system theory – specifically, open systems and the necessary feedback, information, communication and so on required to sustain them, known as negentropy or negative entropy (Bertalanffy 1969). He describes a firm as an open social system, the result of a coalition of stakeholders whose cohesion rests on a variable dose of authority and adherence, and whose cooperation creates the conditions for an efficient, value-creating service to customers. A few years later, Williamson (1975, 1985) analysed the conditions of this efficiency specific to firms, approaching them in terms of transaction cost economics. Controlling transaction costs requires a manager to focus on core activities, and to organise interrelationships in a chain to ensure the security and quality of transactions, as well as their cost management.

This new, implicit managerial model is complemented – completed one might say – by the development of agency theory, where emphasis is on the primacy of shareholder satisfaction: without shareholders' investment and holding of a firm's residual debt, there would be no productive risk taking. This model would reinforce shareholder engagement, that is, their ability to control managers' decisions and, if possible, to persuade them that their fundamental mission and interest are to increase the firm's shareholder value.

We have sketched out the convergent maturation of these four conceptual models; they are articulated, in turn, with curriculum growth in business schools. Alongside functional studies reinvigorated by years of strong economic and entrepreneurial growth, new cross-functional management dimensions emerged and took form after 1975. First, strategic management appeared. Absent from most business school programmes at the end of the 1960s, it had become universal ten years later. It developed managers' ability to react to newly uncertain environments, to construct a sustainable competitive position and to analyse internal strengths and weaknesses along with external opportunities and threats. It also addressed the structure of vast, international networks and groups of companies, designing vehicles for their cohesion and ensuring their ability to manoeuvre collectively.

To achieve this, a second, transdisciplinary current of thinking spread through business schools, more in the United States than in Europe: it extracted findings from other disciplines and applied them to business management. 'Organisational behaviour' drew upon organisational theory, workplace sociology and psychology. European academic circles viewed psycho-sociology ironically, as a mixed-breed discipline that was neither psychology nor sociology. In the United States, the dominant view was operational rather than disciplinary, and teachings in this field quickly became an essential part of management curricula.

At the end of the period under review – the second half of the twentieth century – the outline of a third cross-functional field emerged: information systems management. As cited by the French epistemologist Edgar Morin (1977), Olivier Costa de Beauregard speculated that 'information is potential negative entropy'. Managing firms that had become complex organisations – especially the largest ones – required the circulation of internal as well as external information, to be organised, systematised, controlled and revitalised for operational team use. In this new field, information technology, data digitisation and the internet developed as major innovations, playing a determining role that we will revisit in section 5.2.

Thus, we see that the dominant managerial model had established itself by the end of the last century. On the one hand, years of tremendous growth refined the functional disciplines: production management, marketing, business financing, general management, controlling and so forth. On the other hand, cross-functional disciplines arose from management's need to adapt to the structural changes of the times: strategy, organisational behaviour and information systems. These two versions of management are primarily oriented toward creating value for shareholders. Financial markets do not depend on management, although the market's behavioural and organisational dynamics affect managers' behaviour and have taken on a greater importance. In all, at the end of the twentieth century, business education (knowledge) was characterised by a solid, dominant model that was simultaneously functional and cross-functional. This model feeds on the articulation between the operational requirements needed to master vast corporations (powers) and theoretical contributions that both describe and influence them (discourse). However, the model itself contains disruptive forces that put it in question and offer new prospects for its redefinition. Section 5.2 will address both.

5.2   QUESTIONING THE DOMINANT MANAGERIAL MODEL AND PROVIDING NEW PERSPECTIVES

Even as the dominant managerial model achieved international ortho-doxy, two challenges emerged that inform current debates about retool-ing it. On one hand, the systems framework provided an answer to the structural and geographical expansion of corporations and the increasing power of stakeholders (particularly investors) by elevating the 'corpo-rate' aspect of management. It thus gave priority to the enterprise as an autonomous and international organisation. This line of thinking also crystallised in challenges to the compatibility of actors' 'corporate' and societal commitments, of the company's own aims and society's, and of shareholders' and other stakeholders' interests. Questions about corpora-tions' aims (and those of their managements) arose at every geographical level in the countries where they operated. We will examine this question in more detail by analysing societal perceptions of firms – insofar as we can ascertain them – in some of the countries that have seen the greatest corporate expansion.

At the same time, and despite its renewal following the great post-war growth years, management's functional aspect faced radical changes in the aims of collective action, the collective production project. The increased importance of the services sector in industrialised economies required a redefinition of 'value'. Consequently, so did the management of this value creation – not only for traditional services industries such as transport, banking, insurance, business services, retail and wholesale activities, but also for services especially affected by information technology: education, research, sports and healthcare, along with culture and entertainment. This redefinition poses the second challenge for the current repositioning of management.

5.2.1   From Social Responsibility to Societal Responsibility

In a work that had a strong impact in his home country of France and elsewhere, Michel Albert (1991) contrasted 'Rhenish' capitalism (based on a 'social market economy') with 'Anglo-American' capitalism (based on a liberal market economy). 'Rhenish' refers to the economic model adopted by West Germany after the Second World War, which emphasises non-market patterns of coordination by economic actors, for example engagement by firms, unions and other associations to develop and renew economic institutions, and extensive state regulation of market outcomes. Anglo-American capitalism is linked with the ideas of Hayek and Milton Friedman, inspired by classical liberalism and laissez-faire theory. We consider the dominant managerial model we spoke of in section 5.1 as very much Anglo-American-style capitalism; indeed, we invoked Chester Barnard – an American business executive – at the beginning of the chapter. American universities, joined by the best of the British schools, strongly marked the theoretical landscape of management in the second half of the twentieth century. The supremacy of American business schools – at least the most prestigious ones – is unquestioned; it was reinforced by the Association to Advance Collegiate Schools of Business (AACSB) and the Association of MBAs (AMBA) rankings, even before the European Quality Improvement System (EQUIS) took up the same torch. European business schools follow these ranking trends, and an institution congratulates itself upon receiving an American or British accreditation or a high ranking in the *Financial Times* league tables. At the same time, the relative poverty of business management thought coming out of Europe, Japan or emerging countries is altogether too evident, and bears witness to the spread of the American model. However, new themes, such as sustainable development, diversity and social responsibility, pose challenges to the model, driven by rising awareness of how corporate strategies affect daily life – in jobs, lifestyle and environmental quality. Questions also arise regarding communities' views of the companies they host, their roles and their mission – not to mention the widening gap between corporations and communities.

Views about companies

We will examine three environments that may fairly represent diverse views beyond the dominant Anglo-American model: the German case since Albert contrasted Anglo-American and Rhenish capitalism; views in France, the country where business schools were born; and the climate in Japan, an Asian culture and the oldest of the emerging countries.

The Germans and companies   We can approach the Germans' collective conception of companies by analysing the legislation that established *Mitbestimmung* or 'co-determination'. The concept of co-determination refers to two distinct modes of employee participation: co-determination at local office level, through a works council, and co-determination at headquarters level, on a company's supervisory board. This mode of governance is very particular: we draw on a study by Peter Wirtz (2008) to describe it. The legislation is recent, dating from 1951 and expanded in 1976. Large companies must have both an executive board that makes management decisions and a supervisory board that appoints the executive directors and oversees them. The latter comprises equal numbers of shareholder and employee representatives, usually ten of each. The company's president represents shareholders and has the deciding vote in the event of a tie.

The legislation was enacted after the Second World War as West Germany redesigned its social and political frameworks. In 1949, the DGB – the country's sole trade union, established by the German Federal Republic's constitution – and the Social Democratic Party converted to a social market economy at the landmark Bad Godesberg party conference. Wirtz emphasises two essential features of this reconstruction: first, the fact that it took place in West Germany, cut off from Prussia's influence for the first time in more than a century; second, the Catholic Church's crucial role in securing commitments from Chancellor Adenauer, from the second-in-command at the brand-new DGB trade union and from the Archbishop of Frankfurt, who publicly called for workers to join the union.

Under such conditions, it is understandable that a dual way of thinking about companies would develop. First, employees certainly accept that management aims to enrich shareholders, but also expect it will consult their interests with respect to jobs and remuneration. We can make two observations to support this analysis. In 1976, 25 years after the German parliament voted for the co-determination law of 1951, the same parliament expanded co-determination laws to firms with more than 2000 employees. Moreover, German trade unions favour negotiation; industrial action (strikes) occurs only as a last resort, when talks hit an impasse. We note in passing that this tendency has less to do with the country's cultural tradition (or some 'Germanic' character trait) than with laws designed and passed at a precise moment in the country's history. The legislation's second potential effect is on managers' behaviour. Co-determination has inspired countless studies about its impact on company performance, but no certain evidence exists of its positive or negative effect. These findings at least allow us to conclude that considering employee representative expectations has not measurably harmed companies' development. One might think – although precise investigative work would be needed – that the co-determination configuration has led German managers to favour investments that create added value. In fact, we know that the weight of private research and development in German GDP is high – much higher, in any case, than in a number of developed countries. We also know there is little elasticity in Germany's trade surplus when the euro rises.

Thus we identify German management's important traits: ensuring shareholders' wealth while preserving employees' adhesion to the company, via an active policy of 'high-tech' investment and ensuring industrial jobs through exports. Certainly, co-determination is not the only key to understanding these choices, but it is most assuredly one of them.

The French and companies What do the French think of companies and, consequently, what do they expect of management? The answer is obviously no more simple than for other nations. As with Germany, we will look for answers in France's political history by referring to two texts, one very old and the other more recent. In 1791, the d'Allarde Decree did away with corporations. At the time, 'corporations' meant entities that regulated how and where individuals practised a profession; they often came under fire for hindering competition and the free exercise of professions. A few months later, the Le Chapelier law forbade workers' gatherings, and made coalitions – notably of workers – a crime. The stage was set: France's nineteenth-century social movements would take up the objective – necessarily political, since the law required reform – of legislating coalitions to defend workers' interests.

From a legal point of view – and a political one, if one assumes that the parliament's actions represented the people's will – French companies seem to rest on two contradictory foundations. On the one hand, everyone recognised the importance of free initiative, especially in industry and trade. We have seen how the genesis of business schools reflected a need for trained professionals in these two sectors. On the other hand, it required a nearly hundred-year war for the law to recognise the collective expression of workers' interests. The distance between these two views has diminished but not disappeared: a French manager will be perceived positively if his or her initiatives, with the attendant personal risk, create value for the company owner, while recognising the contribution of personnel working in the company's offices or shops or on the factory floor.

The Le Chapelier law was repealed in 1864, and trade unions were legalised in 1884. Over one hundred years later, the debate continues, with the same aim of reconciling two expectations. A few years after Germany passed its co-determination laws, the French parliament passed, or at least accepted, two Gaullist-inspired ordinances (1959 and 1967). Here we observe another aspect of the intellectual and cultural closeness of General de Gaulle and Chancellor Adenauer. The employee participation formula for sharing the fruits of post-war growth is worth examining, since it reveals the collective logic underpinning it: $P = \frac{1}{2} (I - 5\% \ EC) \ EC/AV$. Participation (P) is an equal share, half to be precise. The amount shared is determined by three things: first, the profit or net income (I), less the 'legitimate' remuneration (5 per cent) of equity capital (EC). This level of remuneration was determined when inflation was low, and equals an average risk-free return of 2 to 3 per cent with a nearly equal risk premium. In the formula, the balance is weighted by the capital intensity ratio needed to create added value (EC/AV). We conclude that, for the French, or at least for their elected representatives, the wealth created by an enterprise should be shared equally between investors and workers. From this perspective, management will be accepted as legitimate if the wealth it helps create is shared accordingly.

The Japanese and companies   The Japanese economy's success in the 1960s led Western analysts to study the wellsprings of its dynamism. Many macroeconomic studies examined Japan's international specialisation, particularly focusing on how the legendary Ministry of International Trade and Industry ensured coordination. Other studies focused on the organisational specifics of *zaibatsus*, the vast conglomerates that came out of Japan's industrialisation during the Meiji era (1868–1912). Just as in Germany, post-Second World War reconstruction – and the need to counter Communist China – limited efforts to break up these cartels. Many studies, especially those by American academics, have queried the mechanisms underpinning Japanese corporate strength. Williamson's analyses stand out for their broader theoretical fruit: examining managerial systems in Japanese corporations fired his interest in internal transactions, organisational forms and network complexities.

We can emphasise at least three findings resulting from studies of Japanese companies. The link between contractors and subcontractors was certainly the first operational factor that struck Western observers. The density of partner-like relationships revealed an organised sharing of economic roles in the quest to conquer international markets, where the contractor is directly linked to a Japanese supplier (and later, more generally, to a South-East Asian supplier). The way large Japanese companies organised their work also influenced Western analysts' views, especially the systematic inclusion of employees' initiatives in the firms' all-important battle against waste and quest for 'total quality', a process now known generically as 'Toyotism'. We must also emphasise another Japanese management characteristic from the 1960s – the strong relationship between employees and their company. Their sense of belonging, which compensates for the individual's involvement in the fight for greater productivity, rests on employment stability and the importance given to internal promotions.

The Japanese model that emerged from the Meiji era, reinforced by the growth of the post-war years, has been shaken by Japan's economic difficulties of the last 25 years: competition from emerging countries, especially neighbouring China; recurring problems in the largest Japanese banks; the effects of large European firms internationalising; and the increasing share of services in national GDP. However, the Japanese model continues to have an influence on management thinking: several studies emphasise the continued importance of organisational identity. We draw on doctoral research by Sakura Shimada (2009) that examines this question through the Japanese approach to knowledge management. She highlights the concept of 'Ba', 'an everyday Japanese word . . . that designates a cultural or physical place shared by individuals for dynamic interaction: a protected space for emerging relationships, a place where people can create individual and collective knowledge'. The Japanese company appears to be 'a collection of social interactions that form around the sharing and creation of knowledge', that is, 'a Ba group'. We can therefore understand why the Japanese were surprised by Carlos Ghosn's far more Anglo-American management style and standards, after the French head of the Renault automotive company took control of the Japanese car manufacturer Nissan. We can also understand why the Japanese question the compatibility of their perception of the corporation, their expectations for its performance and the recent directions it has taken under the 'imported' managerial model.

Depending on the country, the gap between the public idea of what a company is (or should be) and its apparent social utility will prove more or less marked; it is doubtless larger in France than in Germany, and in Europe than the United States. As the gap increases, the public questions the role of managers and management's usefulness to society. This feeling is latent everywhere: managers cannot ignore it, nor can management education programmes, without risking that the acceptance of corporations and their social articulation be called into question. Another rich development also affects perceptions of management: the issue of corporate social responsibility.

Societal responsibility demands new managerial abilities
In recent years, several theories have described the articulation between management's functions and corporations' societal responsibility, renewing discussions about management's operational issues. Douglass North launched a new line of thinking with his work, first developing a historical and economic view of growth. In *Institutions, Institutional Change and Economic Performance* (1990), he argues for the system we now conventionally term 'institutional economics'. This work produced several important currents of thought: awareness of the role of informal constraints in conditioning behaviour; a better understanding of the influence of embedded assumptions, especially legal ones, in managerial decisions; and a demonstration of the collective responsibility of public authorities

at all levels – local, national, continental or global – in organising the functions of markets, trade and therefore commercial enterprises.

The same perspective also impelled a second line of studies on corporate social responsibility. Initially centred on the internal, specifically social aspects of such responsibility, this discourse has lately emphasised ecological dimensions, that is, environment, pollution, public health and so forth. More recently, the literature has included the (systemic) economic responsibility of corporate strategies, illustrated by the 2007–08 financial and economic crises. While such investigations lack an integrated conceptual framework, their influence on international organisations, governments, public opinion and corporations is obvious. Companies – especially the largest ones – have been obliged to embrace corporate social and environmental responsibility, whether to improve their brand, increase stakeholder loyalty, obey laws or renew their business models' conditions for success – as in the case of strategic partnerships between corporations and non-profit organisations, for instance.

A third line of thought now pervading managerial and media discussions highlights the concept of governance. Two complementary theories influence its conceptual framework: transaction cost economics, which views governance as a structure to measure, monitor and verify the ways that the market, contracts or firms execute transactions; and positive agency theory, which focuses on the distribution of rights and authority in a firm as a 'nexus of contracts'. Managers as well as politicians are concerned with governance, which has increasingly expressed the articulation between various stakeholders, including societal interests. This line of thinking initially reinforced the logic of shareholders guiding companies; but in recent years, and in light of the 2007 financial crisis, governance thought has refocused on if not precisely questioned this financial logic.

Since the end of the twentieth century, we have witnessed a strongly renewed interest in the cross-functional and transdisciplinary aspects of management. It arises from the questions citizens and societies pose about the social utility of corporations. Initially, this questioning reflected the difficulty of bridging organisations' strategies: they want to be global while acting locally. The power of theoretical arguments next questions the affected actors – managers, politicians, citizens and scholars. The dominant model of management teaching has begun to integrate these new, transdisciplinary perspectives, as courses on business ethics, diversity and sustainable development spread into curricula. In the same way, management fundamentals, for example economics, law (and not only business law) and sociology, receive renewed attention.

Beyond affirming managers' new transdisciplinary responsibilities, the very purpose of business schools comes into question. Do they serve the nations and people they represent? Historically, states and citizens needed specialists capable of directing the organisations that manufactured and distributed needed goods and services. Have business schools become oriented toward corporations with international as much as national ambitions (so much that Vernon (1971) thought they could endanger the sovereignty of nations), but which play an essential role in economic growth? Are the schools destined to promote managers' interests even as they educate them, in accordance with the questions evoked 80 years ago by Berle and Means? It is up to business schools to answer those questions. The schools cannot avoid the debate; under certain governance conditions – increasing ties with universities, multiplying financing sources, and opening their boards – their practices could support the three stakeholders groups: citizens, corporations and managers. However, if business schools favour only one of the three, especially managers, they will lose their societal legitimacy.

This debate connects with another inquiry: as industry evolves towards services, the functional aspects of the dominant managerial model necessarily come under scrutiny.

5.2.2   From Industrial Management to Providing Services

We have seen that the practice, theorisation and teaching of the functional aspects of management were in place by the end of the nineteenth century. During the post-war years and the 1960s, these aspects were affirmed and transformed in response to 'consumer society' dynamics, which Jean Baudrillard (1970) described as increasingly oriented toward consumption (of goods and leisure), rather than the production of materials and services. At the same time, a very profound change emerged in the practical details affecting economic growth, at least in developed countries. The increasing power of services transformed the existing pattern, which, in its simplest form, articulated households and companies via industrial production, distribution and financing. As with previous observations, we will describe this change by identifying its chief mechanisms, the analytical thought describing it, and its implications for the courses taught in business schools.

'Intangibles' and their business models
A few observations will suffice to describe the growth of services in industrialised economies. The post-war years of strong growth progressively saturated households with durable goods: increasingly, consumers spent money on services that appeared increasingly necessary, such as healthcare, leisure, sports and tourism. In all, the share of services – in

its broadest definition and including food, entertainment and personal services – rose to 80 per cent of GDP in industrial countries, of which healthcare is 10–15 per cent, tourism 5–8 per cent and sports 2–3 per cent, not to mention insurance and financial services.

The expanding use of computers and software increased manufacturing flexibility and made 'industrial craftsmen' possible. Their efficiency shifted focus away from a relatively small number of mainstream products and markets at the head of the demand curve, and toward a huge number of newly economic niches in the 'long tail' of the curve, while completely transforming administrative activities along with communication and leisure habits. From the moment large industrial corporations included a services component – for example, IBM offering technology consulting services in addition to its mainframe computers – company management called for directing the functional and cross-functional missions this chapter discusses. However, implementing these services requires a mastery of profoundly changed functions. Today we see three changes taking place simultaneously. Classic service industries, such as retailing, wholesaling, banking, insurance and consulting, have greatly expanded in recent years. New service industries, tied to the healthcare, well-being and entertainment needs allowed by a higher standard of living, have emerged at the forefront of the economy. At the same time, these service industries – whether classic or new – find their practices very much transformed by the use of computers and communications technologies, as do agriculture and traditional industries, for that matter. We shall use the term 'intangible' to describe this new service economy.

This mutation reaches deeply into the operational practices of all companies: relationships with clients, conditions for creating value, mobilisation of necessary resources and designing appropriate processes. In fact, the whole business model for intangible services comes into question: we should necessarily wonder about these new dynamics. The term 'business model' seems of relatively recent vintage. It is not a business plan, but rather an architecture for converting innovation into economic value or, more simply put, a description of the way a business makes money, using updated classic strategic analysis tools such as value chains and the SWOT matrix. This new term fits well with our approach here, defining a few essential aspects of the (new) production means that service industries require, in order to examine how much they influence management teaching.

One characteristic of new business models is that transactions are intangible. That does not assume that all *services* are intangible, however; simple observation of most business models shows a link between the physical and the intangible. In the sports economy, for example, exercise, which may be considered intangible, represents about half of the sector's spending, while clothing and equipment make up the rest. However, although the intangible share varies, it is essential: consumers have to buy equipment for sports, just as they have to buy medications for their healthcare. Once we posit this 'primordial' character of services as experiences, the implications come into view. The customer cannot evaluate a service before 'consuming' or participating in it. Consequently, the service provider must develop a 'package' of elements that assure the quality of his or her offering: recommendations, brands, ethical codes and various certifications. Likewise, the customer does not buy the service at a prescribed time; he or she consumes it in real time. A service not provided is lost – a sporting event, seminar, game or trip, for example – unless it can be delayed. Value creation comes from use, not purchase; it underpins a spreading economy of access, subscription, fees and intellectual property that, in turn, takes over an economy of production, distribution and consumption.

In Europe, this raises questions about traditional employment contracts, typically inflexible when it comes to minimum and maximum hours and weeks worked, and the extended length of notice required before workers can be laid off. The predominant employment contract used in France, for instance, was developed in the 1930s. It aimed to retain workers coming into the city from rural areas for factory labour, deterring them from returning home for planting and harvests. Addressing the need for work flexibility is especially sensitive and socially crucial, since state-provided social welfare services – healthcare, pensions, and unemployment and family benefits – are paid for by obligatory deductions from payroll, employees paying 20 per cent and employers 80 per cent.

The nature of the relationship between service provider and customer changes in this 'intangible economy'. The apparently trivial but fundamental question becomes: 'What would be sport without an athlete, or higher education without a student?' If the department store is where the customer buys, then the stadium is where the runner trains and the classroom is where the student expands his or her knowledge and analytic ability. Commercialised service provision is obviously 'co-constructed', for example it occurs through the shared participation of the vendor–provider and at least one customer. Therefore, it requires two conditions: the customer must be willing to participate actively in co-constructing the service, and the vendor–provider must be actively present, whether we are speaking of the trainer or the professor of our previous example. The vendor–provider is a key actor who not only has the operational skills to provide the service, but secures the customer's willingness to participate – the vendor–provider is the 'strategist in practice'. We can well understand how this has recently affected management thinking: strategy no longer consists of playing 'organisational Lego' – mergers, acquisitions, offshoring, refocusing, core competency and all the rest – but of co-constructing value creation, whether it has to do with healing, teaching, managing assets, entertainment or physical effort!

A final characteristic of new business models is that they require the cooperation of all colleagues in a company. In the middle of the last century, Friedrich Hayek (1945) had already emphasised the critical importance of employees' 'active cooperation'. It takes on its full meaning in delivering services, where it needs to occur naturally, without coercion. The positive attitude needed for customer service requires employees' active adhesion and commitment, especially for those in direct contact with customers. Michel Crozier and Erhard Friedberg (1977) showed that any employee can establish a free field of action within a collective effort. (In a complementary perspective, the conventional approach enshrines the collective cognitive mechanisms that structure behaviour.) The 'collective production project' that characterised the firm at the beginning of this chapter thus remains at the heart of a company's activity, doubtless even more than it did 200 years ago. But it is henceforth a predominately intangible rather than physical project, requiring the customer's participation and employees' active cooperation.

Managing services

How can the management of services firms be taught? Energising the business models that we have just described requires a combination of aptitudes and skills that no longer correspond to the typical managerial profile, if only because the manager's internal social legitimacy no longer suffices for his or her responsibilities. Must we agree, then, with a work by Gary Hamel (2007), retitled in French as *La Fin du management* [The end of management], or should we try to conceive of the 'future of management', as suggested by the original title? We shall opt for the latter, of course, because collective action obviously will not disappear from the field of economics, and managing it will always be necessary. How, then, do we teach mastery of the projects developing today? The question can simply be reformulated, using the three characteristics of the intangible business models that we have underscored: 'How do we teach experience creation, transaction co-construction, and motivation of coalitions of employees, contractors and partners?'

Some solutions have emerged and spread in curricula. Teaching creative aptitude and innovation poses difficult questions – whether such behaviour can be taught at all, or whether it first must be part of an individual's personality. We are not talking about risk taking so much as a propensity for imagining the future. One common response would require the future manager to acquire research skills. In fact, scientists' methods and those of an innovative manager are very similar. The scientist will ask a question to which he or she does not have a sure answer, then examine all available information on the subject and refine the question; next, the scientist will invent a model representing the answer, and finally try to validate the designed solution in the field. The manager, in a situation of uncertainty, proceeds in the same fashion. He or she will use his or her own experience, and that of colleagues, to design a positioning and a strategy, and then implement it in a sequential way if possible, correcting the direction as real-life results come in.

The parallel between the two methods is clear: teaching about and via research may contribute to the development of a manager's creative aptitude. However, this requires a real effort to conduct research: the professor should have active research projects and the student should have opportunities to learn about them. In this respect, business schools should follow the example of Wilhelm von Humboldt, who sought to link teaching and research in creating the University of Berlin in 1809. Most of the prestigious institutions cited earlier have understood this articulation, keeping their research potential at the forefront of strategy. However, there is a far-from-negligible risk of 'ghettoising' researchers, who, cut off from business realities, seek only to enhance their institutions' reputations through their papers and other publications. In such cases, the schools' research effort will not contribute much to teaching managers in the field. Furthermore, it may trap them in a confined, self-referential and closed academic circuit that has nothing to say to society.

Services delivery also requires a manager to learn relationship dynamics and to co-construct experiences. For this subject, business schools can draw on an old pedagogic tradition – the case study, one of the practices in use by ESCP since 1819. However, systematic use of case studies may make the management student too accustomed to virtual actions, disconnected from reality. Putting students in real work environments answers the growing demand for real operating experience. Business schools increasingly exercise this option, developing many kinds of programmes that allow students to work while continuing their education – apprenticeships, long-term internships, gap years, sabbaticals and so forth. Henry Mintzberg's well-known quip that management strategy could only be taught to experienced managers now applies generally to primary managerial education. However, the exercise will again bear fruit only if the student has frameworks for analysis, interpretation, perspective and formalisation, allowing him or her to form an opinion and organise actions. This presupposes a magisterial, parallel theoretical education. University lectures thus seem to be a necessary counterpart to grounding in operations, particularly in the cross-cutting disciplines that we have shown as essential: law, economics, sociology and history. Once again, Humboldt's insight in organising the University of Berlin along multidisciplinary lines re-emerges as a core strategy in business schools today.

Finally, how can managers be taught to inspire and maintain active cooperation among their stakeholders (especially employees) over time? This question touches on human resources education. Until recently, the prevalent thinking focused on individualising remuneration via a system of 'compensation–benefits'. Finely tuned management of material and non-material inducements would presumably steer employees into desired behaviour. This system is perfectly compatible with the image of the firm as a nexus of contracts, and with agency theory's implications. It has certainly led to managers appropriating corporate aims. However, it poses dangers to the collective aspects of a company that require – once again – active cooperation. Research by business sociologists increasingly shows the importance of a positive psychological attitude (Alter 2009), affirming the recent contributions of Albert Breton and Ronald Wintrobe (1982). In short, active cooperation depends on an intrinsic perception of social justice and fostering relationships of 'active trust' (Dameron 2002). This cooperation cannot become a basic condition unless the manager is perceived as the guarantor of the common good. This is what business schools must persuade and teach the aspirant: the demands of management efficiency have become humanist!

Research, multidisciplinary studies, humanities – in the end, business schools must become universities to teach future managers. Is that a joke or simply a witticism? Neither, really, and my brief conclusion takes a look forward after this long analysis.

5.3   CONCLUSION

First, we must observe that most business schools are integral parts of universities except, alas, in the country of their birth – France – for the historical and social reasons we have outlined. Thus they can readily update their curricula by reaffirming ties with their supporting universities, especially if they know how to sustain real interactions with them.

In this view, a professorial corps specifically dedicated to business schools no longer seems systematically appropriate: management students require access to the structured and critical thinking of lawyers, sociologists, economists, historians and others who think about business with academic independence and their own discipline's logic. That is the measure of a truly multidisciplinary education.

In the same way, management students must confront the realities of a firm. It would be even more constructive if these students could come from different backgrounds and cultures. Once again, the American model seems to have the greatest potential, because it favours a very open curriculum in the first years of bachelor degree programmes. In Europe, and especially in France, the closed circle of five years of business schooling, or preparatory courses plus business school, proves pernicious: it does not open up companies to diversity in background or approaches. It may also reinforce the emergence of dominant models and a single way of thinking.

The debate about teaching functional versus cross-functional courses has lost its centrality. Their complementarity is a given, necessary even, as long as they are reoriented towards providing services and societal responsibility. What is important – urgent, in fact – is business schools' ability to inspire creative, innovative, collective and responsible action. In achieving that, they will re-enact the model first proposed by Greek mythology – Jason's quest with his companions, the Argonauts, for the Golden Fleece. Jason needed the Golden Fleece as a precondition to winning back the throne and exercising legitimate political power in the kingdom of Iolcos. But Jason also signifies a faith healer, and thus we rediscover the foundational insight of Alphonse Lavallée, champion of the original French business school: the manager is, if not the doctor of modern factories, at least their necessary wonder worker.

NOTES

1. The National Convention comprised the constitutional and legislative assembly in France during the French Revolution.
2. ESCP, www.escpeurope.eu, 2010.
3. The group of technicians within an enterprise (or an administrative body) with considerable influence and control over its economy.

REFERENCES

Albert, M. (1991), *Capitalisme contre capitalisme*, Paris: Le Seuil.
Alter, N. (2009), *Donner et prendre*, Paris: La Découverte.
Barabel, L.M. (2002), *Les Grands Auteurs en management*, Paris: EO.
Barnard, C. (1938), *The Functions of the Executive*, Cambridge, MA: Harvard University Press.
Baudrillard, J. (1970), *La Société de consommation*, Paris: Éditions Denoël.
Berle, A.A. and G.C. Means (1932), *The Great Modern Corporations*, New York: Macmillan.
Bertalanffy, L. von (1969), *General System Theory*, New York: George Braziller.

Breton, A. and R. Wintrobe (1982), *The Logic of Bureaucratic Conduct*, Cambridge: Cambridge University Press.

Chamberlin, E. (1933), *Theory of Monopolistic Competition*, Cambridge, MA: Harvard University Press.

Champaud, C. (1962), *Le Pouvoir de concentration de la société par actions*, Paris: Sirey.

Coase, R. (1937), 'The nature of the firm', *Economica*, **4**, 386–405.

Crozier, M. and E. Friedberg (1977), *L'Acteur et le système*, Paris: Le Seuil.

Dameron, S. (2002), 'Les deux conceptions du développement de relations coopératives dans l'organisation', in H. Laroche, I. Dostaler and O. Boiral (eds), *Perspectives en Management Stratégique*, Éditions EMS, p. 101–30.

Fayol, H. (1916), *Administration industrielle et générale*, Paris: Dunod.

Foucault, M. (1976), *Histoire de la sexualité*, vol. 1, Paris: Gallimard.

Galbraith, J.K. (1967), *Le Nouvel État industriel*, trans. J.-L. Crémieux-Brilhac and M. Le Nan, Paris: Gallimard.

Hamel, G. (2007), *La Fin du management* (French trans. of *The Future of Management*), Paris: Vuibert.

Hayek, F.A. (1945), 'The use of knowledge in society', *American Economic Review*, **35**, 519–30.

March, J. and R. Cyert (1963), *A Behavioral Theory of the Firm*, Englewood Cliffs, NJ: Prentice Hall.

March, J.G. and H. Simon (1958), *Organizations*, New York: John Wiley & Sons.

Montmorillon, B. de (1986), *Structure et stratégie des groupes industriels*, Paris: Éditions Economica.

Morin, E. (1977), *La Méthode: La Nature de la nature*, Paris: Le Seuil.

North, D. (1990), *Institutions, Institutional Change and Economic Performance*, Cambridge: Cambridge University Press.

Shimada, S. (2009), 'Le knowledge management au Japon', Master's thesis, Université de Paris-Dauphine, Paris.

Vernon, R. (1971), *Sovereignty at Bay*, New York: Basic Books.

Wikipedia (2010), 'Biography of Vital Roux', retrieved from http://fr.wikipedia.org/wiki/Vital_Roux

Williamson, O.E. (1975), *Markets and Hierarchies: Some Elementary Considerations*, New York: Free Press.

Williamson, O.E. (1985), *The Institutions of Capitalism*, New York: Free Press.

Wirtz, P. (2008), 'Institutionnalisation des régimes de gouvernance et rôle des institutions socles: le cas de la cogestion allemande', FARGO Working Paper, Université de Bourgogne, Dijon.

6. Building more sustainable and responsible firms: proposals for a science of acceptable design

Alain Charles Martinet and Marielle Audrey Payaud

Business policy teaching is 100 years old. Strategic management research is 50 years old. The business policy *raison d'être* was to be reflexive, integrative and synthetical. Born in the 1960s as a research field, strategic management is now, in its mainstream, coloured by analysis, causal explanation, statistical validation, general micro-relations searching and prescription avoidance. In the same period and especially over the last 15 years, there have been an ever growing number of studies and guidelines concerning corporate governance (CG). Whether their focus has been on financial or accounting scandals, self-dealt fat-cat pay cheques, bursting stock market bubbles or even heightened social or ecological concerns, the various suggestions have often boiled down to a series of static, technical measures for the structuring, make-up and running of boards, along the lines of the theory of agency. As a result, business policy looks as though it is lost in translation and divided into two separate fields. On the one hand, there is strategic management *sensu stricto*, which seemed until recently not very interested in governance; on the other hand, there is the corporate governance mainstream, which pays some attention to making explicit the strategic implications of its recommendations and, more generally, the established findings of strategic management research. This chapter aims at showing how it is crucial to re-link these when it comes to establishing corporate governance and to regenerate general business policy in both research and education programmes. It can be seen as typical of this kind of approach that it refuses to choose between rigour and relevance. We can find here the epistemic main requisite of management research. In relation to CG, it goes on to articulate the conditions necessary for CG to work effectively in today's complex world and to be linked with strategic management issues. This argument allows us to create a model seen from an agonistic antagonistic systems theory perspective, which is particularly helpful in the way it gives structure to governance, strategy, management, and the way players can be made responsible for their work.

6.1 THE GRAVE DEFICIENCIES OF A CONTRACTUAL READING OF CORPORATE GOVERNANCE (CG)

The dominant stream of work in corporate governance, which found its greatest expression in the 1990s, can be traced back to organisation theory as seen through the lens of contract, by which is meant what Charreaux (1997) calls the 'interworking' of the theory of agency and transaction cost economics. This can be seen in financial terms, as far as its seminal proponents – Jensen and Meckling, and Williamson – are concerned, but also, and more importantly, in their theory's epistemology, methodology and 'transparency', that is, the desire to come up with simple, universally understood standards.

We start our discussion of CG by using a restrictive definition where CG means all the mechanisms that limit the scope and power to act of the management, who are both representatives of the stockholders, who want them to maximise profits, and opportunist individuals, who are likely to make decisions in their own interests whenever they have information that the stockholders do not (information asymmetry), to fail on their promises and, more generally, to make investments that are idiosyncratic or linked to their place in the firm.

Jensen and Meckling (1994) outlined and fleshed out their 'model of man', whom they placed at the heart of their theory: more than just a simple homo economicus, he comes across as an opportunist, someone who is ingenious and makes the most of his lot and who time after time will make decisions that will improve his own situation without any moral, cultural, social or political considerations.

Therefore, according to this theory, management should be surrounded by control mechanisms so that the stock price is maintained. There is both an internal mechanism, through the intervention of the board of directors, and external mechanisms, through the 'bad' CEO's reduced employability on the job market (he can have his reputation tarnished) and through his making the firm open to a hostile takeover. The problem of CG is basically one of finding mechanisms that are cheap enough while still providing effective monitoring. Of course, this monitoring will be effective only if the board is run well and if the top management's job market or the financial market poses no problems.

As stock market research tends to show, problems in the financial markets are increasingly being ironed out, and almost all papers on CG suggest that boards should be more active and have formal guidelines – such as independent administrators, and audit and pay criteria. However, it is also clear that the senior management's job market is far from efficient. Practically all across the developed world, CEOs in the biggest companies have been successful in earning pay rises, in the form of stock options, bonuses and so on, which have been totally out of proportion and sometimes in inverse proportion to the shareholder value they have contributed to create or destroy.

Thus there is a paradox: CG systems, which were supposedly set up simply to monitor the top management in line with an epistemology and a theory that are difficult to conceive in a more restrictive sense, have in practice shown themselves to be ineffective with regard to that single criterion – maximising stockholder value.

So we have clear proof – or at the very least an extremely strong case for empirical proof – and now the historical demonstration via the financial crisis that contractual theory is gravely deficient when it comes to creating CG mechanisms. Further, these theories are also lacking when a firm tries to operate continuous governance to create sustainable corporate responsibility – which includes financial control – and it becomes impossible to distinguish corporate responsibility from the responsibility of top and middle managers in organisational structures that increasingly differ from the ideal managerial firm as outlined by Fayol, Burnham, Berle and Means, Chandler, Mintzberg and so on.

Responsible corporate governance should not be based solely on shareholder theory with its shareholder–agent relationship, which gives us model managers who are simply there to make money and just in it for themselves. Neither should CG be based on the presupposition of substantial economic rationalism, which was torn apart by Simon back in 1947.

The empirical evidence does suggest that there is a pressing need to create new CG systems and processes wherein governance is based on mutual value creation for the financial organisation and strategic management.

Indeed, these deficiencies and the restricting of the basis of CG to a contractual framework continue to be given credence, all the more since strategic management research has in the main developed from this starting point. This means that the strategic management field has grown further and further away from corporate governance and policy. As a result it has little weight in the core debates over the future of the firm and the future of democratic society. Without allowing for possible developments in the equation, strategic management research already enables us to justify and develop certain hypotheses put forward by organisational finance specialists (Charreaux 2002). So, following Zingales, we maintain that current company structures are moving away from a concept that is stuck in time and adrift from the knowledge inherited from Taylor and Fayol – and given a facelift by Berle and Means, and then by Jensen and Meckling. Today's structures are less integrated, ever changing and more fluid (Martinet and Payaud 2007b); they are open to competition but also to networks, and internal and external partnerships; they put emphasis on knowledge, information and innovation; and they constantly blend the lenses of design and ideas, with decision making coming from the top and initiative coming from the base. Thus, top-level and middle managers are seeing their traditional roles and functions redefined.

Ergo, an epistemological re-examination of the conditions and basis for CG becomes of crucial importance if company policy is to be fully revised (Martinet 2007).

6.2 COMPLEXITY AND CORPORATE GOVERNANCE

We have seen that when CG is reduced merely to the shareholders' monitoring of the top management through control systems inspired by the shareholder–agent relationship it is ineffective from an empirical point of view. So we suggest that it is vain to hope for anything useful from such an approach. A complete remodelling of a company's corporate policy – both internal and external – is what is needed if in the twenty-first century the large corporation is to re-emerge from the current crisis.

CG as defined by contractual theories is not good enough. But at the same time there can be no way forward with a vague idea of governance. Too often it is couched in irenic and asymmetrical rhetoric where the playing field in question – here, the company – is a mere 'ballpark' where free, responsible equals play amiable roles and systematically bat around ideas that lead to a positive conclusion.

In other words, it is the exact opposite of a re-evaluation whereby CG worth its salt builds in the different actors rather than just the shareholder–management relationship. Such CG would be clearly defined with controls and processes that were sufficiently flexible to cope with the dynamic, complex face of the issues in question, but also tight enough when it came to processes and procedures, as well as incentive schemes and disciplinary measures. In this way Montesquieu's higher principle would be restored to its rightful place: 'Any man who is in a position of power is tempted to abuse it; therefore it is in the way of things for power to stop power.'

This re-evaluation of corporate governance has at least three basic premises that can be articulated through the creation of a general model.

6.2.1 Good, Working CG is Necessarily Based on the Stakeholder Theory of the Modern Corporation

At about the same time in both the English- and the French-speaking world, Freeman (1984) and Martinet (1984) clearly established that strategic management, unlike finance, could not be satisfied with shareholder theory, since it was continually having to deal with what lay behind the critical success factors. This meant posing a whole series of questions to find out things such as what the firm's activities, products, techniques, markets, partnerships and organisational structures were.

Any study of company policy should embrace the following principles:

- The company should be seen as an agent of both production and social organisation, as well as a political system.
- The company is part of society and not just in a market, and its stakeholders have both economic transactions and socio-political interactions with it.
- Policy making and strategy gravitate around the top management's strategic intent to make sure that the real company survives and develops.
- The strategic intent should be completed and enriched by strategies coming up from the other levels of the organisation, either directly or through those levels from outside.
- Over time company policy and strategic management should therefore create and regulate favourable economic, financial, technical, social, cultural, political and ecological conditions, so that both the company and its environment might be nurtured.

The top-level management and, to varying degrees, all managers concerned with the strategic planning process should be involved in an inclusive or multidimensional rationalisation process and cannot allow themselves to be locked in by any a priori assumptions. This rationalisation is part of a procedural and networking outlook, since it needs to be regulated by accepted procedures and operated through actor interaction.

In this way the company is continually constructing and deconstructing itself through its changing group of stakeholders, people who have stakes in both the cooperative and the competitive interests of the firm. Thus Perroux's old principle of conflict–mutual support or opposition–cooperation (1961) will be at work. The changes in the role of politics render it even more appropriate.

6.2.2   CG Puts Politics in the Right Place

There have been many recent studies on the economic effects of globalisation, the merchandisation of society, and the decline of politics, and an obvious conclusion can be drawn from them. The barriers which derive from Ancient Greece between economics and politics, between public and private affairs, and between the company and the state are no longer able either to be a basis for or to give legitimacy to a notion of management that shakes off the minimum requirements of the control of its power. Neither are those barriers there to underpin a theory of politics that suggests it is the exclusive characteristic of the state, and thereby gives justification to economic laxity, to which any monopoly is predisposed.

On top of this, there has been the crumbling of the barriers between nation states which also recasts the relationship between the private and public domains, between economics and politics, between administering things and governing people, and between management and political science. Politics has to be careful not to fall foul of 'ubiquitous and pervasive economics' (and by extension 'ubiquitous and pervasive finance'), just as economics has to be careful not to fall into the authoritarian or discretionary power trap that politics lays for it (Viard 2004). Today this reciprocal warning comes as much from recognising political power in the company as it does from seeing state or public organisations remodelled. The political scientist (Revault d'Allonnes 1999) invites us not to be content to see politics in decline, something which suggests that management should start realising and embracing the fact that politics is also (and perhaps primarily) about governing people. But this governing of people needs to be remodelled, since it must avoid the easy options of domination, uniformity, and imposing strict rules designed so that autonomy, diversity and process complexity (where there is interaction between different mobile players working in different places and organisations and within complicated hierarchical, network and market set-ups) can be included or even fostered. As the political scientist also tells us, it is the framework of politics that has changed (Viard 2004). Today it is less a case of organising and arbitrating in power struggles between various groups, and more one of promoting linkages between people – something that is a necessary condition of, but also the goal of, organised collective action, whether it be for economic, cultural or humanitarian purposes.

This complex world pushes us to think again about CG with a heuristic close to Luhmann's political sociology: any system can be defined as a search for identity that maintains itself within a complex and changing environment through stabilising a moving dividing line between the interior and the exterior, the known and the unknown (Luhmann 1999). This concept was greatly enriched by Maturana and Varela's theory of autopoietic systems (1980).

6.2.3 In Responsible CG, Ethics Must Be Omnipresent

With such complexity, focusing exclusively on static rules for CG can be a smokescreen when it comes to ethics, since they can be a way of hiding their real goal: maximising profit (Pesqueux 2002; Martinet and Payaud 2007a).

Such can be the case made for a functional treatment of ethics which imposes values on individuals so that their moral resources can be put to better use. A similar case can also be made for a reading of ethics that refrains from undermining the moral basis of corporate practice.

The change in the role of politics mentioned above, together with the crumbling of the power of the law and the growing fragility of human organisations, means that the questions arising from an ethical standpoint naturally seep into managerial practice and decision making. In this way things like social responsibility, sustainable development and procedural justice should in no sense be reduced to management's playthings; rather they should become core questions. Because the whole decision-making process is at stake here, decisions about scope, criteria, working conditions and the siting of work all include questions about profitability and viability, the short and long term, the economic, social and ecological perspectives, and the relationship between the individual, the small group, the division and the group.

Further, all real desire to improve CG will necessarily be translated by new readings of ethics, decision makers' responsibility, and interindividual and organisational strategy-making processes (Martinet and Payaud 2007a).

6.2.4 Four Principles for the Responsible Company

The following general model forms a theoretical framework that gives guidelines for a whole range of actions and decision making, and all of these guidelines will – to varying degrees – help create a responsible company. The model aims at assisting both top-level and middle managers to improve the way in which they steer responsibility-delegating processes.

Before outlining some of these processes, let us go back to the underlying principles which give them coherence and which the responsible firm must incorporate if it wishes to see its chances of becoming a sustainable company improve (Martinet and Payaud 2008).

P1: the ethical principle

The idea of corporate amorality is no longer a tenable mantra, since over the last few years in particular it has been used as a smokescreen for a lot of immoral business practices. As far as management research is concerned, corporate amorality has helped the development of a positivist reductionism that removes the praxeological *raison d'être* of management and that fosters an unquestioned state of what the French have coined 'rule by management' (*ordre gestionnaire*).

Ethics cannot by sidelined either in practice or in management research. On the other hand, it cannot be used to form a universal and radical criticism of the 'capitalist system'. Rather ethics should be part and parcel of practice and research, since it is the key to the future of free society.

P2: the political principle

Recognising the political dimension of management and creating the necessary conditions for it to work are the logical extensions of having power in the hands of big corporations, which can be seen not only through their business practice but in the way the world is structured.

Things like measurement and performance indicators, the goal-setting process, the inclusion or rejection of a given dimension or stakeholder, and the rewarding or sanctioning of managerial responsibility or irresponsibility are part of a whole range of critical success factors that must not be passed over or merely paid lip service. For instance, while there has been massive and dazzling press coverage of EBITDA[1] that extols its virtues as both a corporate performance indicator and a salary assessment tool, has the way it has influenced strategic decisions been enough studied?

Whenever politics is explicitly embraced within and outside the company, questions – such as the following – will be raised regarding both the style of politics and the mode of governance. How much control, negotiation and coordination should there be? And what should be the balance between command and influencing?

P3: the organisational principle

Today the large corporation can no longer be run just by hierarchy and top-down decision making any more than it can be content with direct supervision and short-termism that are continually being challenged.

The structure needs to be flexible and likely to stimulate an organising process rather than embody the organisation. The more the critical resource becomes knowledge, the more politics will flourish. The more

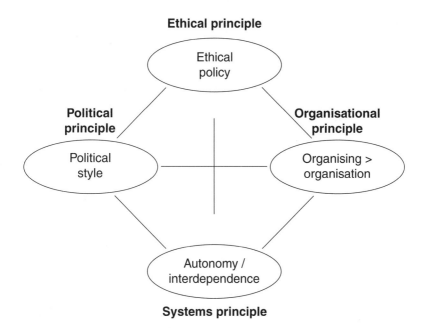

Figure 6.1   Four principles for the responsible company

autonomy and player coordination become decisive, the more functional structuring and process management need to encourage dynamic learning.

P4: the systems principle
The systems principle is epistemological. Our conviction is that corporate responsibility takes time to build up and that this is done by many inter-related actions. Consequently leverages must be sought, as well as making coherent the sort of learning spirals that agonistic antagonistic systems theory tends to produce. It is primarily the continual research into the architecture of autonomy and interdependence that characterises this systems principle.

6.3   A MODEL OF GENERAL POLICY

6.3.1   Epistemological Presuppositions of the Model

When taken as a whole, strategy appears in conflict with Boolean, uni-polar and disjunctive logic – as its rich history shows, particularly if one delves beyond the confines of the corporation (Martinet 1990).

Strategy has a much wider and more pragmatically applicable significance, a significance that can be found in the epistemology of complexity and dialogical method (Morin and Le Moigne 1999) and more precisely in an agonistic antagonistic systems science (AASS) developed by the French endocrinologist Elie Bernard-Weil for over 30 years; and we have also made a contribution in applying AASS to strategic management (Bernard-Weil 1988, 2002; Martinet 1997).

Let us quickly summarise the principles of the main epistemology used for AASS models in different fields:

- Phenomena are viewed as agonistic antagonistic couples in that they react in one way for some receptors and in the opposite way for others.
- These couples are live processes where a dynamic equilibration needs to be maintained within a certain bandwidth, but without one element ever crossing another out.
- These agonistic antagonistic couples can be seen in a fractal or even holographic way at every level of the organisation.
- The model should enable forces that are generally considered opposites to be viewed together so that they prove to be both open and shut, and synchronic and diachronic, at the same time.
- Taking its inspiration from the psychoanalyst Lacan, who talked of 'constituent division', the model should not look for illusory synthesis but keep the live elements in play but separate.
- Whether explicitly or not, any model refers to a meta-model and cannot stand on its own, and is thus a variation on Gödel's famous theorem published in the 1930s.

Elie Bernard-Weil has been able to get these epistemological models to work together, even though they cover a whole range of fields, from the natural to the social sciences. In particular, he agrees with us that management research can benefit from AASS (Bernard-Weil 2002, 2003).

6.3.2   The Main Agonisms and Antagonisms

In general, the complex relationship between the various elements that make up strategy assumes that there will already have been a priori consideration, so that the company will be able to implement a durable policy instead of letting events dictate what it does.

Adopting the AASS view, the company needs to articulate agonistic antagonistic elements and sub-systems and allow them to interact (Bernard-Weil 1988). This is necessary if it is to cope with the paradoxical dictates. In a planning approach, a strategy and guidelines are earmarked so that a durable policy may be implemented. But a learning approach is just as necessary: the location's subtleties and uniqueness, as well as its sociological, ecological and economic dimensions, all have to be considered.

Thus, we believe that what very often appear to be opposing forms of logic are, in fact, compatible. Further, we posit that they need to be articulated and allowed to coexist if the company is to be robust, responsible and durable. The agonism antagonism of planning versus learning implies both top-down and bottom-up processes. Top-down processes are ones where a team of managers – who are inspired by past experience and a knowledge of the sector, structure and trends – come up with new strategies (teleology), and these new strategies help macroscopic uncertainty to be absorbed (Martinet and Payaud 2006). These new global strategies are then enriched at local levels by middle managers, who are held responsible for making their unit fit into the corporate system.

The second sort of process is bottom-up. Here the local teams are led by middle managers, who have to adapt the corporate strategies to the local conditions. They absorb microscopic uncertainty at the negotiating table and in joint ventures (what Argyris and Schön called 'single loop', 1978), and they contribute to corporate strategies whenever their local conditions are brought to an organisational level (or Argyris and Schön's 'double loop', 1978). This knowledge creation follows the phases of evolutionist dynamics: variation, selection and retention (Nelson and Winter 1982). Teams that develop a network of relationships and a knowledge system with their local stakeholders allow ideas to emerge. This is called the inspiration zone – or 'variation' zone by evolutionists – and it is where problems are raised and tentative answers put forward. Thus what Nonaka et al. (2000) call 'Ba' is found: places where a shared context for knowledge creation can be formed through originating, interacting within and systematising relationships. Not only is there is knowledge of strategy, competencies and global solutions, but also embedded, contextualised knowledge of the market and the players who form it. The knowledge thus generated is then sorted and submitted for acceptance or rejection in the respective phases of selection and retention.

The agonistic antagonistic planning/learning system brings out two further agonisms and antagonisms: teleology and ecology, and the dialectic between continuity and change. The company should be viewed as a system of interdependent entities that create, share and apply knowledge (organisational ecology) in order to pursue strategic goals (organisational teleology) (Lovas and Ghoshal 2000). This approach can allow us to get rid of the classic distinction between strategy formulation and implementation in favour of a spatio-temporal strategy making that integrates both continuity and change.

There are agonisms and antagonisms that are derived from the main agonistic antagonistic systems (planning/learning, teleology/ecology, continuity/change). These so-called 'spin-offs' embody the sustainable company's frame of reference (Martinet and Payaud 2008). Such a company does not base itself simply on economic performance. Instead it tries to be responsible and responsibilising in its search for effectiveness and efficiency; there cannot be economic performance without social and ecological performance in the long run.

This new definition of the company and its performance finds form in new strategic action: strategy making where different dialogics are possible. These dialogics include planning/emergences, corporate/local, know-how/ relationships, factors/actors, technico-economics/socio-politics. One pole will not inhibit the other, but have a constructive relationship with it. As a consequence, the coexistence of these poles and paradoxes helps the subtleties and complexities of situations to be harnessed, with the company taking responsibility at the same time as it gives responsibility.

6.3.3   Responsibilising Processes

The top management team and the stakeholders
According to our general model of strategy development, where a teleological and ecological dialogic seems necessary, it cannot function without the development of relationships and know-how with the stakeholders who are the wellspring of information, and it becomes a means of adjusting, owning and sharing the organisation's ambitions, means and constraints, at both an individual and a corporate level.

Consequently, the top management team should help promote inter- and intra-organisational relationships so that a balance – a sort of corporate compromise – can be struck. The team's governance style is thus of great importance. Indeed, it gives enough weight to negotiating and organised activity to allow time and space for discussion and strategic conversation, and to foster putting issues on the corporate agenda. By encouraging these times of sharing, the senior management team shows that it is sensitive to the world around it. This is the 'corporate level', which should listen and thereby match the sources with the various different interests – all of which should lead to a learning organisation. More than just giving voice to the idea, there should be a real desire to adopt a mode of governance that is likely to embrace the stakeholders. That might mean keeping tabs on and developing human resource competencies. Or it might mean taking on board what customers, suppliers, shareholders and/or other stakeholders are asking for. At the same time, all the social, ethical and environmental principles and goals that have been fixed need to be adhered to and/or have their criteria transformed appropriately. All this remains possible only if the mode of governance practised by the strategic top does not impose rules and regulations that stifle the negotiating drivers between the different hierarchical levels – and with the world outside. By the same token, the mode of governance can no longer be primarily founded on dictating financial objectives that replace the logic of organised activity and negotiation, both of which are necessary if there is to be fruitful strategic dialogue. In this set-up, the middle manager can only play the part of 'financial controller' and cannot be part of strategy development, as success is measured only by meeting financial goals. In such conditions, there is no point in middle managers taking part in strategy. Yet there are two very logical reasons why they should: organised activity means allowing individuals to be dynamic within corporate strategic lines, and negotiating encompasses all strategic channels and means (Payaud 2004).

In organised activity individuals use the means at their disposal to make the group vision work, and at the same time they modify and bring new ideas to it to improve the strategy that is being developed. This logic is not just about nurturing unit-level autonomy and following a group image risk reduction policy at the expense of imposed, highly coordinated corporate strategy. It is also about enriching corporate strategy by giving details and tactics developed in local contexts.

In this situation, both objectives and means are negotiated. As a result, strategic planning makes room for qualitative discussion and the justification of micro-strategic decisions and decentralised strategies. The logic of negotiating enables discussion of strategy that is born out of a more or less formalised process of stakeholder interaction.

Whether organised activity or negotiation, the firm's logic in relation to its stakeholders should generate criteria that are justifiable for and appropriate to every party's existence – criteria that take account of both individual and corporate interests and that are negotiable between the firm and the stakeholders. These criteria promote sustainable corporate performance.

Learning and planning

Learning and strategic planning are frequently said to be opposites, but they are reconciled by agonism antagonism, as shown also by Brews and Hunt (1999). Thus instead of pitting them against each other, we should see the benefits of each and in this way find it easier to accept that each can both endorse and put constraints on the other. Consequently, the idea of 'learning planning' calms the stormy debate. Some are likely to retort by asking if learning can really plan. To answer this, we have to use nuances: the company can indeed promote and facilitate learning in whatever form, whether – in Agyris and Schön's words (1978) – it be single loop learning (adaptive learning whereby people react to change by adapting their actions), double loop learning (meeting goals means questioning the organisation's action plan itself to subject it to critical scrutiny) or deutero-learning (learning to learn). The concept of learning is one that is dynamic and one that explains why organisations change. But it is also one that regroups several levels of analysis – the individual, the unit and the company (Crossan et al. 1999) – and thereby allows one to review the nature of organisational cooperation. An interdisciplinary approach to learning also prevents us from taking too introspective an angle on it. The dynamics between these three forms of learning are at the foundation of strategy making in that they enable bottom-up ideas to be embraced and information and knowledge to be institutionalised. These dynamics are anchored in structures that facilitate organisational learning.

Thus, an idea is born out of knowledge that in turn is the foundation, conceptual framework, and guide for everyone. Any idea about improving a competency or adding value cannot come into being without understanding a whole host of other things about the company, including its commitments, politics, objectives, vision, culture and competencies, and the way it operates and adds value. In this way an idea will be 'on the same wavelength', connected to the rest of the organisation. Nor can the outside world and its rules, practices and requirements be left out of the loop; otherwise the initiative will not tally with the activity or job. Knowledge at both a macro- and a micro-level, together with inter- and intra-organisational relationships, broadens individual and organisational understanding and allows one to build mental models that admit variation. When these spaces for exchange are fostered, companies can then take on board all those bottom-up, local characteristics and fine-tune their planned strategy. Therefore, the players within these relationships must have considerable knowledge of the organisation's activity, business, and absorption capacity – or, in other words, of 'shared models' (in the sense Kim uses, 1993).

This knowledge is built on strategy dissemination, articulation and monitoring, as well as on meetings that resemble communities of practice. Firstly, to develop learning there need to be mental models and operational and conceptual knowledge so that individuals can fit what they are doing and where they stand within the organisation. Only then will individuals know and understand what the structure allows and forbids them to do so that they work within it and can improve or renew it. Disseminating desires, articulating the objectives and monitoring what is done all lead to the company's logic being owned. When planned strategy is disseminated it will echo company policy, inform about new goals or reiterate the old ones, and it will present the objectives within an agreed timeframe. In this way everybody in the organisation knows what they are aiming at. Next the articulating phase will hone this knowledge by adapting company commitments to local contexts and by carrying out a policy with operational- and individual-level objectives. This knowledge will later be reinforced through a monitoring phase which places where the company, the location and the personnel are within a wider context. These stages can be seen simply as spaces for sharing knowledge and experience.

Further, knowledge hangs on inter- and intra-organisational relationships. Stress can be placed on 'communicating best practice' and on shared learning of the specifics of certain locations, since the experience can be useful for other locations in a similar context. The aim is identical to that found in communities of practice – groups of people linked informally and fired by a passion for the same work (Brown and Duguid 1991). Thus, the capacity for individual and corporate learning is core to performance in its broadest sense. 'Continuous improvement', through successive, cumulative little steps, is a potential source of considerable efficiency, and it is dependent on an empirical analysis of real work rather than on theoretical a priori formulations.

Links between information and knowledge creation

The model we offer directly leads to further questions about knowledge – how it is created, what form it takes and what it is based on. The epistemological principle – the agonistic antagonistic systems approach – as much as the anthropological bias suggests a broad conception of this knowledge, far beyond mainstream knowledge management.

Furthering Polanyi's seminal studies (1958, 1967), Nonaka and Takeuchi (1995) brought two fundamental sets of opposites into play – explicit/tacit and individual/organisational – and they developed the conversion processes relating to them. More recently (Nonaka et al. 2000) they have expanded the model where stress is placed on 'Ba', space where interpreted, negotiated information interacts and is likely to be transformed into knowledge.

Using the same matrix, Lam (2000) schematised four types of knowledge:

- Embrained knowledge is individual explicit knowledge that is embedded in the brain.
- Encoded knowledge is organisational explicit knowledge that is codified and proceduralised.

- Embodied knowledge is individual tacit knowledge that is assimilated through experience.
- Embedded knowledge is organisational tacit knowledge that is shared by the whole community through relationships.

This typology, where each of these categories is part of an organisational ideal, can be developed so that the main epistemological paradigms can be articulated. These paradigms are North American expertise positivism, logical positivism taken from Roman legalism (such as is found in Latin countries like France), the experimental pragmatism of network cultures (for example, the West Coast of the United States and NICT), and the epistemological and social constructivism of community cultures (for example, Japan).

It is obvious that we need to take into account the four categories to enrich the corporate governance and strategic management research areas. The *raison d'être* of these domains is mainly to produce guidelines and frameworks which enable top and middle managers to elaborate business policies and strategies.

By no means can the explanation of what has worked ('if A, then B') be seen as sufficient, *ex ante* actionable knowledge. We have to produce concepts and tools which are relevant for virtualising, sense making and enacting. These concepts and tools are often elaborated in the dialectics between knowledge and knowing (Hatchuel 2005), as it is supported by pragmatist philosophers. This scientific work is a kind of 'generative dance' (Cook and Brown 1999).

6.4   CONCLUSION

Business policy teaching is 100 years old. Strategic management research is 50 years old. Corporate governance research and the dominant ideology stream are mainly coming from Jensen and Meckling's financial foundations.

The business policy *raison d'être* was to be reflexive, integrative and synthetical and to produce *ex ante* knowledge like Porter's famous frameworks. As a research and academic field, business policy is dominated by analysis, statistical validation of stable and general relations and prescription avoidance. These epistemological and methodological choices have created on one hand an increasing gap between the academics and actionable knowledge. On the other hand this so-called neutral position is producing poor critical insights into bad practices and their meso- and macro-consequences.

The major crisis that started with subprimes in August 2007 is a crisis in the banking system, and also a crisis in financial theory and engineering; but it can be seen too as a crisis in strategic management research, which was balancing between keeping silent and loyalty vis-à-vis financial prescriptions.

In the context of today it seems necessary to produce new strategic theory with a clear critical and actionable purpose, that is to say, business politics able to point out wrong ends/means couples and to help people involved in organisational sense making and enacting. This effort does imply epistemological openness and methodological pluralism (Avenier and Schmitt 2007). In every case, producing actionable knowledge to design and build a sustainable and responsible company seems to be the core object and project of this new scientific work (Martinet 2009), that is to say, corporate policy – governance and strategic management – as a science of acceptable designs.

NOTE

1.   Earnings Before Interest, Taxes, Depreciation and Amortisation.

REFERENCES

Argyris, C. and D. Schön (1978), *Organizational Learning: A Theory of Action Perspective*, Reading, MA: Addison-Wesley.
Avenier, M.J. and C. Schmitt (eds) (2007), *La Construction de savoirs pour l'action*, Paris: L'Harmattan.
Bernard-Weil, E. (1988), *Précis de systémique ago-antagonisme*, Limonest: L'Interdisciplinaire.
Bernard-Weil, E. (2002), *Stratégies paradoxales en bio-médecine et sciences humaines*, Paris: L'Harmattan.
Bernard-Weil, E. (2003), 'La science des systèmes ago-antagonistes et les stratégies d'actions paradoxales', in V. Perret and E. Josserand (eds), *Le Paradoxe: Penser et gérer autrement les organisations*, Paris: Ellipses, pp. 25–56.
Brews, P.J. and M.R. Hunt (1999), 'Learning to plan and planning to learn: resolving the planning school/learning school debate', *Strategic Management Journal*, **20**, 889–913.
Brown, J.S. and P. Duguid (1991), 'Organizational learning and communities of practice: toward a unified view of working, learning and innovation', *Organization Science*, **2** (1), pp. 40–57.
Charreaux, G. (1997), 'Le statut du dirigeant dans la recherche sur le gouvernement des entreprises', in G. Charreaux (ed.), *Le Gouvernement des entreprises*, Paris: Economica, pp. 471–93.
Charreaux, G. (2002), 'Variation sur le thème: à la recherche de nouvelles

fondations pour la finance et la gouvernance d'entreprise', *Finance Contrôle Stratégie*, **5** (3), 5–68.

Cook, S. and J. Brown (1999), 'Bridging epistemologies: the generative dance between organizational knowledge and organizational knowing', *Organization Science*, **10** (4), 381–400.

Crossan, M.M., H.W. Lane and R.E. White (1999), 'An organizational learning framework: from intuition to institution', *Academy of Management Review*, **24** (3), 522–37.

Freeman, R.E. (1984), *Strategic Management: A Stakeholder Approach*, Marshfield, MA: Pitman Publishing.

Hatchuel, A. (2005), 'Towards an epistemology of action', *European Management Review*, **2**, 36–47.

Jensen, M.C. and W.H. Meckling (1994), 'The nature of man', *Journal of Applied Corporate Finance*, **7** (2), Summer, 4–19.

Kim, D.H. (1993), 'The link between individual and organizational learning', *Sloan Management Review*, **35** (1), 37–50.

Lam, A. (2000), 'Tacit knowledge, organizational learning and social institutions: an interactive framework', *Organizational Studies*, **31** (3), 487–513.

Lovas, B. and S. Ghoshal (2000), 'Strategy as guided evolution', *Strategic Management Journal*, **21** (10), 875–96.

Luhmann, N. (1999), *Politique et complexité*, Paris: Cerf.

Martinet, A.C. (1984), *Management stratégique, organisation et politique*, Paris: McGraw-Hill.

Martinet, A.C. (1990), 'Épistémologie de la stratégie', in A.C. Martinet (ed.), *Épistémologies et sciences de gestion*, Paris: Economica.

Martinet, A.C. (1997), 'Pensée stratégique et rationalités: un examen épistémologique', *Management International*, **2** (1), 67–75.

Martinet, A.C (ed.) (2007), *Sciences du management: Épistémique, pragmatique et éthique*, Paris: Vuibert/FNEGE.

Martinet, A.C. (2009), 'Management stratégique et libertés', *Management International*, **13** (3), 85–98.

Martinet, A.C. and M.A. Payaud (2006), 'Absorption d'incertitude, enrichissement des stratégies et cadres intermédiaires: une modélisation ago-antagoniste', *Management International*, **10** (2), 29–42.

Martinet A.C. and M.A. Payaud (2007a), 'Complexification des stratégies et modes de gouvernance', *Revue Française de Gouvernance des Entreprises*, **2**, 9–35.

Martinet, A.C. and M.A. Payaud (2007b), 'Frénésie, monotonie et atonie dans les organisations liquéfiées: régénérer les formes et rythmes en politique d'entreprise', *Management International*, **11** (3), Spring, 1–16.

Martinet, A.C. and M.A. Payaud (2008), 'Le développement durable, vecteur et produit d'une régénération de la gouvernance et du management stratégique: un cadre théorique intégrateur', *Management International*, **12** (2), 13–25.

Maturana, H.R. and F.J. Varela (1980), *Autopoiesis and Cognition: The Realization of the Living*, Dordrecht: Reidel.

Morin, E. and J.L. Le Moigne (1999), *L'Intelligence de la complexité*, Paris: L'Harmattan.

Nelson, R.R. and S.G. Winter (1982), *An Evolutionary Theory of Economic Change*, Cambridge, MA: Harvard University Press.

Nonaka, I. and H. Takeuchi (1995), *The Knowledge Creating Company*, Oxford: Oxford University Press.

Nonaka, I., R. Toyama and N. Konno (2000), 'SECI, Ba and leadership: a unified model of dynamic knowledge creation', *Long Range Planning*, **33** (1), 5–34.
Payaud, M.A. (2004), 'Le middle manager dans la formation de la stratégie: repère théorique et précision empirique', in B. Quélin and L. Mezghani (eds), *Perspectives en management stratégique*, Cormelles-le-Royal: Éditions EMS.
Perroux, F. (1961), *L'Économie du XXe siècle*, Paris: Presses Universitaires de France.
Pesqueux, Y. (2002), 'La politique responsable de l'éthique dans le capitalisme', in D. Dupré (ed.), *Éthique et capitalisme*, Paris: Economica, pp. 175–203.
Polanyi, M. (1958), *Personal Knowledge: Towards a Post-Critical Philosophy*, Chicago: University of Chicago Press.
Polanyi, M. (1967), *The Tacit Dimension*, London: Routledge.
Revault d'Allonnes, M. (1999), *Le Dépérissement de la politique*, Paris: Champs, Flammarion.
Simon, H.A. (1947), *Administrative Behavior: A Study of Decision-Making Processes in Administrative Organizations*, New York: Free Press.
Viard, J. (2004), *Le Nouvel Âge du politique*, Paris: L'Aube.

7. Relevance and irrelevance of management research: some European hope[1]

Peter McKiernan[2]

7.1 INTRODUCTION

Management research may have lost its relevance. Pfeffer's[3] rhetoric, though controversial, may contain some grains of truth. Briefly, he asserts that:

> management scholarship has (a) lost contact with the real issues facing the main audiences that it is meant to serve (primarily business practitioners, their consultants, policy-makers and generally anyone who is interested in aspects of how business organizations are, or should be, organized and managed), (b) lost the (always relatively modest) interest it once had in the social implications of managerial decisions and actions, and (c) reached such a deep degree of institutionalization that it is becoming enormously difficult to change the established norms and remedy this situation. (Zollo 2009)

Pfeffer's plea for regaining relevance may be easier to accomplish in Europe than in the United States. History and progress have made Europe a different place, where rich but different scholastic antecedents have produced an eclectic array of research approaches in a multicultural setting. But such heterogeneity is in danger of dilution by powerful US research hegemony unless individual and concerted action is taken soon. This thesis offers some hope for a distinctive European response once we have digested quite what the concept of relevance is and whether the accusation of 'irrelevance' is either true or important.

7.2 PFEFFER'S THESIS AS SYSTEM BALANCING

The evolution of modern management has been slow but very successful. Management and business schools flourish, even in recession, as international products, conferences, journals and networks proliferate on the strength of strong demand. Researchers have created a language, culture, narrative and identity that allow managers to cope with change, growth and survival in complex organisations (Clegg et al. 1996). As a marriage of disciplines, management has made substantial progress, with its own teaching activity ranging from undergraduate to doctoral programmes, its own academic labour market and its symmetric labour exchange with other social sciences (Wensley 2007). The supply chain has been professionalised through the generation of a peer-regulated body of knowledge, the control over access quality and status through research degrees and publications, and the emergence of energetic institutions like academies and accreditation agencies (Spender 2005).

But this social recognition is at odds with perceived weaknesses in management theory and research, notably: 1) a lack of scientific unity; 2) the limited efficiency of its educating institutes; and 3) a lack of action-ability or a 'relevance gap' (Hatchuel 2005). For the latter, Pfeffer makes a constructive plea for regaining relevance, however defined, based upon the non-trivial assumption that the research became irrelevant in the first place. Pfeffer's thesis describes a domain that has shifted from its 'close to practice' origins towards theoretical dominance by embracing economic outcomes and shareholder well-being. Arguably, in the pursuit of scientific legitimacy, such a shift has disenfranchised practical stakeholders. Problematically, this shift has grown rigid, as it has fallen victim to an 'Icarus paradox' whereby career progression based upon research citation is caught and reflected in institutional structures and results in the 'wrong' type of article. Consequently, the domain is deprived of data-driven articles in respected practical journals, and the safety of replicative testing of content relevant to the welfare of society and its policy makers is denied.[4]

These warning bells are the natural 'checks and balances' built into any intelligent system that runs best when there is harmony between countervailing forces and excesses at the margins are prevented. For the case of rigour and relevance, then, too much theory and the practice stakeholders begin to bark; too much practice and the 'theory police' start to shriek. Despite management's disciplinary youthfulness, these warning bells have been rung long and loud by some pretty experienced operators (Simon 1967; Livingston 1971; Hayes and Abernathy 1980; Lataif 1992; Hambrick 1994; Locke 1996; Starkey and Madan 2001; Mintzberg 2004; Pearce 2004; Bennis and O'Toole 2005; Ghoshal 2005; Hatchuel 2005; Spender 2005; Wensley 2007), of whom Pfeffer (1993, 2009; Pfeffer and Fong 2002, 2004) has been the bell master. The majority may be US-based management academics who have used the *Harvard Business Review* as their music sheet, but many Europeans, notably from the UK, have joined the chorus. Place despair aside as these sounds are echoed in other domains, for example engineering, medicine, law, the clergy (Spender 2005), economics and English language (Wensley 2007), so we should live to expect them and apply our critical talents to teasing out any 'truths' in the rhetoric.

7.3   RELEVANCE OR ENGAGEMENT?

Cynically, given the power and authority of this 'industry' of writers, we may have started to believe our own hyperbole and so the tune has meta-morphosed into our 'music memory'. So now we believe a 'problem' exists whether it does or not. More practically, the annoying repetitiveness of these chimes suggests that 1) the 'problem' is so severe that the domain is about to self-destruct; 2) we know the 'problem' and have not bothered to rectify it; or 3) the 'problem' recognition, and thereby the warning bell, is faulty. Self-destruction is not an option in a system with plenty of product and an expertise made flexible and sharp by the challenges of international market exposure. Capacity constraints within the system (for example labour shortages as the 'baby boomer' generation retires) may slow growth, but will not stop the system holistically. Certainly, industries die, but university education has endured in Europe for nearly a thousand years in one shape or another as other sectors, empires, wars and renais-sances have come and gone. So there is every chance it will continue and, if the world continues to be made up of organisations, then some form of administrative science will be in its educational portfolio. Clearly, we recognise a 'problem' of sorts and, clearly, many institutions (see below) are addressing what they perceive it to be. The key to our understanding might lie in the notion of problem recognition or perception, as Weick (2001) has surmised:

> The much lamented relevance gap is as much a product of practitioners wedded to gurus and fads as it is of academics wedded to abstractions and fundamen-tals. The gap persists because practitioners forget that the real world is actually 'a' world that is idiosyncratic, egocentric and unique to each person complain-ing about relevance ... joint practitioner–academic effort devoted to how events come to be seen as 'real' could re-bridge a gap whose nature has been mis-identified.

This dual-sided problem suggests that the practice of self-flagellation should be tempered as we gather better evidence of the phenomena about which we complain. The jury is still out, sifting what evidence exists on the 'relevance gap', as for many years this was anecdotal and filled with rhetorical, reflective ramblings. This was corrected partially by Pfeffer and Fong (2002), who perceive clearly that a problem exists. It is countered by Baldridge et al. (2004), who perceive quite as clearly that it does not. Some (for example Grey 2001) question whether relevance should be an evaluative criterion at all given that objectivity and independence could be damaged by too much emphasis on it. Others critique the use of the outmoded concept of 'convivial' relevance in management research (convivial to one particular set of stakeholders), rather than focusing on 'critical' relevance (critical about asking the right questions of phenomena in the first place) (see Eldridge 1986). Such definitional issues plague our interpretation and, until we solve them, make any decent measures of relevance to either practice or policy (and the measure can be different for each) tough to assign and operate. This is especially true if we acknowledge that much of the relevance concept is wrapped up in fads and, maybe, fashions (as suggested by Weick above), which makes the role of 'scholar versus management guru' difficult to untangle. Wensley (2007) calls for a 'back to basics' approach by asking the question 'What informs management action?' This moves us beyond the old rigour/relevance conundrum, which was an asymmetric relationship originating in academia, to tackle the symmetrical notion of 'engagement' with policy and practice, where knowledge transfer can begin in either source. Engagement falls short of a full marriage but assumes that the partners, academia with policy and practice, share a genuine, communicative relationship where mutual respect develops into a deeper trust, so allowing the sharing of the innermost secrets of each. That way, a richer understanding of the needs, wants and desires of each is realised, and the co-production of knowledge (mode 2) can bear fruit. Taking the relation forward into a full marriage would be a failure scientifically, as the partners' embrace might be damaging to the cognitively constructed notion of perceived 'objectivity'. In particular, this new conception of engagement raises the questions: engagement with whom, why, what for and for how long?

7.4   DIRECT RELEVANCE

A focus on 'engagement' allows us to see the total outputs of management and business schools rather than focus, somewhat guiltily, on a small part of the restrictive field of management research that has entered so-called top-ranked journals. We note above that schools and their faculties have succeeded in providing a number of 'engagements', including 1) teaching products, for example suites of proven undergraduate courses replete with student exchange packages, MBAs in all modes (running at 100 000 per annum in the United States), hundreds of new Bologna-driven specialist master's programmes across Europe, executive short courses, conversion master's degrees, professional doctorates, and critical and non-critical textbooks; 2) policy reports for public and third sector organisations; 3) practitioner-oriented articles in academic journals (for example in the *Harvard Business Review*, *Sloan Management Review* and *Long Range Planning*), in professional journals (for example house magazines for management institutes like the Chartered Institute of Management in the UK); 4) regular commentary in newsprint and TV/radio commentary (for example Hatchuel in *Le Monde*); 5) consultancy services; 6) the formation of academies, some of which influence policy significantly (for example the British Academy of Management); 7) market-facing institutes and centres; 8) internships and practical student dissertations; and 9) a fair share of global management 'gurus'. More, management academics have contributed significantly to other influential centres in adjacent domains, for example healthcare and public policy, in a manner that Pfeffer acknowledges openly.

7.5   INDIRECT RELEVANCE

The above might be seen as direct engagements. Indirectly, there are other derived impacts from the activity of these schools that are crucial to clarify Pfeffer's stance. First, any claim for the 'significant' role played by consultants and others in generating the useful practical management tools identified by survey research ignores the prior education of many consultants in management schools. Good schools embody research-driven teaching and so provide the knowledge and inspiration for students to produce their practical output in other employment. Practical material and policy advice does not have to have its immediate origins in university management research to have that source as its root. Consultants have been the brokers of much management research, playing an important translation role between high science and action implementation to a discriminating clientele. As testament, many scholarly academics continue to work alongside former students on fee-paying project work. Second, the system produces much first-class management research in high-status journals of underlying basic disciplines. This masks a number of crucial issues, not least the debt this research owes to prior management research and the test bed of conferences and workshops in the world of management academe. Proudly and politically, it is evidence that such output can equate to that of the best subject specialists and, perhaps, position itself in journals that may have a better policy impact. In Europe, examples include the impact of management researchers in healthcare research, where evidence-based, replicative studies have been de rigueur for over a decade.

Taken together the direct and indirect 'engagements' of management plus the broad range of theoretical contributions that have emerged from management research from agency theory to the resource-based view of the firm that have metamorphosed into management advice and practice (see Zollo 2009) are extensive. We make no judgement on its quality and admit to some dysfunctions along the way, but such doubts would be natural ones in a developing domain. But the increasing volume of outputs seems to belie Pfeffer's slightly provocative charge that management theory and administrative science have produced little of practical value to broader society and its welfare. To be fair, Pfeffer makes this charge against a certain segment of research in high-impact journals, but his thesis skips over the fundamental question about the purpose of such research. The answer, whether to be relevant or to be critical, or a rich variety of each, might help shape our interpretation of its contextual setting and meaning.

7.6 CUSTOMERS

The argument above posited a strong and broad range of 'engagements' from the supply side, and from it we can infer that the demand side must be fairly segmented in order to digest it. Perhaps the largest stakeholder communities are three:

1. public, private and third sector practitioners;
2. policy makers and their advisers; and
3. academics themselves.

For academics, the search is to challenge existing, and inform new, theory, build a sound stock of knowledge and develop the domain through further research. There is a good sense that existing outputs deliver. But, because entry barriers to high-impact journals (usually US based) can be both dominated and wounded by a specific epistemological approach to both rationality (and there are many others; see Townley 2008) and empiricism that is cloaked in, and driven by, a cameralist[5] context, the copy-science outputs are less accessible and so less understood by practitioners. Alone, this does not make them 'irrelevant' to the academic audience for whom they are scripted. A certain approach to theory building and theory building itself are improved, a stock of knowledge is generated, and there seems to be no limit to the advice for further research. Perhaps Pfeffer's issue relates to the direct relevance of that research to the other two groups for whom other outputs are targeted and delivered. Directly, he is correct, but indirectly, as we have shown above, some of this research will make its way through lectures, textbooks, practical articles and the translating minds of consultants to the other user groups. Until further exploration is conducted, we can't say what proportion, but we can assume it makes a valuable contribution or we would witness massive market failure in the supply chain. Besides having 'engagement' with its own captive market and so long as the translation chain remains intact, some of the high-impact work in top journals will have further 'engagement' down the channel.

7.7 INSTITUTIONAL CAPTURE

This chapter did not begin with the intention of condoning management research in high-ranked US journals. It is just that, if we place that work in the globe of outputs from management *and* alter our perception through the lens of 'engagement' rather than 'relevance', the picture becomes a little clearer. Management has been successful in delivering a host of outputs to its audience group down a broad set of channels. Now, that does not mean that things could not be better and/or that we should not strive for *aggiornamento*. Pfeffer is correct in saying that we may have trapped that high science research tract in institutional mechanisms which, if allowed to persist, could lead to the sort of system imbalance that could foretell market failure. We fear the trap is greater, as the institutional capture has bred clever 'game-playing' behaviour on career progression that has become embedded psychologically in influential actors in the system. An acquaintance with the perceived top-ranking journals (mostly US based), the tenure track system in the United States, the legacy of five research selectivity exercises in the UK and the concomitant reward structures in both environments will serve to testify.

As a cameo example, scholars in the UK have been driven hard for 25 years by their institutions to gain greater shares of the government's research monies. These are distributed after peer-reviewed research audits (termed RSE, RAE and REF) of a school's research activity conducted every five years or so. Clearly, this system has advanced both the quantity and the quality of the research output in the UK, but the unintended consequences have been significant. For example, this quest has brought defined journal ranking lists which have influenced an active academic transfer market, the ascendancy of the article over the book and the individual over the academic community, significant 'game playing' by institutions and individuals, distortions in the academic labour market (for example retention promotions) and a transformation of value systems that can privilege research over teaching and service and so the replacement of the academic all-rounder with the journal specialist. Ambitious specialists target top journals for rapid career advancement and monetary reward. Pfeffer is correct in asserting that their output can eschew the longer distillation processes involved in good empirical research with its closer liaison to policy and practice. That is a pity, as strong and influential researchers may be lost to a particular segment directly. This situation is not unique to the UK, as isomorphic compliance means that other European countries and Australasia will follow suit and develop such stringent auditing regimes without clear thought as to the balance they might bring or upset.

7.8   EUROPEAN HOPE

If there is a system imbalance problem or the anticipation of one, then any corrections to the system may be executed more easily in Europe than in the United States. At bottom, our best chance of rectification is to tackle 'institutional capture' head on by influencing both individual scholar behaviour, by adjusting the 'rules of the game', and organisational behaviour, by adjusting the 'rules of funding and accreditation' that surround the game. Tinkering within the system, for example by launching new journals or tweaking existing ones in the hope that new 'relevant' output will be forthcoming, will strengthen outlets but is unlikely to be enough to force the seismic change in management research demanded within the Pfeffer thesis. Further, hoping that continuous warnings in the system will make any difference once the pattern of complaints is lodged in the 'musical memory' may be overtly optimistic.

7.9   INSTITUTIONAL CHANGE

So how do we make progress and why does Europe represent a better context in which to accomplish this? Progress through behavioural change is no easy matter, even in Europe, but a key lies in tapping into the mechanisms of the very institutions that push the system in one direction or another.[6] Ironically, 'game playing' by individuals and organisations for the regular research audits like the UK's Research Assessment Exercise (RAE, to become REF) depends on the 'rules of the game' announced during each round. During five rounds over 25 years, UK academia has become used to significant behavioural change, both individually and collectively, in response to these changing rules. By altering the rules constantly, the audits have promoted a system which has an adaptable mechanism or 'requisite variety' built in. For the next audit in 2012, the salient change concerns the 'impact' of management research – mainly on policy and practice, though impact waits for a fuller definition at the time of writing. To be sure, individuals and their directors of research who engineer a path quickly towards impactful research and outputs before 2012 will be focused far more on the interface with society and a practical/policy audience than they have been before. That progress will probably continue through the audit round thereafter. Hence journal editors and publishers will have to respond if they are to capture the high-level output that will ensue. Five years might be a long time for management research to readjust, but mechanisms exist to encourage it (or force it?) to do so.

Probably the UK's is the closest fully developed research assessment system to that of the United States that exists in Europe. But it, and similar audit systems in Europe (for example the Netherlands, Spain and Italy), could respond to the plea for more relevance quickly if the cause were ignited. If there is a real desire for change in the system, both government civil servants and the academics who perform the peer review are in a prime position to make their voices heard. In the United Kingdom, at least, the process of change is facilitated by having a national academy, the British Academy of Management (BAM), which is a strong influencer of policy and close to government bodies, and an Advanced Institute of Management (AIM), which was set up with £20 million of public funds, to address issues of rigour and relevance in UK management research. Significantly, the research findings are disseminated in easily digestible forms to policy makers and practitioners. Similarly, Germany (with 19 billion euros in its Excellence Initiative, though this is not wholly for management) and the Netherlands (where 12 per cent of revenues are for applied research) have created incentives for 'relevant' research. Perhaps Pfeffer's institutional capture is specific to, and informed by, particular rigidities in the US system, whose systemic nature may be harder to adjust and which, as he argues, traps even those senior members (for example journal editors) who should be capable of leading the way out.

This strategy of accessing the power base of institutions to enable change could be addressed at the major accreditation bodies (for example AACSB and EQUIS) whose rules include a strong need for members and potential members to internationalise and for their researchers to publish in highly ranked journals. Research (Durand and Dameron 2008) suggests that most top European schools (for example in the Netherlands, France, Spain, Portugal, Sweden and the UK) see publications in top-ranked journals as key to their internationalisation as they pursue the

American model. This is reinforced through an EQUIS kitemark, despite this process requiring having a distinct category for practice-orientated research. This reinforcement of 'what impresses' in the United States in business and management[7] may become problematic as lesser European schools with fewer resources strive for the same identity. Such powerful hegemonistic pull controls behaviour, and Europe is in danger of succumbing to US mimicry and destroying the best parts of its own heterogeneity in the process. But there is hope. Usefully, in Europe, EQUIS accreditations come under the schools' (or deans') organisation – the European Foundation for Management Development (EFMD). EFMD has an influential scientific committee and works closely with the umbrella organisation for European academies, the European Institute for Advanced Studies in Management (EIASM), which enjoys a similar structure. The common denominator for both EFMD and EIASM is a strong representation of thousands of active academics. If the academics perceived a need for rule changes, then both organisations would have to listen carefully to their fee-paying constituents. There is good evidence that they have listened to market voices in the past, for example with demand for new programmes (for example EFMD for the deans' and directors' programme) and for new academies (for example EIASM in the case of the European Academy of Management – EURAM).

Ironically, management theory might suggest that decentralised systems (for example the United States) might enable change better than more centralised (for example European) ones. But rule-altering behaviour change within a concentration of institutions might have a better chance of getting change faster and more effectively, especially if the context in which the latter institutions are placed can act as an additional facilitator. The fertility of the European scene could be a clue to its potential response.

7.10 *TEXERE*[8]

Contextually, the historical progress of Europe provides a rich opportunity to reflect a stance closer to policy and practice. There are four reasons why this might be so. First, the role and diversity of its heritage have provided a challenging variety in business and management. University programmes in applied management[9] can be traced to the University of Oxford in the UK in the fourteenth century (Richardson 1940), and the oldest formal school was established at the University of Coimbra in Portugal in 1759, as a school of commerce. Today, schools have multiplied into a colourful rainbow ranging from the elite schools following the 'dominant' US model (for example INSEAD, IESE, HEC, ESSEC, LBS and Bocconi) through to those based upon the social sciences, humanities and professions and to niche schools focusing on specialisms like finance or technology. Many schools emerged from universities with deep traditions in sociology, psychology, political economy and philosophy, making approaches to management research diverse and mainly qualitative and providing pockets of strong critical management scholars. Consequently, Durand and Dameron (2008) argue that the soil is more fertile and relevant to practice:

> One would argue that this European management is more transverse, somehow more integrated and systemic [than the North American way]. Also, one would argue that it pays more attention to intercultural issues, ethical concerns, sustainable development and corporate social responsibility etc. This does not mean that North America ignores such matters. It simply means that Europe seems even keener to deal with these issues.

Second, harmonisation in the European education process, with common levels of degrees and diplomas, credit transfers and growing strategic partnerships between institutions (for example Community of European Management Schools – CEMS), encourages student mobility and enables scholarship to thrive in a multicultural setting, laying the foundations for potential international management careers, especially in multinational corporations. Further, internship and research links to employers in some countries are very close, especially in Scandinavia (for example Copenhagen, Stockholm School of Economics and Gothenburg), France (for example the *grandes écoles* like ESCP Europe or EM Lyon, or leading universities such as Paris Dauphine) and Germany (for example Technical University Munich). In Scandinavia, the culture privileges the content of new ideas over repetitive articles concerned with scientific methodology and 'ranking mimicry' that tend to champion process over content (Hopwood 2008). Substantial interaction with the business community (for example Nokia, IKEA, Skandia and Ericsson) ensues. Though Hopwood warns: 'But while others should replicate these strengths, a danger is that the Nordic schools imitate the rest, as they seek rankings more commensurate with their merits.'

In France and Germany, pedigrees are built upon backgrounds that blurred the distinction between engineering and management and created a harmony and respect between business and practice. Germany is distinct again, with chairs being closer to science and engineering chairs in the UK and United States rather than conventional business ones, where career paths follow a well-trodden 'medieval guild' model and where managers are likely to have completed a doctorate and so have a value and respect for the productive capacity of academe.

Third, Europe has several active and influential academies and associations that play a key role in articulating a particular European approach to management education. EIASM houses several functional societies with academics who are close to practice (for example marketing and accounting). EURAM champions practice-related research in its conference tracks, and its house journal (the *European Management Review*) is welcoming of the sorts of articles Pfeffer calls for in a management version of 'Health Affairs and Foreign Affairs'. Similarly, the European Group on Organisation Studies (EGOS), through its house journal *Organisation Studies*, eschews deductive research for qualitative reasoning and action (Durand and Dameron 2008). Finally, besides the Bologna experiment, the EU is active in funding other projects (for example Tune) to help harmonise curricula to aid student transfers. It has significant further roles to play in faculty transfers between academic institutions and in creating symmetrical flows between academia and employers. For example, many of its research projects are conducted by such mixed teams, for instance the current 'Anticipation and management of change in the EU automotive sector' programme involves suppliers, original equipment manufacturers, unions, academics and politicians.

7.11 CONCLUSION

Of course, this does not mean that Europe has a monopoly on the context for change, but at this moment sufficient cultural and institutional difference exists in business and management education between it and the United States to enable several approaches to thrive. Noted, the drivers and the drive to copy the US model are strong in Europe and, if change is needed, time is of the essence. However, one of the reasons for the establishment of EURAM, alongside EGOS, was to help champion inclusively this variety in the general management domain. That includes both nomothetic and idiographic designs (Tsoukas 1989), whether high theory or high engagement, in Europe and elsewhere.

But we have left ourselves with an output puzzle. A good deal of the research behaviour of academics is captured within institutional frameworks, and we have argued that one way to galvanise the change process is to alter the rules of the game, especially where this involves funding. But the exit valve of this research lies with journal editors, and Pfeffer has warned us that many editors (especially in the United States) of high-ranking journals may be captives of the system in which they are entwined. Change here is essential if the academic community wants good 'engagement' work to be 'perceived' as valuable research. Kogut (2009), a former editor of the *European Management Review* (*EMR*), identifies a typology of journals thus:

> there are association and taste journals. Association journals, such as *EMR*, the *American Sociological Review*, the *Academy of Management Journal*, or the *American Economic Review*, have a responsibility to give a broad voice to the diversity of research and researchers. They are, in many ways, democratic. Taste journals, such as the *Quarterly Journal of Economics* or the *American Journal of Sociology*, have the freedom to be more arbitrary, often somewhat autocratic, but all justified in creating an interesting and elitist forum of published researchers. For me, the third category has always appeared as illogical, namely the journals that have no organisational allegiances and yet choose not to exercise a pronounced taste ... and yet, the choice of reviewers and the power to persuade and to override [reviewers] are fully within an editor's purview.

Clearly, editors have a power that may not be exercised fully for one reason or another, for example younger academics who might owe their career status to the system in which they are now a major gatekeeper. But association journals, though technically independent of their parent (for example *EMR* and EURAM), still bear an obligation to that community (Kogut 2009). If that community feels that it has a major issue over 'relevance' then it has a duty to change things at association AGMs (for example AoM, EURAM, EGOS), including putting pressure on, or changing, editors. In turn, the latter have a duty to instruct or replace reviewers. Perhaps the editorial system has grown to be too comfortable.

We have argued that the mechanisms for change in Europe may be easier to activate than in the United States, yet it is infinitely sad for European academics wedded to variety to be surrounded by mechanisms of our own creation that may prevent a balance within our own system and force it in a homogeneous direction. Pfeffer strives to make us aware and, in terms of solutions, he has a point; the worst crime may be our own inactivity.

NOTES

1. A previous version of this chapter appeared in the *European Management Review*, Autumn, **6**, 2009, 149–56.
2. I am grateful to comments from my colleagues – Chris Carter, Alan McKinlay and Barbara Townley – for their valuable comments on earlier drafts of this chapter. Any errors are mine alone.
3. Jeffery Pfeffer provided a keynote speech to the European Academy of Management's (EURAM) annual conference in Liverpool in 2009 entitled 'Renaissance and renewal in management studies: relevance regained'.
4. Though this seems to be the main thesis in the first few pages, there are some contradic-

tions. Later, Pfeffer (2009) ponders: 'Thus, it is not the case that management research has little or nothing useful to say to help us understand and possibly even avoid many contemporary problems.'
5. The German science of administration that influenced early US business schools.
6. Academics will chase money 'like swarms of bees'. If funding is made available to address the political topic of the day, for example productivity, identity or entrepreneurship, it is surprising how quickly academics with little pedigree in an area become engrossed in it.
7. Note that European business and management are not alone in facing such a power base. We see similar patterns in sociology.
8. *Texere* is the Latin verb stem 'to weave' (as in a network or structure).
9. Estates management.

REFERENCES

Baldridge, D.C., S.W. Floyd and L. Markoczy (2004), 'Are managers from Mars and academicians from Venus? Toward an understanding of the relationship between academic quality and practical relevance', *Strategic Management Journal*, **25**, 1063–74.

Bennis, W.G. and J. O'Toole (2005), 'How business schools lost their way', *Harvard Business Review*, **83** (5), 96–104.

Clegg, S.R., C. Hardy and W.R. Nord (1996), *Handbook of Organization Studies*, London: Sage.

Durand, T. and S. Dameron (2008), *The Future of Business Schools: Scenarios and Strategies for 2020*, Basingstoke: Palgrave.

Eldridge, J. (1986), 'Facets of "relevance" in sociological research', in F. Heller (ed.), *The Use and Abuse of Social Science*, London: Sage.

Ghoshal, S. (2005), 'Bad management theories are destroying good management practices', *Academy of Management Learning and Education*, **4** (1), 75–91.

Grey, C. (2001), 'Re-imagining relevance: a response to Starkey and Madan', *British Journal of Management*, **12**, S27–S32.

Hambrick, D. (1994), '1993 presidential address: what if the Academy actually mattered?', *Academy of Management Review*, **19** (1), 11–16.

Hatchuel, A. (2005), 'Towards an epistemology of collective action: management research as a responsive and actionable discipline', *European Management Review*, **2**, 36–47.

Hayes, R.H. and W.J. Abernathy (1980), 'Managing our way to economic decline', *Harvard Business Review*, July–September, 67–77.

Hopwood, A. (2008), 'The rankings game: reflections on Devinney, Dowling and Perm-Ajchariyawong', *European Management Review*, **5** (4), 209–15.

Kogut, Bruce (2009), 'Rankings, schools, and final reflections on ideas and taste', *European Management Review*, **5** (4), 191–4.

Lataif, L.E. (1992), 'MBA: is the traditional model doomed?', *Harvard Business Review*, **70** (6), 128.

Livingston, J.S. (1971), 'Myth of the well-educated manager', *Harvard Business Review*, January–February, 79–89.

Locke, R.R. (1996), *The Collapse of the American Management Mystique*, New York: Oxford University Press.

Mintzberg, H. (2004), *Managers not MBAs: A Hard Look at the Soft Practice of Managing and Management Development*, San Francisco, CA: Berrett-Koehler.

Pearce, J.L. (2004), 'What do we know and how do we really know it?', *Academy of Management Review*, **29**, 175–9.

Pfeffer, J. (1993), 'Barriers to the advancement of organization science: paradigm development as a dependent variable', *Academy of Management Review*, **18**, 599–620.

Pfeffer, J. (2009), 'Renaissance and renewal in management studies: relevance regained', *European Management Review*, **6** (3), 141–8.

Pfeffer, J. and C.T. Fong (2002), 'The end of business schools? Less success than meets the eye', *Academy of Management Learning and Education*, **1** (1), 78–85.

Pfeffer, J. and C.T. Fong (2004), 'The business school "business": some lessons from the US experience', *Journal of Management Studies*, **41** (8), 1501–20.

Richardson, H.G. (1940), 'Business training in medieval Oxford', *American History Review*, **46**, 259–73.

Simon, H.A. (1967), 'The business school: a problem in organizational design', *Journal of Management Studies*, **4**, 1–16.

Spender, J.-C. (2005), 'Speaking about management education: some history of the search for academic legitimacy and the ownership and control of management knowledge', *Management Decision*, **43** (10), 1282–92.

Starkey, K. and P. Madan (2001), 'Bridging the relevance gap: aligning stakeholders in the future of management research', *British Journal of Management*, 12 (**S1**), S3–S26.

Townley, B. (2008), *Reason's Neglect: Rationality and Organizing*, Oxford: Oxford University Press.

Tsoukas, H. (1989), 'The validity of idiographic research explanations', *Academy of Management Review*, **14**, 451–561.

Weick, K.E. (2001), 'Gapping the relevance bridge: fashions meet fundamentals in management research', *British Journal of Management*, **12**, S71–S75.

Wensley, R. (2007), 'Beyond rigour and relevance: the underlying nature of both business schools and management research', *AIM Research Working Paper Series*, 051-January-2007.

Zollo, Maurizio (2009), 'Taking on board (*cum grano salis*) Pfeffer's call for relevance in, and renewal of, management scholarship', *European Management Review*, **6** (3), 156–8.

PART III

Redesigning the institutional setting of management education and research

8. Evaluating management education and business schools in context
9. Evaluating programmes of management education: the EFMD perspective
10. Journal rankings and evaluation of faculty performance

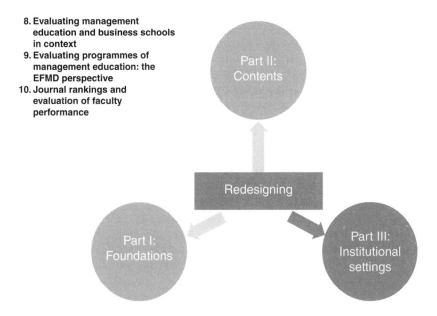

Part III deals with the current evaluation and regulation mechanisms of business schools' strategies and teaching programmes, and contributions by individual faculty members. This part begins with a strong argument in favour of changing the ways business schools face stakeholders' expectations. Olivier Basso, Philippe-Pierre Dornier and Jean-Paul Mounier argue that the management education and research system is characterised by a high degree of standardisation, which goes against the academic ideals of freedom of thought, discovery, and the creation of knowledge.

They analyse the mechanisms that participate in reproducing a single model and maintaining one particular system, and conclude by proposing a few rules of actions to help business schools become more entrepreneurial and dynamic. In turn Eric Cornuel presents a way of evaluating a business programme through the example of the EPAS scheme. This chapter adopts EFMD lenses to illustrate – and advocate – the role played by the external programme accreditation system and the quality improvement philosophy behind the evaluation process. Part III ends with a discussion of how individual faculty members are being evaluated, in particular through journal rankings. Dennis Tourish analyses the pernicious effects of performative pressures on faculty freedom and creativity; he argues that those pressures may be counterproductive, as they confound the means and purpose of knowledge production.

In a way, Part III addresses the issue of how current institutional settings tend to limit the ability of business schools and faculty members to innovate and differentiate from one another.

8. Evaluating management education and business schools in context

Olivier Basso, Philippe-Pierre Dornier and Jean-Paul Mounier

Is life's ultimate goal to auto-reproduce (survival), or is it to metabolise (in other words, to enjoy life)? Do we live to survive, or do we survive to live? There's no possible answer since survival and living . . . are reciprocally a means and an end to one another.

Edgar Morin (1999)

Education is one of the greatest and most difficult challenges that man is faced with. Indeed, enlightenment depends on education, which in turn depends on enlightenment.[1]

Immanuel Kant

The development, strengthening and multiplication of socially minded business men is the central problem of business.[2]

Wallace B. Dunham, Dean of Harvard Business School, 1926

8.1 INTRODUCTION

The current chapter is entitled 'Evaluating management education and business schools in context': what do we mean exactly by 'context'? Two different definitions of the term are possible. Firstly, it can refer to a particular space–time location that a person or process is necessarily embedded within. In this sense, we are concerned primarily with industrialised countries, which appear to represent today's world in its globalised state. However, a 'context' can also be understood as a force field that expresses the expectations and actions of different stakeholders. Hence, the society as a whole, businesses, students and faculty are actors whose network precisely defines the context (as the Latin etymology of the term suggests: *contexere*, meaning literally 'to weave together') or 'fabric' of management education.

Central to our inquiry is how the teaching of a particular discipline in a given physical, geographical, historical and institutional location is positioned. Any examination of a particular educational event seems to raise two questions simultaneously: what is the aim of the teaching in question, and how is the subject matter approached? This leads us to distinguish three, not necessarily exclusive, approaches based on different conceptions of knowledge of management, the subject being taught.

Business education institutions[3] – universities, business schools, engineering and technical schools, and so on – can set objectives[4] to:

- Train technical experts. The aim is to train individuals in technical expertise in order to allow them to fulfil a particular role in a company or organisation. Knowledge is therefore focused on acquiring tools and know-how. It allows for specialisation in a specific company function (marketing, finance, accounting and so on) and eventually occupying positions in this area of expertise according to a well-defined division of labour for the assigned tasks. For example, think of job descriptions for a product manager, price-setting manager, or survey conductor for a marketing department.
- Educate managers. Individuals educated in this way are expected to become team leaders in a given organisational context[5] (companies, non-profits, NGOs, public administration and so on). Managers therefore seek to influence others' behaviour in order to instigate collective action. They have to know how to divide and delegate the work to do by allocating the resources at their disposal as best they can. Managers are by definition organisers.
- Prepare future leaders. This added objective refers to instruction for those who will directly influence the construction of the society. The idea is no longer simply to train managers to work for corporations and large-scale organisations, but to encourage the emergence of leaders. The explicit goal of leading business schools, especially in the United States, is to contribute to the 'making of great men' in the Hegelian[6] sense. The examples they give in their mission statements are proof of this (for example, Kofi Annan for MIT).

Our thesis is simple. It seems to us today – and the financial crisis of 2008–09 reinforces this perception – that most business schools claim to have ambitions to educate managers and leaders, though ultimately the level of instruction provided remains essentially very basic. Are we going too far? Let's formulate this conviction in another way and more emphatically (a typically French approach, as the reader might know). Schools and universities, generally speaking, should be places of creative problem solving, bold experimentation, and elevated thought relative to the 'real world' or social status quo. Yet the most influential business education institutions – according to the numerous international rankings – are content merely to participate in reproducing a single model and maintaining one particular system. This system is characterised by a high degree of standardisation, which runs counter to the very concept of diversity that civil society and businesses now so insistently claim to promote. Let's recall a few elements of a process that turns out to be an organised way of diminishing variety:

- Business education in major international business schools (as ranked by the *Financial Times* or *Businessweek*) mostly consists of case studies and books, predominantly based on large public companies ruled by American managerial principles.
- The business school ranking system is defined by journalists from the business world, with a major weight given to the average salaries of alumni, which reinforces the tendency of schools to cater to the demands of the job market.
- The quality of academic research is measured by articles published in a limited set of listed journals and formatted to meet standard criteria that explicitly encourage mimetic and cross-referencing habits.

As it stands, management education therefore seems to be prisoner to a model that leads to identical reproduction – a thousand miles from what characterises an academic place and its ideals of freedom of thought, discovery, and the creation of new knowledge.

To support our thesis and clarify a few essential arguments, we suggest a threefold approach. The first step, in section 8.2, involves analysing the structural constraints facing educational institutions, such as the reigning values of the times and stakeholders' expectations. In section 8.3, we outline the positions and concepts that result from this system. In section 8.4, we offer a few rules for action to render the model under study more entrepreneurial and dynamic, and reintroduce a degree of freedom of action.

8.2   A MODEL WITH LIMITATIONS

In this section, we look at the various forces that exert pressure on management education institutions, especially business schools. What is the nature of the force field they are surrounded by? Their context operates on several structural levels. We have identified two types of tendencies: some, such as the values of the times and the society, are built upon fundamental characteristics of our civilisation, while others may prove to be more ephemeral.

8.2.1 Relationship to the Modern Paradigm

May the reader forgive us for the apparent digression, but this relationship occurs within the wider context of a major trend in our civilisation identified by Max Weber as a shift towards increased rationalisation of social activities.[7] This trend originated in Europe, then spread to the United States, and is now being imposed on the rest of the world. This zeitgeist was perceived in contrasting ways, either as a liberation movement (especially by nineteenth-century utopian thinkers, 1980s post-modernists, and so on) or as a harbinger of the decline of humanity[8] (see the esoteric works on the Kali Yuga age, works by early-twentieth-century German existentialists, and so on).

The external characteristics of this phenomenon seem well established. Once led blindly into the dominant logic of productivism (thus the Marxist critique of capitalism is subject to the same glorification of productivity), the trend towards the division and specialisation of labour was established, affecting even the production of knowledge.[9] The shift also ushered in the reigning conception of reality where quantifiable data are the sole measure of any reality (Guénon 2004) and the guarantee of its being tractable.

The social fabric also seems to have become a numbers game. The Foucauldian belief that social sciences were born out of a drive to control populations with the reigning biopower (Foucault 2004) dovetails with the emergence of the manipulation of large groups (see Desrosières 2002). Democracy simultaneously opened the door to both individualism and political strategies involving mass movements, making the definition of shared goals and collective decision making very difficult. Today, even the limits of the United States' legitimacy seem to be challenged by overarching and transverse phenomena, including international trade, the development of multinationals, the globalisation of NGOs, the expansion of mass tourism, the omnipresence and increased mobility of information systems such as the internet and mobile phones, and so on. This situation introduces new uncertainties for possible forms of organised collective action on a global scale. We are now living under a system of governance that is still in the process of being defined. In other words, while an international government still proves to be impossible, there are an unprecedented number of attempts at international coordination (for example, the United Nations Global Compact is a strategic policy initiative for businesses that are committed to aligning their operations and strategies with ten universally accepted principles in the areas of human rights, labour, environment and anti-corruption).

As a discipline dealing with how organisations function, business education is very much part of this dynamic of theories and actions that seems to define a practically autonomous model for a civilisation (Western civilisation?). All the more, the institutions where management is taught are penetrated by these forces, which extend far beyond their walls and are largely responsible for shaping their behaviour, as is demonstrated in section 8.3).

8.2.2   Relationship to Society

Since educational institutions play a major role in enlightening future citizens, do they have responsibilities to society?

Today, there are two opposing views in the academic world on this issue, and the debate essentially concerns business schools. One side insists on the need for a place that, by definition, escapes social conformity, since its purpose is to educate enlightened people: according to Kant, to teach individuals to 'think for themselves'.[10] Ultimately, when the time comes, they participate in the construction of the social reality and contribute their skills to society as they wish. The opposing argument, resulting from increased concern for employment and social uncertainties (recession, school drop-outs, and so on), leads many to demand that educational places guarantee a level of conformity among students in order to turn out 'job-ready' graduates. The goal is to secure students' future careers.

For this reason, the fundamental question that arises is what position to take. Is the business school a place dedicated to teaching conformity, or is it an arena where debate and opposing views can be heard? The financial crisis of 2009 demonstrates the first position: business schools were receptacles of demand, and provided the technicians that the economy required. To stretch this logic further, business schools came up with theories explaining the main economic events of the 1980s only after the fact. Faculty and researchers justified financial regulation by providing modelling elements (the capital asset pricing model) which pre-supposed the efficiency of markets. Using efficiency as a rationale, they then produced arguments that explained the major shifts accompanying the expanded role of institutional shareholders and the multiplication of takeover bids. These shifts, including the idea of value creation and the insistence on strictly financial returns on investment, are based on economic concepts developed in the 1970s (Michael Jensen (Jensen and Meckling 1976) and the theory of agency, and so on). The scandals associated with corporate executive compensation are also a direct result of this theory that the main goal of managers should be to increase shareholder value. Managerial thought has therefore drawn on the history of economic scholarship (resorting to selected quotes from Adam Smith, whose moral perspective is judiciously neglected (Smith [1759] 2002, and reiterating the Friedmanian view (Friedman 1970) on the 'social' responsibility of enterprise) to gain legitimacy and find the most relevant theories in order not only to justify the practices adopted by the corporate world, but to encourage their proliferation.

Even today, in the shadow of the collapse of major pillars of the financial world, when the prospect of an extended financial crisis is still looming, how many business schools have stopped to rethink their curriculum to imagine a new reality and prepare for a change in attitude?

8.2.3   Relationship to the Business World

The same line of questioning applies to businesses. What are their expectations regarding management education? Where a company falls on this issue depends on two factors. The first is size: a small or medium-sized company has very different expectations and less capacity for action compared to a major multinational corporation. Multinationals genuinely take part in the construction of the civil and political landscape (see the shift from government to governance evoked above), while small and medium-sized companies possess less capacity to influence their surroundings.

The second factor is geographic. Depending on the country, the corporate level of interest in and expectations of management education varies greatly. Thus, in France, interest is minimal, since there is still little confidence in management education.[11] In contrast, in Germany, professors are widely represented on corporate boards of directors, and academic programmes that combine management and economics are prevalent.

What do companies expect of business schools? In short, access to a preselected talent pool. The situation is close to caricature in France: the admissions selection system effectively filters the good from the bad, which saves companies a lot of time and energy. They have bought a model that is admittedly simplistic – the pool is not particularly diverse – but very efficient. The second implicit expectation is the extension of natural conditions in the different countries for doing good business. Diffusing good practices and sharing a common set of references and managerial concepts will help to globalise the corporate world. In such an environment a Chinese MBA student in Luoyang is expected to be able to exchange views, communicate and collaborate smoothly in business matters with, say, a Peruvian MBA student in Cuzco. Finally, it seems that companies have no expectations in terms of research on management. Their own experiences by trial and error and a constant stream of consulting firm interventions apparently answer all their questions on the changes they must make to reinforce their competitiveness. The different ways they help business schools strike us as often calculated marketing (employer branding) to students and future employees, more than a real concern for investing in knowledge production that they consider useful for their development.

8.2.4   Relationship to Students and Alumni

Though students have diverse profiles, ranging from those with no prior experience and young professionals to managers in continuing education and executives changing career paths, career advancement seems to be the common motivation for choosing to enrol in a management education programme. In France, students in preparatory classes are warped by the system: it is so difficult to get into a business *grande école* that entrance nearly equals the validation of the curriculum. Accordingly students have little interest in the course contents once admitted, because there is no real stake and the topics (technical expertise) differ too strongly from their previous learning experience (social sciences and modern humanities are taught during the preparatory class). MBA students have made a significant financial investment, and their criterion for choosing a school is based on its ranking (largely dependent on average post-graduation salaries), the technical contents of the programme, the reputation of the school's name, and the quality of its alumni network.

Continuing education students can be driven by various motivations. Therefore they look for different components for various goals: to acquire technical expertise, to legitimise a new position in their company, to gain the opportunity to reassess their career, or to have a chance to tear themselves away from their job to get some perspective (often to the detriment of their holiday time). Similarly, their expectations can vary from a ticket to enter the job market, to field-specific course contents, or even just a way to climb the social ladder (the *grandes écoles* in France, ESADE in Spain, or Bocconi in Italy).

The relationship with alumni establishes the link to social networks. The goal is to manage the school's brand capital. Alumni events are occasions for former students to meet, exchange ideals and ultimately maintain their business networks. One's time at the school is temporary, but belonging to a network of 'old boys' is a lifelong benefit. Alumni often either directly or indirectly influence their school's governance and future by underscoring the need to reinforce its brand name and reputation.

8.2.5   Relationship to Faculty

How is the term 'faculty' defined? Should we consider it an institutional asset? Or should we focus on career trajectories and the identity crisis facing the professor–researcher–teacher–published author?

A closer look at faculties reveals the growing importance of temporary and part-time instructors, including affiliated professors, adjunct faculty, visiting fellows and so on. Owing to the growing number of students and the explosion in the number of programmes (BA, MBA, MSc, DBA, PhD, executive education degrees and so on), courses are no longer taught by so-called permanent faculty. The frenzied rush to publish articles in leading journals has even led some institutions to subcontract this task to visiting professors, who teach just a few days a year and allow schools to flaunt a high publication rate by taking advantage of their dual-institutional affiliation. Now a real market exists for professors for the world's top 100 business schools based on their number of publications and reputation. Professors are therefore confronted with identity crises – research versus teaching, undergraduate versus executive education, and so on – making it difficult to discern any coherent expectations. Further, their naturally individualist behaviour limits the possibilities for collaborative reform initiatives.

8.3   IMPOSED POSITIONS: THE CONTEXTUALISED EFFECTS

The contextual elements identified in section 8.2 help shape a certain number of criteria that define business education: the status of educational institutions, the material taught, and teaching methods all converge to paint a portrait of a very coherent system. In the process, this contextualisation leads to a series of difficulties that attest to the issue's extreme complexity.

8.3.1   The Status of Educational Institutions

The ambiguous status of schools that teach management is even evident in the designation most use: 'business school'. Are they academic institutions that adhere to values associated with recognised ideals, such as the independent spirit of higher education and the notion of unbiased objective knowledge? Or are they just a particular type of business, in other words flourishing economic structures fully integrated (Locke 1996) into the education market?

The issue is further complicated by the choice of a particular economic model that relies on alumni donations and revenue provided by executive education activities. This has made business schools a major source of financing for universities, particularly in Great Britain and the United States.[12]

Country-specific choices include the predominance of public university programmes in Germany, the tuition-paying model in England with business schools providing support to universities, and the coexistence in France of tuition-paying consular schools with engineering schools and public university programmes. However, beyond these differences, at the heart of our debate lie independence of thought and the capacity for autonomy that makes it possible for schools *not* to systematically meet existing demand.

8.3.2   The Status of the Academic Content

The nature of the knowledge and skills taught in management science proves to be problematic. As a direct consequence of current trends, all faculty researchers must now obey the dictates of research methods based on a dominant mainstream scientific model directly borrowed from the natural sciences. The goal is to isolate behavioural laws and identify causal relations that make it possible to predict events.

The hidden side of this positivist standpoint is the implicit universality of management science. In other words, teaching methods can vary according to educational traditions, but the body of knowledge remains the same.[13] Consequently, the scientific framework for management set forth in this way can justify existing practices without having to explain their *raison d'être* (see the genesis of works on market efficiency).

Nevertheless, there is a fundamental hesitation regarding the nature of management science course content. Is it about teaching basic techniques (such as the four Ps of marketing, Porter's five forces, and so on) such as those taught in vocational or professional schools (the *Hochschule* in Germany, the engineering school in England, or the IUT degree in France)? Or can management claim the status of a science, an academic discipline on the same level as other social sciences? Stated otherwise, is it an action-based art, a collection of rudimentary recipes and tools that help practitioners, but one that retains a tacit irreducible component that can be mastered only through experience in the field? Or are we talking about real technical know-how with an established model informed by aspects of the 'hard' sciences? The current debate on the tension between rigour and relevance reflects the difficulty we have described.

8.3.3   Teaching Methods and Purpose

Contrasting teaching methods augment the sense of disarray. What is there in common between the abstract, practically axiomatic formulations specific to market finance, and so-called quantitative marketing and the analytic methods used in the field of organisational behaviour? Should we favour a deductive approach that formalises the coherence of articulated knowledge (in keeping with French and German trends, for example), or an inductive approach associated with experience and field-based learning? The diversity of programmes (BA, master's, MBA, EMBA, executive education, and so on) and their various formats (full-time, part-time, work-study, and so on) add to the confusion.

Beyond the disparity in practices, what does management teach? Does it standardise behaviour? The question might seem much too provocative, but can't we compare business schools with Microsoft's global platforms? Most business school students go on to work for leading multinationals.

Multinationals are built on the same model, with a number of employees equivalent to the population of a large city, often more than 100 000, large-scale operations, business activities dispersed worldwide, listed shares, and so on. They strive to standardise their business practices in order to simplify the complexity involved in managing large-scale, international operations. Business schools thus function as useful go-betweens to smooth out the historical differences in trade and production modes[14] and to implement a single, collective organisation of labour (language, reflexes, key concepts, and so on) in the name of improving operational efficiency on a global scale. If we add the fact that the majority of MBAs join management consulting firms,[15] the universality effect is even greater. The claim that management universality is the only 'catholic' (whose Latin etymology reveals it is synonymous with 'universal') practice echoes the claim of certain researchers in the field to have attained scientific knowledge on a par with that of the natural sciences in terms of both method and content.[16]

8.3.4   Modelling a Coherent System

Today, the system appears stable and therefore shielded from forces of internal change. It seems to function according to the following mechanisms. Students pay business schools so they will be guaranteed to find a job when they graduate. Companies participate in financing the schools or their teachings because they want to attract talent, train, or reward their managers in order to gain a degree of legitimacy (knowledge) and prestige (the Harvard effect) from the university. The instructors are torn between the need to teach students managerial realities, and the pressures of competition to produce highly standardised research.

Consequently, a dual 'stock market' assessment process has been established. The rankings published in the business and financial press (the *Financial Times, Businessweek* and so on) evaluate how well the instruction matches corporate expectations, with alumni salaries reflecting the perceived quality of the programmes. On an academic level, indexes of collective productivity (the ranking of Jiao Tong University in Shanghai[17]) and individual productivity (the h-index) make it possible to gauge the activity of 'publishing faculty'.[18] There is a disjunction between the two systems of evaluation, one by companies and the other by the academic community. Along with the complaint sometimes expressed that there is a lack of professors capable of teaching practical realities, this problem is deftly circumvented by relying on affiliated or adjunct faculty and experienced professionals to teach executive education programmes and certain MBA courses. This can go in the other direction, too, through the use of visiting professors who simultaneously credit the flow of their numerous publications to two institutions. The quality accreditation processes (AACSB, for example) validate formal coherence by looking only at adjustments made between the stated objectives and resources implemented, without ever examining the relevance or thoroughness of the options chosen. They assign a common destiny to schools and companies, two variations on the same theme, with a productive activity and subject to the canons of rationality and finality so dear to Max Weber and characteristic of our modernity.

Can a system like this break down, or is it an inevitable part of a societal process that extends beyond individual or collective action? In our view, the only way to leverage change resides in a return to the critical question: what is the purpose of a business school?[19] Is it only to help students find a job, or should it also advance the noble ideals intrinsic to any educational project?

More specifically, two perspectives can be considered. According to the first perspective, companies define the specifications for the programmes that business schools peacefully consent de facto to teach like any other supplier confronted with its customers' requirements. The function of business schools is thus to accustom future employees to an 'acceptable serfdom' and instil in them the rules of the game of the current economic climate without making an effort to foster a capacity to think and act in any other way. According to the contrasting perspective, a school's independence is determined above and beyond strict immediate utility. The goal is not just to educate students to be competent future organisational actors – technicians, managers and leaders – but also to be responsible citizens capable of contributing to positive changes in the company as a whole, its operating modes and its place in society.

The recent financial crisis reveals the incapacity of management education institutions to influence views on the economic system or to formulate analyses and propose alternatives in any articulate way. Do their contexts condemn them irrevocably to this degree of powerlessness?

8.4   CONCLUSION: A FEW ICONOCLASTIC SUGGESTIONS

In conclusion, we offer a few suggestions to reboot the system to allow professors of management science to realise their ambition to contribute their efforts to a carefully planned construction of social reality.

The measures we suggest are not aimed at destabilising a system that is solidly set in place, but to shift the direction a few degrees from its programmed trajectory. Introducing a small difference can make it possible to consider other changes and expand the range of their effects.

The goal of the first suggestion is to breathe new life into research. It is time to revive the tradition of the major European competitions held in the eighteenth century to encourage real creativity. For example, think of the Académie de Dijon's initiatives in 1749 to wonder 'if the restoration of the sciences and the arts contributed to moral purification', raise the issue of 'the origins of inequality among men, and whether it is justified by natural law' and award a prize to Jean-Jacques Rousseau. When might a prize be awarded by the city of Berlin, Madrid or Paris for, say, an essay on the evolution of organisational structures, or a practical solution to a governance problem? Awards like this would make it possible to gain wider recognition and give rise to outstanding works in management science while escaping the reductive formalism of scientific articles. Business school directors could initiate projects like these.

A second idea would consist of diversifying the assessment criteria used to evaluate business schools' performance. It would aim to take into account the variety of careers of alumni. How many of them are in charge of a cultural institution, an NGO or a public administration? How many of them have become political leaders, artists or thinkers?

Bear in mind that, currently, encouraging professions in the non-profit sector negatively affects rankings, since it lowers the post-graduation salary average. The qualitative recognition of an educational programme would then not be reduced to just how much alumni are paid. A core group of schools could suggest new ranking procedures and engage in a real debate on the subject.

A third promising track is to enrich the ways major managerial topics such as change management or leadership are broached. A typical approach could combine three different angles to fully comprehend the complexity of the issues. Firstly, a technical session could provide students with a contextualised toolbox and a repertoire of associated behaviours, and then an applied workshop would prompt them to evolve in real-world situations and experience the very difficulties of playing managerial roles. Eventually a more interpretative session would equip them with an understanding of the nature of the phenomenon (with, for instance, some reflections upon the historical background, the hidden assumptions behind the tools, their unintended consequences within different contexts, and so on).

Let's take an example with leadership. The new curriculum could encompass the following learning modules: 1) a study of the models currently identified by scholars of the field; 2) the real practice of leadership art during virtual or real projects (see IMD MBA students who were asked to launch and implement assistance projects for Sarajevo some years ago); and finally 3) a collective conversation on great historical figures (see the yearly class 'The art and adventure of leadership' which was taught by Warren Bennis and Steven Sample at the University of Southern California[20]) or on the portraits we have been given of classical authors (think of Charles Handy[21] with his students from the London Business School attending Shakespeare's plays and debating upon the intricacies of the human soul confronted with power).

Resorting to such a diversified approach to leadership we would be far from the sole use of the case method. Cases provide readers with stylised situations and put them in the shoes of advisers or consultants: the method is consistent with the wish of its makers, the American law schools at the end of the nineteenth century that intended to educate legal advisers. It appears to be less relevant to the making of future leaders, who are often invited to find inspiration in short-lived performing models.[22]

Finally, it might be wise for business schools to adopt the model currently used by Médecins sans Frontières (MSF) (Doctors without Borders). To protect against any abuse, the NGO has an internal strategic council that constantly analyses the real social utility of the organisation's actions. Its Centre de Réflexion sur l'Action et les Savoirs Humanitaires (CRASH) meets two main objectives: it encourages discussion and critical reflection of humanitarian efforts within MSF, and it provides a forum for public debate on MSF's own questions on humanitarian action in general. This way of challenging authority allows MSF regularly to subject its actions, programmes and operations to thorough investigation and make sure its voice is heard.

Couldn't some business education institutions adopt a process like this with the sole purpose of raising the question at the end of the year: have we accomplished anything of real use?

NOTES

1. Kant, *Treaty on Education*, Ak. IX, p.446.
2. As quoted by Khurana (2007, p.116).
3. We often deliberately refer to 'business schools'. The term means different things in different countries, but the American business school model has gained considerable influence upon the other players. See Basso et al. (2006).
4. 'If its purpose is to train "hands," or technicians, or merely successful money-makers, in my judgment the course has no place in a graduate department of a university. On the other hand, if its purpose is to train "heads" or future leaders in business, it has no difficulty in justifying its existence or place' (C.P. Biddle, Assistant Dean, Harvard Business School, 1926, quoted in Khurana 2007, p.5).
5. Far from dealing exclusively with the corporate world, management extends to the art of managing all kinds of organisations (governmental structures, museums, opera companies, hospitals, non-profits, institutions and so on), as Peter Drucker pointed out starting in his earliest works.
6. Hegel (1995, Chapter II).
7. In brief, this can be defined as the expansion of activities completed according to a logic dictated by the calculation, prediction, assessment and drive to increase efficiency: 'The fate of our times is characterized by rationalization and intellectualization and, above all, by the disenchantment of the world. Precisely the ultimate and most sublime values have retreated from public life either into the transcendental realm of mystic life or into the brotherliness of direct and personal human relations. It is not accidental that our greatest art is intimate and not monumental' (Weber [1948] 1994a).
8. For a more global perspective on the evils of the Occident, read the prophetic work of Pierre Thuillier, *La Grande Implosion* (1995).
9. Weber clearly saw the end of the lone researcher as an artisan of knowledge, and the emergence of laboratory research teams (see Weber [1948] 1994b).
10. For example, '*To think for oneself* means to look within oneself (i.e. within one's own reason) for the supreme touchstone of truth; and the maxim of thinking for oneself at all times is *enlightenment*' (Kant 1991, p.249).
11. In French society, management is too often confused with 'managerialism' and rejected as a threat for individuals or perceived as something one can learn only on the job. See Basso et al. (2006).
12. The English example is particularly clear: see Starkey and Tiratsoo (2007).
13. The work of Pierre Legendre makes it possible to gain perspective on this one-dimensional approach: 'Modern experts, impregnated by American and continental Weberianism, consider power and organisational phenomena – let us think about consulting firms that sell management techniques and executive education to Islamic countries, for instance – as available and easy to handle, thanks to scientific objectivisation, assessed through post-Weberian codification' (Legendre 1989, our translation). For non-French readers, see Legendre (1997).
14. Consider the diversity of the economic models that still exist in Europe: German companies and *Länder* still often work together, united by a capitalistic bond to defend labour; in France, the historical mix between the strategic-entrepreneurial state and major corporations remains powerful, while in England the two universes still insist on remaining separate and the mercantile tradition is now focused more on seeking a competitive advantage in the financial industry, far from any 'industrial nationalism'. Added to these national business culture elements are moral perceptions. Thus we can

roughly distinguish a Latin block (Spain, Italy, Portugal and France) characterised by strong opposition to wealth accumulation, often perceived as resulting from reprehensible or even illegal schemes (see Balzac: 'behind every fortune, there is a crime'). The royal paths to social recognition in these countries are therefore not those of business and commerce.

15. Between 1965 and 1985, the number of Harvard Business School graduates who chose to work in finance and consulting rather than as corporate executives had already gone from 23 to 52 per cent.

16. We should say here that it is a mark of our times that social sciences aspire towards objectification as a sign of rigour and scientific legitimacy. Based on the artificiality of human constructions, the conclusion seems to be that man himself is artificial (see, for example, the prologue by Supiot (2007).

17. http://www.arwu.org.

18. Read the scathing article by Grégoire Chamayou, 'Petits conseils aux enseignants-chercheurs qui voudront réussir leur evaluation', online on the Contretemps website (http://contretemps.eu/interventions/petits-conseils-enseignants-chercheurs-qui-voudront-reussir-leur-evaluation).

19. This is also the only leverage point that Rakesh Khurana has found to justify his critical approach to business schools. He believes they have failed to meet their purpose of educating a community of professionals united by a shared belief in independent experts committed to providing a service (like doctors and lawyers). As such, the 'professional managers' are obliged to manage a new type of organisation (the multinational corporation) and be the guarantors of its smooth functioning, while also making sure that it does not damage the economic and social foundations of the society that created it (Khurana 2007, p. 10).

20. Drawing from several academic disciplines, the course explored leadership in theory and practice, and examined the lives of leaders such as King David, Socrates, Cesare Borgia and Elizabeth I.

21. See Handy (2002, pp. 47–8).

22. Think about the destinies of such iconic CEOs as Percy Barnevik (ABB) or Jacques Nasser (Ford), highly praised leaders in their time and afterwards strongly criticised for their behaviour and the negative effects of their previously extolled leadership virtues.

REFERENCES

Basso, O., P.-P. Dornier and J.-P. Mounier (2006), *'Tu seras patron, mon fils!': Les Grandes Écoles de commerce face au modèle américain*, Paris: Village Mondial.

Desrosières, Alain (2002), *The Politics of Large Numbers: A History of Statistical Reasoning*, Cambridge, MA: Harvard University Press (originally published as *La Politique des grands nombres: Histoire de la raison statistique*, La Découverte, Paris, 1993).

Foucault, M. (2004), *Sécurité, territoire, population: Cours au Collège de France 1977–1978*, Paris: Hautes Études, Gallimard.

Friedman, Milton (1970), 'The social responsibility of business is to increase its profits', *New York Times Magazine*, 13 September.

Guénon, René (2004), *The Reign of Quantity and the Signs of the Times*, 4th edn, Hillsdale, NY: Sophia Perennis (originally published as *Le Règne de la quantité et les signes des temps*, 1st edn, Gallimard, Paris, 1945).

Handy, Charles (2002), *The Elephant and the Flea: Reflections of a Reluctant Capitalist*, Boston, MA: Harvard Business School Press.

Hegel, G.W.F. (1995), *Reason in History*, trans. Robert S. Hartman, Upper Saddle River, NJ: Prentice Hall.

Jensen, M. and W. Meckling (1976), 'Theory of the firm: managerial behavior, agency cost and ownership structure', *Journal of Financial Economics*, **3**, 305–60.

Kant, I. (1991), 'What is orientation in thinking?', in I. Kant, *Political Writings*, ed. H.S. Reiss, trans. H.B. Nisbet, Cambridge Texts in the History of Political Thought, Cambridge: Cambridge University Press.

Khurana, Rakesh (2007), *From Higher Aims to Hired Hands: The Social Transformation of American Business Schools and the Unfulfilled Promise of Management as a Profession*, Princeton, NJ: Princeton University Press.

Legendre, Pierre (1989), 'Droit, communication et politique', *Hermès*, **5–6**, 21–32.

Legendre, Pierre (1997), *Law and the Unconscious: A Legendre Reader (Language, Discourse, Society)*, ed. Peter Goodrich, New York: St Martin's Press.

Locke, Robert R. (1996), *The Collapse of the American Management Mystique*, New York: Oxford University Press.

Morin, Edgar (1999), *Amour, poésie, sagesse*, Paris: Points, Seuil.

Smith, Adam ([1759] 2002), *The Theory of Moral Sentiments*, Cambridge: Cambridge University Press.

Starkey, Ken and Nick Tiratsoo (2007), *The Business School and the Bottom Line*, Cambridge: Cambridge University Press.

Supiot, Alain (2007), *Homo Juridicus: On the Anthropological Function of the Law*, London: Verso (originally published as *Homo juridicus: Essai sur la fonction anthropologique du droit*, Seuil, Paris, 2005).

Thuillier, Pierre (1995), *La Grande Implosion: Rapport sur l'effondrement de l'Occident 1999–2002*, Paris: Fayard.

Weber, Max ([1948] 1994a), 'Politics as a vocation', in H. Gerth and C.W. Mills (eds), *From Max Weber: Essays in Sociology*, London: Routledge, p. 155.

Weber, Max ([1948] 1994b), 'Science as a vocation', in H. Gerth and C.W. Mills (eds), *From Max Weber: Essays in Sociology*, London: Routledge, p. 131.

9. Evaluating programmes of management education: the EFMD perspective

Eric Cornuel

Business schools should ask themselves about their methods of preparing their participants to become the next generation of business leaders. In the context of a free economy, business schools have a crucial role to play to optimise the way institutions, private as well as public, are managed, with the objective of ensuring the best possible level of growth and thereby, we all hope, a dramatic improvement in people's lives.

The last two decades have seen the extension of the World Trade Organization from 90 to 153 members and the greater integration of global markets, allowing goods, services, capital and technologies to spread across the world. For less developed countries the period has also led to a reduction in poverty, allowing people to live a better life, especially in Asia.

These dramatic improvements, however, should not hide the deep problems and injustices that remain and the massive problems of poverty, ignorance and disease that many countries still face. Almost 40 per cent of the world's population lives on less than two dollars a day, and a child dies every 15 seconds owing to lack of access to safe water and adequate sanitation. Since the beginning of the global era, we have also seen a much stronger polarisation of wealth and economic growth, not only among countries but also within nations.

Within this framework, what sort of intellectual contribution are business schools able to make to private and public decision makers – and, more generally, to society as a whole? Management education has an important role to play on at least two levels. First, the techniques and methods of management that are taught and the research underlying them should lead to a general improvement in managerial efforts and therefore to optimised economic growth. Second, the 'soft' elements increasingly integrated into curricula should raise awareness of the role of managers in society in creating more social cohesion inside and outside private, public and not-for-profit organisations.

The economic problems we are facing today have created a situation in which companies and organisations generally try to limit their expenditures. This implies restrictions on the number of managers being employed, and a more limited utilisation of outside consultants. Alongside this, tasks have become increasingly complex, and individuals are having to cope with increasing stressful situations, not knowing which principles (or leaders) they can turn to. It is precisely this type of challenge that our schools should be trying to overcome, so that they have something to contribute to firms' profitable growth but also to society as a whole.

The successful business schools of the future will ensure that they offer their students innovative programmes, with an excellent faculty body, international experience and a multicultural environment. They will not only implement changes to remain competitive but will pursue quality improvement programmes and accreditation to prove to the market that they are committed to excellence and innovation. Above all, quality will become an ever growing concern for business schools, in particular with regard to measures for determining and improving the quality of programmes.

This chapter looks at the quality improvement and quality assurance of programmes along two dimensions. First is the need for a formal internal management system for the pursuit of excellence and the management of quality improvement. This should lie alongside other management systems for research, teaching and learning, marketing and financial management. Second is the role of external programme accreditation systems, in this case the EFMD Programme Accreditation System (EPAS) launched in 2005, in assisting and promoting that process.

Business education today is a global industry. The days of relatively cosy local markets with captive student populations are disappearing fast as international competition comes to our doorsteps. There is only one way to survive in such competitive markets, and that is to offer very high-quality products or programmes.

So what does high quality mean to a business school? Current wisdom suggests that a business should 'delight' its customers, so perhaps a business school should delight its stakeholders. This can only be done by having a high-quality culture or ethos that pervades all the activities within a school. It has to be a way of life and not a one-off project for the quality department or even for those responsible for accreditations such as EQUIS or EPAS. The development of a quality culture can only come from the dean and his or her management team leading, promoting and supporting it.

A key way to do this is to establish a formal management system that should specify standards, set key performance indicators, have a measurement system for these and require regular reporting. Management should also ensure it is taken seriously by publicly celebrating success and taking remedial action in less successful areas.

Of course, the concept of achieving high quality is a moving target. It can never be finally achieved. The management system should therefore be designed to take the school to ever higher levels of quality.

A number of significant quality assurance issues arise in each key phase – design, delivery, outputs and review – of such a management system.

9.1   CRITERIA FOR EVALUATING PROGRAMMES

9.1.1   Programme Design

Programme initiation

A faculty member with a particular interest in the subject area will often initiate a programme, but it is unwise to let that one person design and run it. Apart from the 'falling under a bus' syndrome, programmes based on 'bees in bonnets' can often look odd when viewed from outside. They may even not have a real market or may not produce employable graduates.

Programme design process

A wide range of stakeholder views should be brought into the design process. Stakeholders include faculty members, potential students (market research), potential employers, and the parent school and university. A robust process for gathering those views and debating how they should be translated into a sound academic programme probably needs some form of formal programme committee. It should also be tasked with overseeing the running of the programme and its reviews.

Aims and learning outcomes

There should be clearly stated aims and intended learning outcomes (ILO) for the programme. These will make clear who it is for and what the graduates will know and be able to do at the end of it. These become the basis for quality assurance of the delivery and the outputs of the programme. Initially they are the basis for the design of the curriculum and assessment processes.

Programme approval

Programmes should have to be approved not only by the programme committee but also further up the organisational framework. This is to ensure that the programme fits with a school's or institution's strategy and programme portfolio, that it is seen to be academically rigorous, that there is likely to be a market both among students and among employers, and that there are sufficient resources to promote and run the programme. In some institutions and countries, approvals have to be obtained at university and state level as well.

Programme changes
After periodic review, programmes will need some form of change, major or minor, usually undertaken by the programme committee. However, major changes should also be approved at a higher level.

9.1.2 Programme Delivery

Student quality
The quality of the student intake should match the target market and be able to achieve the ILO for the programme, which in turn means that they should meet employers' expectations. One of the problems of management education remains its continuing (though reduced) emphasis on the trappings of functional disciplines when in reality managers work in a cross-disciplinary, even multidisciplinary, world. So many different elements interact each with the other that managers must be capable of a broader view.

Developing the competencies, capacities and attitudes required for the next generation of leaders requires more than relying solely on the simple acquisition of knowledge. Experiential, presentational, propositional and practical ways of learning must be integrated into the curriculum. The top business schools of the future will train their students to meet the demands of an increasingly complex world, and in doing so they will use challenging and innovative approaches to management education. They will implement substantial changes in the ways they prepare the next generation of leaders.

In particular, I believe they will, and should, put globally responsible leadership and corporate responsibility at the heart of the business school curriculum. This will also present the schools with an opportunity to expand and enrich their academic offering and to employ new pedagogical approaches.

Teaching quality
Teaching should be evaluated not only by students but also by some programme management oversight, which may involve peer observations, staff–student forums and individual discussion with faculty.

Assessment quality
While faculty members are capable of setting assessments of an appropriate standard, it is necessary to have some management oversight to ensure consistency of standards and either to agree planned overlap or to remove duplication. Furthermore, there should be some oversight of the marking or grading process to ensure consistency and fairness. This might mean some random sample second marking or even, as in the UK, total blind double marking and the use of external examiners. The assessments should test whether the programme aims and ILO have been achieved.

9.1.3   Programme Outputs

Student work quality
A formal quality assurance system for the assessment process should ensure that the quality of student work is appropriate to the level of the degree and that the ILO are met. The quality of projects or theses can be an issue here. An examination board should be established to manage the process of deciding progression from one degree stage or year to another and for the degree award. This allows for transparency and can take care of special circumstances.

9.1.4   Programme Review

Annual review
All programmes should go through some form of annual review overseen by the programme committee. This enables small changes to be made for continual improvement of the programme.

Periodic review
Programmes should also be subject to major review involving all stakeholders on a periodic basis (say five years). This will ensure that the programme stays relevant to those stakeholders and that major changes in the environment are reflected in the programme design. Major changes should undergo a higher-level approval process. Such reviews should also allow for the fact that the programme may no longer be viable or relevant to the stakeholders and should be removed from the school's portfolio.

Quality improvement in a higher education institution, in short, is concerned with an ongoing cycle of agreeing on a set of standards and/or goals, gathering relevant information, evaluating feedback and ensuring the implementation of change.

A higher education institution involved in a strong and effective quality improvement process will be characterised by the following:

- an institutional culture that is open to constructive evaluation and to change;
- a high level of satisfaction from students, employers and external customers;
- institution-wide embracing of the concept of quality improvement, including a commitment to participate in institutional improvement and growth;
- evidence of ongoing measurable improvement in institutional performance in agreed areas of need;
- open communication within and between different areas of operation;
- self-confidence in the institution's ability to manage its own future, and evidence of its success in doing so, particularly in relation to any external accreditation bodies.

As the last point suggests, institutions will also increasingly be looking at some form of external programme accreditation in order to validate and demonstrate their commitment to quality improvement and quality assurance.

The most competitive schools are already looking for benchmarking opportunities as well as quality improvement programmes that will provide them with an opportunity to gain a thorough understanding of their strengths and weaknesses, to develop new and better programmes, and to prove the level of their offerings to the market through accreditation.

9.2   THE EFMD PROGRAMME ACCREDITATION SYSTEM (EPAS)

9.2.1   Why EPAS Was Needed

It was to respond to this need (coupled with concerns that the Bologna process might create some confusion within European education systems and that the European Foundation for Management Development, EFMD, ought to provide thought leadership in this area) that in 2005 EFMD launched the EFMD Programme Accreditation System (EPAS), a system that accredits individual programmes.

At the time, the European Quality Improvement System (EQUIS), the leading international accreditation for business schools launched by EFMD in 1998, was already well established and undoubtedly perceived to be a catalyst for continuous quality improvement. EQUIS was, and is, targeted at those business schools around the world that show outstanding performance on the basis of the EQUIS framework of quality dimensions and standards. Schools that have gone through the EQUIS process have acknowledged the improvements created by it. This has been signalled by schools not only when they receive EQUIS for the first time but also when they go through the process for a second or third time to renew their accreditation. Even those schools that initially have failed to gain accreditation have acknowledged the contribution the EQUIS process made in terms of guidance and challenge. Many succeeded in gaining accreditation subsequently.

In 2004, EFMD considered that this approach needed to be supplemented. At the same time, it wanted to protect EQUIS standards, not soften them and thereby dilute their value. The answer was EPAS, which provides a direct contribution to quality improvement not in an entire school but in the more focused area of one or two of its degree programmes. This broadens the direct impact to schools that for some reason cannot benefit directly from EQUIS.

Following two successful pilot phases in 2006, EFMD Quality Services embarked on an ambitious 'Scale Up' initiative to expand the portfolio of accredited programmes.

9.2.2 What Is EPAS?

To an extent, the EPAS process reflects the philosophy and methodology of the EQUIS approach. It involves an in-depth review of individual programmes through international comparison and benchmarking. It also includes an evaluation report with strategic advice on how a programme may be improved to compete more effectively in international markets. Where it is appropriate, focus may also be put on the programme's compatibility and/or conformance with the Bologna structure.

The EPAS accreditation process centres around a guided self-assessment and peer review service to help programme providers assess, benchmark and improve their programmes.

The EPAS scheme focuses on institutions of higher education offering business- and management-related programmes (or sets of programmes) that aim to meet international levels of quality. However, the assessment criteria can also encompass all formalised business- and management-related programmes, including for example those offered within corporate universities and management learning centres.

The main stages of the EPAS process are the following:

- Stage 1: application;
- Stage 2: clarification;

- Stage 3: eligibility;
- Stage 4: self-assessment;
- Stage 5: peer review;
- Stage 6: accreditation;
- Stage 7: follow-up and continuous improvement.

Most institutions complete the process from Stage 1 to Stage 6 in six to nine months. Stage 7 is followed until such time as re-accreditation is sought.

EPAS reviews generic institutional aspects only to the extent that they affect the quality of the programme under review. Unlike EQUIS, it is not a whole-school accreditation, and its criteria and standards are therefore different in focus. EPAS and EQUIS are separate systems and are not equivalent, although schools aspiring to EQUIS accreditation may find that undergoing EPAS for key programmes will be a beneficial first stage.

9.2.3   How EPAS Developed

The development of the EPAS process has provided useful insights into the quality of such programmes around Europe and also produced some concerns that validate the need for a procedure such as EPAS. For example, during pilot stages it became apparent that programme design was often left to programme teams and that there was little or no involvement of stakeholders such as corporate partners, other faculty, students or alumni. Some programmes were not as academically rigorous as might have been expected, and the academic depth of some master's programmes did not match the level expected of such a qualification.

In addition, the degree of internationalisation of the student experience could, and should, often have been stronger. Quality assurance processes were frequently informal and weak – teaching quality was too often assessed only by student feedback on 'happy sheets', and the feedback loop to the students on actions taken was rarely closed.

EFMD believes that the EPAS accreditation process has a number of benefits that address these shortcomings. They include:

- international market recognition of a programme;
- potential for cross-border recognition by national quality agencies;
- international benchmarking and comparison;
- advice on programme definition, particularly in the Bologna context;
- strategic development of a programme;
- facilitation of a process of reflection by the programme team on the key attributes of the programme.

As at June 2010, there were 43 accredited programmes from 34 institutions in 17 countries. Considering all EPAS accredited and EPAS eligible programmes, the market coverage for EPAS extended to 77 programmes from 55 institutions based in 23 countries covering all five continents. Of the total, 32 per cent were (E)MBAs, 27 per cent were master's programmes, 25 per cent were bachelor's programmes, 4 per cent were doctoral programmes and 12 per cent were non-Bologna country-specific programmes.

Interest in EPAS is expected to remain strong in the years to come. In total, 21 programmes from 15 institutions were discussed in the three EPAS Committee meetings in 2009. While most institutions submitted only one programme for review during the pilot phases, applying with two programmes or programme suites has now become the more typical case. In 2009, 24 peer reviews took place.

9.2.4 What Impact Is EPAS Having?

EPAS accreditation provides value in five distinct areas:

- by ensuring a 'quality first' approach;
- by increasing brand recognition by key stakeholder groups of accredited programmes;
- by acting as a 'proof of concept' for successful internationalisation;
- by providing network value for accredited programmes (EPAS accreditation strengthens the partnership between the member institution and an increasing number of regular EFMD network events);
- by potentially serving as a substitute for mandatory national accreditation (EFMD Quality Services is talking to accreditation authorities with the objective of obtaining national recognition. Any such effort, however, is conditional on a fit of national accreditation standards with EFMD's general philosophy of developing a relationship of mutual trust rather than providing a detailed public rating of a programme).

However, the most immediate benefit of EPAS accreditation is also the one most often overlooked by programme, and possibly even institutional, management. EPAS is based on a unique value model embedded in its standards and criteria that enforces a 'quality first' approach at all levels without infringing on an institution's prerogative to differentiate itself from its competitors (and also any implicit market standards).

The overall programme assessment is put into the context of the institutional as well as the national and international environments. A programme is evaluated on the basis of its design, delivery and outcomes and, in addition, by appraising the supporting quality assurance processes. The assessment philosophy is designed to add value to a school and not to take an auditing approach.

Academic programmes often involve a lot of pragmatism. Programme officials may focus too much on marketing issues and may apply myopic short cuts when it comes to the fundamentals of quality management, often driven by the need to respond quickly to market dynamics in the presence of tight budget constraints.

EPAS, however, puts quality issues at the forefront and thereby enforces principles that ensure the creation of long-term value for the organisation as a whole. It can ultimately create a halo effect for the entire institution and can therefore act as a catalyst for change, enabling a business school to reach a state of 'EQUIS readiness' much more quickly than otherwise.

In this context, organisational learning takes place in two stages: preparing the self-assessment report during the accreditation phase; and dealing with specific weaknesses identified by the peer review team after having completed the initial accreditation.

In sum, EPAS has developed into a valuable accreditation service for EFMD members. It adds immediate brand value by recognising the achievement of educational excellence and successful internationalisation at the programme level.

9.2.5   EPAS – European *and* Global

EFMD was founded on the principle of linking the world of academia with the world of business, and in our view corporate connections are as important for business schools as hospital connections are for schools of medicine. Strong corporate connections that facilitate students' development and allow them to deal with the realities of their intended profession are a cornerstone of the EFMD philosophy which necessitates that a balance between academic knowledge and managerial skills be sought in everything a business school provides. A distinctive feature of EFMD is closely related to its European origin: appreciation for diversity. One might presume that the EFMD accreditation systems would be based on the typical European business school. However, there is no such thing. In fact, many of those who have analysed Europe looking for commonalities reach the conclusion that the basic common feature of Europeans is the ability to live with the idea that diversity is a source of richness and that, while there may be value in certain convergence, diversity should be preserved. This idea is embedded in EFMD, and it has practical implications in the way EFMD assesses schools and programmes.

While the fundamental objective of EPAS, linked to the mission of the EFMD, is to raise the standard of management education in Europe and beyond, both individually for schools and faculties and systemically for national management education structures, it has also been designed to help prospective students and recruiting companies from one country to identify those institutions in other countries that deliver high-quality education for international management.

EPAS is European in the sense that Europeans have designed it and Europeans, from a broad range of countries, manage it. Its scope, however, is global in that it provides a framework for assessing programme quality in highly diverse institutional and cultural contexts. In this sense it is also more adapted to the world outside Europe than other national or regional accreditation systems.

Some institutions with programmes in the EPAS pipeline are aiming for EQUIS accreditation as their ultimate ambition. In this context, EPAS also provides a benchmark for the school's general EQUIS readiness and frequently acts as a catalyst for institutional change, in particular in the areas of internationalisation, quality assurance and academic rigour.

EPAS development is, however, not about numbers. In line with the EFMD's overall mission, EPAS has been designed to award accreditation to academic programmes that are internationally recognised as being positioned in the premium segment of their respective markets. It has also been set up as a framework in support of a school's efforts towards continuous quality improvement.

In line with these aspirations, EFMD Quality Services will maintain its focus on further strengthening the EPAS standards and criteria as well as the supporting processes. As a consequence, rising application numbers are expected to be accompanied by greater selectivity at all stages of the accreditation process.

Just as EFMD is rapidly expanding into the rest of the world, EPAS can be expected to attract rising interest from non-European business schools. This was already reflected in the geographical mix of programmes applying for eligibility in 2009. From the 15 institutions that put forward applications in that year, four were from outside Europe. The non-European share of newly accredited programmes was expected to rise to at least 25 per cent by 2011 and should certainly continue to grow thereafter. Of the 14 initial accreditations in 2011 at the date of writing, three were non-European, thus reaching almost 25 per cent. By widening EPAS's geographical base, business schools within the EPAS system will be able to expand their international reach and to benefit from greater networking opportunities with institutions of similar standing.

Providing network value to EFMD members in support of institutional internationalisation efforts was one of the motives for setting up the EPAS system. Tangible benefits already realised by institutions with accredited or eligible programmes clearly verify the relevance of this approach.

9.3 CONCLUSION

As stated at the beginning of this chapter, the quality of programmes provided by business schools and other institutes of higher education is of growing importance and is already a key factor in the competition between them to attract high-achieving students and faculty and to protect and enhance their reputation and prestige in a crowded marketplace.

The internal measures to ensure and improve programme quality set out above (which draw on the accumulated expertise and experience within EFMD) plus the support, encouragement and validation offered by external accreditation systems such as EPAS can together do much to ensure that those goals are achieved.

10. Performativity, metatheorising and journal rankings: what are the implications for emerging journals and academic freedom?

Dennis Tourish

10.1 INTRODUCTION

I want to consider the future of emergent journals and academic freedom in the context of what I see as the performative pressures now endemic in the higher education sector. The first challenge is the proliferation of journal ranking systems. These seek to list journals which are in some way approved and are then viewed as a proxy measure of article or faculty quality. For example, the *Financial Times* lists 45 journals, and considers faculty publication in them as one measure of MBA quality.[1] Others assign rankings to individual journals. In the UK, for example, the influential Association of Business Schools journal rankings in 2010 list 821 journals, and utilise the RAE system (shortly to be reincarnated as the Research Excellence Framework) to give an overall score to individual journals.[2] A similar approach is followed in the rankings produced by the Australian-based Association of Business School Deans.[3] Ranking systems have also been developed in South Africa, Mexico and New Zealand (Nkomo 2009). I will argue here that these systems are increasingly appropriated within universities as performative tools to limit academic freedom, particularly by pushing people to prioritise publication in a select band of supposedly elite journals above others. This has significant consequences for emerging new disciplines and sub-disciplines, and for those journals which seek to champion distinctive or innovative approaches to particular topics.

The second challenge is equally compelling. Increasingly, 'elite' journals stress that all articles must make an 'innovative theoretical contribution', rather than, for example, contributing to practice, identifying a problem or offering a rich description of an interesting phenomenon. The result is an intense specialisation. Many of our journals are overly focused on narrow issues, frequently of only marginal relevance to the plentiful problems afflicting the world, and all too often inaccessible and unreadable. I want to argue that these two issues are connected. In particular, I see the focus on 'theory' above all else as part of an ultimately doomed campaign to capture similar levels of prestige to those enjoyed by such elite US journals as the *Academy of Management Review*. The chief result is a narrowing of academic inquiry. Many of the concerns I express here are widely discussed among academics, mostly informally. My suggestion is that these discussions should become much more formal and that in our roles as researchers, reviewers, readers and editors we should strive to address them – that is, to make a difference.

10.2   THE PERFORMATIVE IMPACT OF JOURNAL RANKINGS

It is self-evident that academics have grown more obsessed with journal rankings over the past decade, and in more and more disciplines, including the sciences (Lawrence 2008). I suspect that this tendency is particularly acute in business and management. As cash cows in many institutions, undergraduate business programmes and MBAs are subject to penal levels of classification, comparison and rankings. Most publicised systems, as Adler and Harzing (2009, p. 74) have noted, 'claim to measure what is labelled as research productivity, with the definition of productivity often reduced to simply counting publications in high impact-factor journals along with citations in the limited set of journals that such systems recognise'. The effects on scholarship are profound, and largely iniquitous.

For example, the *Financial Times* list of top 45 journals (up from an even more paltry 30 just a few years ago) is but a tiny sample of high-quality journals. Despite this, many 'top' or aspiring-to-the-top business schools use publication in the journals listed as a key criterion of appointment and promotion. The ABS journal rankings list 821 journals, but an analysis conducted by Mingers et al. (2009) shows that, in the UK RAE 2008, papers were published in a further 825 journals not listed in the ABS rankings. It is thus far from exhaustive. Regardless, academics are pushed towards publication in ABS-listed journals, and within this they are increasingly urged to focus their energies on the 93 journals designated as four star. It is now quite common to see job advertisements which specify such publication as a key part of the selection process. Moreover, it is widely recognised that, within this four-star category, there are what the ABS guide itself describes as around 22 'world elite' (that is, mostly US-based journals), which 'are recognised worldwide as exemplars of excellence within the business and management field broadly defined and including economics' (ABS Journal Guide, 2010, p. 8). While some business schools now insist on publication in four-star journals, still others privilege this double-starred 'world elite', disparaging other outlets and forms of publication, such as books or book chapters.[4] It is likely that this approach will be more widely emulated, since the increased importance of business school rankings encourages those further down the ranking lists to copy the behaviours and approaches of those nearer the top (Starkey and Tiratsoo 2007).

This has serious consequences for scholarship. Singh et al. (2007, p. 321) have argued that many top articles appear in what are not regarded as top journals, and many poorer-quality articles are published in top journals. Interestingly, several contributors to a key text devoted to theory development (Smith and Hitt 2005), in which some of the best-known management scholars describe their theories and the processes by which they were developed, reveal that they had huge difficulty in publishing their work in leading journals. For example, Barney (2005), in discussing his development of resource-based theory, had what is now regarded as his seminal paper rejected multiple times, before having to accept it himself for a special issue of a journal he was editing (Barney 1991). This paper currently registers almost 20 000 citations on Google Scholar!

Leadership, a journal I serve as an associate editor, is a further excellent example. Despite its being a fairly new journal, launched in 2005, Mingers et al.'s (2009) analysis of the last RAE suggests that 14 papers from it were submitted for consideration, and that all of them achieved a ranking of three star, corresponding to work that is internationally excellent in terms of originality, significance and rigour. This is a remarkable achievement for a journal which had only three years of publication behind it at the RAE census date. It would appear to confirm *Leadership* as a leading-edge journal in the field, and the value for scholars and their careers of publishing in its pages. By contrast, the more established and US-centric *Leadership Quarterly* is designated a four-star journal in the ABS rankings. But the Mingers et al. (2009) analysis found that only four papers published in it were entered in the RAE. Moreover, none of them appear to have been awarded a four-star score – three got a three star, and one a two star. Of course, there is a margin of error in this analysis, but it does suggest that many supposedly top journals had a wide variation in the scores attached to their papers, with papers in many supposedly lower-ranked journals doing better. Yet the slavish devotion to the ABS rankings, and journal rankings more widely, encourages a false view that the outlet in which one publishes is more important than the quality of the ideas contained in papers. In turn, this handy metric ('How many four-star papers have you published?'), when used by selection and promotion panels, is a performative tool that skews effort into outlets and sometimes subject areas that are often devoid of intrinsic interest to the academics concerned. Academic freedom is diminished.

This has implications both for the impact of the work and for the development of specialised journals. In the first instance, specialised journals often speak more directly to the core academic audience in the field. However, they are often ignored by developing researchers, since they may have a lower citation score and thus reside outside the top-tier categorisations in formal ranking systems (Segalla 2008). Most ranking systems, including those of the ABS, also place a great deal of weight on a journal's impact factor. This further constrains the possibility of new journals in emerging fields establishing themselves. Journals must wait for three years before being considered for inclusion in the ISI Social Science Citation Index. They then have a further three-year 'waiting period' before a score is awarded. This means a minimum period of six years from a journal's inception to receiving its first impact score. The implications are stark. The ABS, in determining its journal rankings, decided that, 'with few exceptions, journals not carrying a citation impact factor were graded at 2 or lower. The exceptions to this rule are journals with an established reputation and previously graded 3 in the Guide' (ABS, 2010, p. 8). As a result, and despite its excellent showing in the 2008 RAE, *Leadership* currently has a rating of one star – not because of its quality, but simply because it did not have an impact factor when the rankings were being compiled, or a lengthy record of publication to compensate. Adler and Harzing (2009) suggest that such rankings discourage people from publishing their work in new and innovative journals, since appointment and promotion panels tend to place more emphasis on a journal's formal ranking than the evidence would suggest is wise. It is obvious that this can become a self-fulfilling prophecy. People may avoid publishing in a journal because it does not yet have an impact factor or feature highly in journal ranking lists, but this then ensures that it will ultimately receive only a modest impact factor and thus struggle to establish itself in 'official' journal rankings.

The consequences for individual scholarship are also serious. There are major differences in approach between elite US journals and their counterparts elsewhere (Grey 2010). Here are two examples. An editorial statement in the *Academy of Management Journal* in 2004 asserted encouragingly that 'Qualitative research is important to *AMJ*' (Gephart 2004, p. 454). It was so important that, in the journal's then 47-year history, qualitative papers won its best article award only three times, with one further best paper combining qualitative and quantitative methods. The US-based Academy of Management publishes influential literature reviews each year in the *Academy of Management Annuals*. A recent edition has a paper that explores the mechanisms of theory development within the field of leadership (Glynn and Raffaelli 2010). This paper reviews academic articles over a 50-year period, but they are all drawn from just three 'top' US journals – the *Academy of Management Journal, Administrative Science Quarterly* and *Organization Science*, plus a further 'specialist' journal, the *Leadership Quarterly*, which also just so happens to have a mostly North American orientation. Few non-US scholars publish in the first three of these outlets in particular, and few issues or methods outside those sanctioned by Ivy League institutions and their graduate studies training programmes find traction in their pages. It is difficult to imagine a similarly themed article by an African, European or Australasian management association affecting a similar bias in its source material.

To accept the hegemony of such journals, as the journal ranking lists would suggest we should, is to mean that we must accept their dominant intellectual, theoretical and methodological paradigms. This means that one can't simply pursue a research agenda in supposedly 'top' journals without it being affected by the traditions, and biases, that dominate those journals. Thus, Grey (2010) points out that contributors to *Administrative Science Quarterly* are almost exclusively drawn from the United States. The few non-US contributors that it publishes tend, of necessity, to embrace the positivist and functionalist orthodoxy of US scholarship in order to be included. There are, of course, exceptions, but they are not sufficient to disturb the general trend. The more pluralistic agenda of journals such as *Leadership* requires outlets such as, well, *Leadership* in order to thrive. But it is precisely this that formal journal ranking systems put in jeopardy, creating the possibility of an academic discourse that is theoretically constrained, methodologically pinched and conformist in its topic coverage. None of this matters, of course – unless there are pressures within the higher education system to internalise the approach of the journal ranking systems. It is this possibility that I now wish to consider further.

10.2.1 The Pressures of Performativity

Performativity is commonly understood as a technocratic preoccupation with maximising the outputs that flow from inputs (Lyotard 1984). Critical management studies (CMS) scholars have focused a great deal of their critique of management practice on this construct. In particular, they explore how the power relationships that underpin organisational life become utterly taken for granted. It is assumed that a performative intent expresses a unitary purpose and advances an unquestionable common good, even as it prioritises in practice particular sectional interests within organisations and society (Spicer et al. 2009). I suggest here that journal rankings have become precisely such a performative tool. Moreover, academics themselves have become complicit in this process – including many of those who identify with the CMS project, and who robustly critique performativity when it is manifest in non-academic settings.

I have noted, above, how publication in particular journals is now privileged above 'lower'-ranked journals, not to mention such outlets as books or book chapters, and has become a common criterion in assessing job candidates or applications for promotion. But the damage goes beyond this. Gabriel (2010) has noted how journal editors have become imprisoned by the performative language of strategy, tactics and positioning that are often critiqued in corporate settings. The aim becomes to improve the standing of 'their' journal in the face of competition from detested 'rivals' – rather than the advancement of a scholarly agenda for its own sake. As Giacalone (2009, p. 122) puts it, this is 'competitiveness in its saddest manifestation'. Critically oriented journals, regardless of mission statements, are also caught up in this game.

One means of pursuing higher standing is to emulate the practices of those journals that have already secured top-dog status, which generally means those based in the United States. Since rejection rates of 90 per cent or more are common in such journals, this becomes a target for others as well. (It must be only a matter of time until a journal can proudly boast a rejection rate of 100 per cent: its standards are so high that nothing by anybody is considered good enough to grace its pages.) This demands an increasingly critical tone towards contributors. Gabriel (2010) has highlighted a trend which many of us have experienced – a deterioration in the tone of reviewer and editor comments, towards sharper, sometimes personal criticism, and an increasingly pedantic tone that is often demoralising to the recipient. The process of submitting one's work to many journals means we must traverse a formidable obstacle course, dodging the bullet of desk rejection, overcoming the hurdle of reviewer comments, crawling through a long process of revisions, before resubmission, only to face another barrage of wounding criticism. Those publications that emerge from this – bloodied, misshapen and usually far too long – have not always been improved by it.

While much of this is driven by the desire of editors to rise up the journal rankings, people rarely question the extent to which these rankings – so objective, numerical and precise in appearance – merely reproduce the inequalities and power differentials in our wider society. Yet Özbilgin (2009) tellingly observes that the panel of 11 reviewers who at that point determined the ABS journal rankings had only two female members, and none from any ethnic minority. It is scarcely representative of the academy let alone our wider society, yet this highly unrepresentative sample has acquired an enormous proxy influence over academic behaviour. However, I also want to suggest that this chase for rankings has created what I see as yet another problem in our academic landscape – the fetishising of theoretical innovation by many journals and editors, and the consequent neglect of other equally valuable goals for academic inquiry.

10.3 THE FETISH OF THEORY DEVELOPMENT

Theory development is explicitly cited by many top-ranked journals as one of their key priorities. This encourages journals building their reputations to do likewise. Increasingly, papers are refused publication – however insightful their content – on the grounds that they 'don't create new theory'. The performative effect is clear: scholars seeking to advance their careers embrace the journal's imperative to engage in theory development, often at the expense of other goals, such as replication (Madden et al. 1995). Here, I want to consider the negative effects that this produces.

Journals rarely offer a rationale for the priority they place on theory development. They do not, for example, insist that all papers must be interesting, well written or relevant for practice or offer a rich description of an important phenomenon. It seems to me that this trend is largely driven by a desire to emulate the practices of elite US journals, in the forlorn hope that some of their reputational shine will rub off on the copycat journal. But the effects of all this are far from benign. A study of papers in the *Academy of Management Journal* over five decades highlighted a growing emphasis on theory development, leading to construct proliferation, even when such constructs differ little from what is already there (Colquitt and Zapata-Phelan 2007). This hinders the accumulation of empirical information about issues for which no theory yet exists, however pressing a problem may be in the real world of management practice (Hambrick 2007; Davis 2010; Edwards 2010). Moreover, Kacmar and Whitfield (2000) found that only 9 per cent of the theoretical models in articles published in the *Academy of Management Review* are ever tested. This suggests that theory development has become an end in itself (McKinley 2010). Given the productivity norms that now prevail in higher education, theories, or refinements of theories, seem to breed like rabbits, but whether they are a blessing or a curse remains largely unknown. They are produced primarily as a means of career enhancement. Hence, most are instantly sidelined, even by their own authors, since the only goal that matters – publication – has already been achieved. No wonder that 'Most of what we publish isn't even cited by other academics' (McGrath

2007, p. 1372), let alone noticed in the wider world. This is a situation that is simultaneously underwhelming and pernicious. It is underwhelming because theories that hardly anyone notices are of little real benefit, and pernicious because it squeezes out other perhaps more worthwhile publication goals that we could be pursuing.

An additional problem is that, as Sutton and Staw (1995) observed, there is no real consensus on what theory is. While Weick (1995, p. 386) asserts that 'Theory belongs to the family of words that includes *guess, speculation, supposition, conjecture, propositions, hypothesis, conception, explanation, model*' (italics in original), the elasticity of these terms suggests that it is not always clear when a contribution offers new theory, tinkers with well-established theory, attaches new descriptive terms to already existing theory, or passes on the opportunity to use an already established theory that might illuminate the issue in more depth. Genuinely new theories are rare. Those with wide-ranging explanatory power are rarer still. Knowing this, but frogmarched in the direction of 'theory development', scholars can only enter into higher states of specialisation. Their work becomes more mechanised and industrialised, whether they intend this or not. They find themselves engaged in alienating displays of metatheorising, about issues of less and less importance. This requires ever more elaborate ways to state the blindingly obvious – but in prose so tortured by the desire for theoretical differentiation that it is accessible to only a tiny band of specialists. In consequence, a plague of bad writing has been unleashed on the academy (Grey and Sinclair 2006), one that threatens to rot all our syntactic structures.

This may also help to explain why so few papers in major management journals address really big issues in either management or the wider world, such as race, ethics or exploitative working conditions (Dunne et al. 2008). Insights that rival those of Darwin or Einstein are difficult to obtain within the timescales of a Research Assessment Exercise. If one's main or only goal is 'to develop theory', the only solution is a retreat to marginal topics where a minor insight can be more easily camouflaged as a major theoretical innovation. Whether this is in the interests of academics, not to mention the world of organisations that we study, is a different matter entirely. The question is therefore raised: what should be done?

10.4 IMPLICATIONS FOR EMERGENT JOURNALS AND ACADEMIC FREEDOM

I have been critical, here, of journal ranking systems. My argument is that they are increasingly employed for performative ends. Whatever the formal intent, they are used to shoehorn the academic effort down channels more concerned with prestige and power than open-ended academic inquiry. Careers thrive or perish depending on one's skill at playing this particular game. As more journals chase reputation by emulating the practices of those that are already successful, the choice of acceptable methods, theories and topics is limited. In time, we may come to resemble emasculated peacocks ostentatiously displaying threadbare feathers. The overwhelming stress on theory development that has accompanied these developments has damaged our field. It is absent in other more established social science disciplines, has led to the neglect of important topics in favour of smaller issues that can yield at least the impression of that vital theoretical contribution, and rendered academic life and publishing a much more emotionally and intellectually fraught undertaking than it needs to be. Nor is it at all clear that those non-US journals chasing the cherished badge of 'world elite' status have much chance of success. As Grey (2010, p. 689) has suggested, 'The very act of a marginal player competing in a space in which it cannot win legitimizes the notion that that space is the only one that matters, that it is, indeed, the "centre".' There is thus little sign of even the most successful non-US journals, such as *Organization Studies* or the *Journal of Management Studies*, achieving the same level of recognition as say the *Academy of Management Review*.

I believe that there are alternatives, and that both emergent journals and authors should strive to follow a different path. Gabriel (2010, p. 758) offers a value framework to approach this task, asserting that journals can be 'places where ideas arrive, settle and meet each other, sometimes fight it out or, more often than not, decide to coexist in a civilised and polite way'. I want us to turn this ideal into reality. Specifically:

- Adler and Harzing (2009) have advocated a temporary moratorium on journal rankings until better methods for genuinely assessing quality are developed. I frankly doubt whether such a method can or should be developed. However, an end to rankings is a desirable goal. In the UK, this obviously means an end to the ABS rankings. I suggest that we should all lobby towards that end, individually and collectively.
- It is vital that journals seek to maintain a commitment to methodological and theoretical pluralism. Pfeffer (1993, p. 615) famously registered his objections to what he saw within the field of organisation studies as 'the proliferation of theoretical perspectives ranging from feminism to conversation analysis and radical humanism . . . in which fundamentally any theoretical perspective or methodological approach is as valid as any other'. His suggestion was that particular

methods and perspectives should become the gold standard, with others relegated to the margins. The implication that what constitutes an acceptable paradigm should be determined by some authoritative body or individual has been characterised as an attempt to 'close down debate outside narrow parameters' (Learmonth 2008, p. 284), parameters that in all probability would bear a functionalist and positivist imprint. This might be consistent with the performative processes I am criticising here. I believe it should be resisted. The study of organisations, management, leadership and human behaviour more widely is too multifaceted, ambiguous and contested to be understood by using only a few canonised methods and theories. The pluralism of our field is a strength not a weakness. It should be celebrated and encouraged.

- Theory development should be one of our goals – but not the only, or even always the most important, one. We should prize insight, imagination, creativity and interesting ideas above the kind of 'rigour' or metatheorising which often produces what Mintzberg (2005, p. 366) has characterised as 'banal results, significant only in the statistical sense of the word'. The drive for rigour is in danger of becoming rigor mortis. Adopting a different approach might not always deliver a paper in a highly ranked journal, but it is more likely to leave a trace in the world of ideas, and maybe even of practice.

- We should aspire to good writing and plain speaking in our work. There are few ideas in the social sciences that can't be expressed in language accessible to an educated layperson. Writing about our work intelligently does not mean writing about it obscurely. This might also mean that reading our journals becomes a pleasure rather than an ordeal, only to be attempted by those who have had all their aesthetic senses surgically removed.

- Dunne et al. (2008) raise the interesting question of the role of intellectuals working within a business school environment. As they suggest, this must mean more than career building, securing an affiliation with a 'top' business school, or even publishing extensively in 'top' journals. I have no objection to such publication. My point is simply that, when it is the main or only thing that is valued, academics become complicit in our own subordination to the performative norms imposed on us by others. As a result, critical intellectual responsibilities become neglected, including the obligation to ask interesting questions, resist conformity and speak truth to power.

- We should publish in established, emergent or semi-established journals, if we believe that they are the best outlet for our work, speak to a community we value and encourage iconoclastic, challenging, multifaceted, interesting work of real significance to what we do. As Rynes (2007, p. 747) put it: 'when we, as academics, plead powerlessness in choosing what we research . . . because of incentive and reward systems . . . we dehumanise our careers and our lives'. Meekly accepting performative constraints on where we publish has a similar belittling effect. Recognising this means that, as a minimum, we should not always make targeting a 'top' journal our only, or main, priority. It is time to reclaim academic freedom, and a greater degree of autonomy in what we research, how we do it and where we publish.

10.5 CONCLUSION

None of us can completely escape the performative pressures I have critiqued. I have, for example, focused on *Leadership* at times, as an example of an emerging journal that I think has huge potential. By the performative measure of the UK's RAE, it has done well. This suggests that publication in such journals can be a sound career move, rather than an abstract good that can only be satisfied by self-immolation. There is room for optimism, especially if it is fortified with determination. It is difficult for new journals to attract high-quality contributions, and an audience willing to engage with its agenda. I have sought to discuss the value of such outlets in the context of the pressures faced by all journals, and imagine what else we can all do to ensure that they are maintained. But even where virtue and self-interest do not coincide as well as they do in my exemplar, we need to carefully consider the medium- and long-term negative consequences involved in wholly embracing the norms imposed on us by pernicious journal rankings.

It is evident that these issues go beyond the fate of any one journal. Rather, they embody the tensions within the university sector throughout the world between open-ended, scholarly inquiry, on the one hand, and performative pressures which seek to corral our research and publication practices within tightly regulated spaces, on the other. In responding to these pressures it is worth considering what brought most of us into academic life in the first place, and reminding ourselves what the purpose of a university is. We do not write only to satisfy the demands of research assessment exercises, nor do we value only scholarship published in purportedly four-star journals. The poet John Masefield, in a 1946 address at the University of Sheffield, described the university as a place where those who hate ignorance may strive to know, where those who perceive truth may strive to make others see; where seekers and learners alike, banded together in the search for knowledge, will honour thought in all its finer ways, will welcome thinkers in distress or in exile, will uphold ever the dignity of thought and learning and will exact standards in these things.

These words are a rebuke to the performative practices now endemic in academic life. They did not appear in an ABS four-star journal, but they express an enduring set of values that should guide each one of us in our career choices, our publication practices and the ambitions that we hold for many good journals which fall outside the domain of North America.

NOTES

1. The *FT* requires registration to access this list. However, it can be found at http://library. mcmaster.ca/find/ft-research-rank-journals.
2. See http://www.the-abs.org.uk/?id=257.
3. See http://www.abdc.edu.au/3.43.0.0.1.0.htm.
4. Theoretically, this process could go on forever. Why not have a world, world elite set of journals within the world elite, but a further world, world, world elite within that (and so on indefinitely)?

REFERENCES

Adler, N. and A. Harzing (2009), 'When knowledge wins: transcending the sense and nonsense of academic rankings', *Academy of Management Learning and Education*, **8**, 72–95.

Association of Business Schools (ABS) (2010), *Academic Journal Quality Guide: Version 4*, C. Harvey, A. Kelly, H. Morris and M. Rowlinson (eds), London: Association of Business Schools.

Barney, J. (1991), 'Firm resources and sustained competitive advantage', *Journal of Management*, **17**, 99–120.

Barney, J. (2005), 'Where does inequality come from? The personal and intellectual roots of resource-based theory', in K. Smith and M. Hitt (eds), *Great Minds in Management: The Process of Theory Development*, Oxford: Oxford University Press, pp. 280–303.

Colquitt, J. and C. Zapata-Phelan (2007), 'Trends in theory building and theory testing: a five decade study of the *Academy of Management Journal*', *Academy of Management Journal*, **50**, 1281–303.

Davis, G. (2010), 'Do theories of organizations progress?', *Organizational Research Methods*, **13**, 690–709.

Dunne, S., S. Harney and M. Parker (2008), 'The responsibilities of management intellectuals', *Organization*, **15**, 271–82.

Edwards, J. (2010), 'Reconsidering theoretical progress in organizational and management research', *Organizational Research Methods*, **13**, 615–19.

Gabriel, Y. (2010), '*Organization Studies*: a space for ideas, identities and agonies', *Organization Studies*, **31**, 757–75.

Gephart, R. (2004), 'From the editors: qualitative research and the *Academy of Management Journal*', *Academy of Management Journal*, **47**, 454–62.

Giacalone, R. (2009), 'Academic rankings in research institutions: a case of skewed mind-sets and professional amnesia', *Academy of Management Learning and Education*, **8**, 122–6.

Glynn, M. and R. Raffaelli (2010), 'Uncovering mechanisms of theory development in an academic field: lessons from leadership research', *Academy of Management Annals*, **4**, 359–401.

Grey, C. (2010), 'Organizing studies: publications, politics and polemic', *Organization Studies*, **31**, 677–94.

Grey, C. and A. Sinclair (2006), 'Writing differently', *Organization*, **13**, 443–53.

Hambrick, D. (2007), 'The field of management's devotion to theory: too much of a good thing?', *Academy of Management Journal*, **50**, 1346–52.

Kacmar, K. and J. Whitfield (2000), 'An additional rating method for journal articles in the field of management', *Organizational Research Methods*, **3**, 392–406.

Lawrence, P. (2008), 'Lost in publication: how measurement harms science', *Ethics in Science and Environmental Politics*, published online 31 January, 1–3.

Learmonth, M. (2008), 'Evidence-based management: a backlash against pluralism in organizational studies', *Organization*, **15**, 283–91.

Lyotard, J. (1984), *The Postmodern Condition: A Report on Knowledge*, Minneapolis: University of Minnesota Press.

Madden, C., R. Easley and M. Dunn (1995), 'How journal editors view replication research', *Journal of Advertising*, **24**, 77–87.

McGrath, R. (2007), 'No longer a stepchild: how the management field can come into its own', *Academy of Management Journal*, **50**, 1365–78.

McKinley, W. (2010), 'Organizational theory development: displacement of ends?', *Organization Studies*, **31**, 47–68.

Mingers, J., K. Watson and P. Scaparra (2009), 'Estimating business and management journal quality from the 2008 Research Assessment Exercise in the UK', Working Paper No. 25, Kent Business School Working Papers Series.

Mintzberg, H. (2005), 'Theory about the development of theory', in K. Smith and M. Hitt (eds), *Great Minds in Management: The Process of Theory Development*, Oxford: Oxford University Press, pp. 355–72.

Nkomo, S. (2009), 'The seductive power of academic journal rankings: challenges of searching for the otherwise', *Academy of Management Learning and Education*, **8**, 106–12.

Özbilgin, M. (2009), 'From journal rankings to making sense of the world', *Academy of Management Learning and Education*, **8**, 113–21.

Pfeffer, J. (1993), 'Barriers to the advance of organizational science: paradigm development as a dependent variable', *Academy of Management Review*, **18**, 599–620.

Rynes, S. (2007), '*Academy of Management Journal* editors' forum on research with relevance to practice. Editor's foreword. Carrying Sumantra Ghoshal's torch: creating more positive, relevant, and ecologically valid research', *Academy of Management Journal*, **50**, 745–7.

Segalla, M. (2008), 'Editorial: publishing in the right place or publishing the right thing', *European Journal of International Management*, **2**, 122–7.

Singh, G., K. Haddad and C. Chow (2007), 'Are articles in "top" management journals necessarily of higher quality?', *Journal of Management Inquiry*, **16**, 319–31.

Smith, K. and M. Hitt (eds) (2005), *Great Minds in Management: The Process of Theory Development*, Oxford: Oxford University Press.

Spicer, A., M. Alvesson and D. Karreman (2009), 'Critical performativity: the unfinished business of critical management studies', *Human Relations*, **62**, 537–60.

Starkey, K. and N. Tiratsoo (2007), *The Business School and the Bottom Line*, Cambridge: Cambridge University Press.

Sutton, R. and B. Staw (1995), 'What theory is not', *Administrative Science Quarterly*, **40**, 371–84.

Weick, K. (1995), 'What theory is *not*, theorizing *is*', *Administrative Science Quarterly*, **40**, 385–90.

PART IV

How to proceed from here? Illustration with two SFM position papers

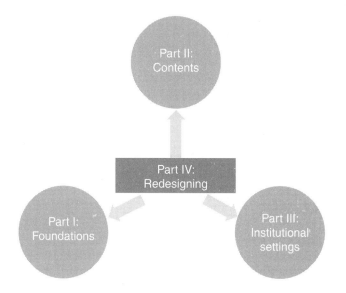

How to proceed from here? How do we contribute to the redesign of our field, the way our community operates, the governance and evaluation processes, and the institutional setting?

We firmly believe that collective strategies are needed to unlock the lock-in situation described in the previous parts of the book. This is what SFM is about.

Founded in 2001, the Société Française de Management (SFM) (the French Academy of Management) gathers professors and researchers in management to contribute proactively to shaping the institutional setting of their academic field. The goal is to act as a creative and autonomous body in the area of management research and education in order to participate in its governance. Ad hoc SFM working parties are dedicated to key topics, such as discussing requirements for PhDs in management, evaluating publications or setting quality requirements for academic contributions. The working parties produce green papers that summarise a diagnosis and present recommendations. Initial drafts are discussed within the SFM membership and then made public after revision and validation. As a result of this process, SFM generates 'soft law' and thus contributes to shape the academic field of management.

This final part, Part IV, borrows from the work conducted at SFM to offer preliminary contributions illustrating how debates among European management academics could help. Two examples of SFM position papers, or green papers, are presented here as a way of giving ideas for collective action. More specifically, these two examples aim at suggesting that a European initiative, similar to SFM but designed to fit the specificities of the diversity of the European context, is needed.

11. What about books in the evaluation process?

Julienne Brabet and Thomas Durand[1]

This SFM green paper looks at the role of books and monographs, and their evaluation in scientific production in the field of management. Can a published book by a researcher in management be considered to be a scholarly production or even a scientific publication? If yes, under what conditions, to what extent and how?

In other fields, for example history or sociology, such a question may seem surprising. Nonetheless, it is nowadays being asked seriously in management. Some institutions and some evaluating authorities assess the production of their faculty solely based on articles published in preselected lists of journals. Such assessment processes exclude, either explicitly or implicitly, the publication of books.

Yet the forms of scholarly production can vary. Indeed, research findings span a wide range (highlighting a new practice, presenting a new theory, articulating a case study around a new issue, and so on) and may require different means of publication (for example article, thesis or book). Self-contained books can themselves take various forms: research monographs, collations of chapters gathered around a common theme, essays, textbooks, compilations of case studies, and so on.

The issue of taking into account the publication of books in evaluating the scientific production of a management researcher is intrinsically tied to the wider issue of evaluating publications and teaching material.

It is, however, difficult to look at evaluating means without considering the economic and cultural aspects of the production, publishing and circulation of scientific books. The evaluation is not merely about distinguishing *ex post* the best productions in order to select, promote and reward the best academics and their institutions; it is not merely a 'beauty pageant', whether one is pursuing rankings or subsidies. It is also about a way of indirectly encouraging, supporting and highlighting the production of high-quality scientific works. Books, like any other product of management research, are also public goods able to contribute to the structuring, organising and functioning of economies and societies.

In other words, raising the question of the legitimacy of management books as scientific publications in their own right, we also inquire into the wider issues of means of evaluation and their impact – for certain productions are discouraged as such, while others are wholly encouraged.

This green paper is structured as follows: nine observations are made, on the basis of which nine recommendations are proposed.

11.1   OBSERVATION 1: EVALUATION HELPS STRUCTURE THE PRODUCTION OF RESEARCH

Evaluation's role is not solely to measure the quality and quantity of scientific production. It is a management device which has concrete and symbolic effects, and as such it contributes to the orientation of research and publication. A part of management sciences has concentrated on the means of evaluating, and their design, as well as on the implied or explicit representations guiding, and thus legitimising or structuring, evaluation processes. Yet, paradoxically, the same management sciences have hardly found a way to cast an eye over the evaluating process of their own research, and particularly that of books.

Books are de facto evaluated by publishers, reviewers and readers. Refusing them an evaluation by the academic community and ignoring them in the management of people and institutions simply imply that they are considered useless – and so would be the time spent in producing them. Acknowledging the role of high-quality books, on the other hand, would require in-depth reflection on the evaluative devices which may facilitate their production, circulation and use.

11.2   OBSERVATION 2: THE PUBLISHING OF BOOKS BY MANAGEMENT RESEARCHERS IS BEING DISCOURAGED

The pressure of rankings has led to a publication race aimed at starred journals. Books no longer have any value in the eyes of most evaluating bodies dealing with management research publications.

Evaluation of scholars, teams, units and institutions is now primarily concerned with journals and articles. In France, the academic research evaluation body, AERES, although they deny it, give more weight to the evaluation of articles, as they are a lot more explicit about evaluating articles than they are about evaluating other forms of academic contributions. Evaluation processes in private or semi-private business schools offer significant financial rewards for authors of articles published in starred journals (and none for authors of books). Worse yet, books are hardly taken into account, if at all. Indeed, articles rank the school higher.[2] Similarly, the French research funding agency, the ANR, ranks the production of books indiscriminately in its all-encompassing 'miscellaneous' category, while it gives articles and communications special mentions. This move towards an article-centred view is most likely due to a mimicking of hard sciences, as well as to the more homogeneous nature of traditional evaluation of articles by journals' reviewing committees, and to the simplification it brings to the evaluation process that is now externalised, for most of the evaluating work is then handed over to journals and their reviewers.[3]

All in all, the evaluation processes in management sciences try to imitate those of the fields of hard sciences and economics. The grounds for importing such processes are not always legitimate, and lack an in-depth consideration of the very specific nature of books in social sciences.

11.3   OBSERVATION 3: THERE IS A NEED FOR MANAGEMENT BOOKS

Encouraging researchers to write research articles has a significant impact on their works. Their productions tend to be fragmented and isolated, as research results are difficult to contextualise within the bounds of the article format. The knowledge produced is therefore hyperspecialised and hardly accessible outside a very limited community of peers.

For certain endeavours, only the longer format of a book allows the development of one's thought and the spelling out of wider conceptions. In addition, when it is a collaborative work, a book gives room for debates between specialists but also with the practitioners who were observed. Whether one is pondering over or transforming paradigms and management models and/or suggesting directions or actionable methods, a book is a very useful means of communication. Indeed, in social sciences, books have always played an important part in publications, and their role was essential in the spreading of French and European thought.

It is also worth noting that the founding fathers of management have, on the whole, circulated ideas through books. What impact would Frederick Taylor, Henri Fayol, Peter Drucker, Igor Ansoff, Karl Weick, Michel Crozier, Henry Mintzberg or Michael Porter have had without the considerable leverage that the circulation of their works through books gave them? Let us point out with Déry (2007) that in over 20 years of publication of the *Strategic Management Journal* (*SMJ*) 18 of the 20 most quoted references were books.

One should not deny the importance of concise and narrow articles, but it is necessary to acknowledge the role of books in the production and circulation of knowledge in management. The community of scholars paradoxically generally agrees on the relevance and importance of books. One can only, however, note that, through ineffective encouraging and evaluating mechanisms, the publishing industry has trouble keeping up.

11.4   OBSERVATION 4: THE BUSINESS MODEL OF PUBLISHING IN SOCIAL SCIENCES IS IN TROUBLE

As highlighted by the title of Sophie Barluet's noteworthy work 'Publishing social sciences: the heart is threatened' (2004), the sector is in trouble. This is the case in France, despite the strength of a model putting together private publishers and public funding from university presses which enabled true encouragement of publishing high-quality books as well as support towards production and circulation. This model was made unstable by the change in reading practices, particularly those of students who nowadays tend to focus on reading utilitarian handbooks, when they do not stop at summaries found on Google; but the change in teachers' reading requirements is also notable. They demand less reading and recommend fewer essential books. Authors too have changed their habits, since evaluating mechanisms have turned them away from writing books. Publishers on the other hand cannot escape economic factors that impose minimum volumes of sales for break-even. In addition the model was shaken by the development and increase in use of new technologies.

Often, such changes are also opportunities for actors in search of new models in publishing. Digitisation opens new spaces for publishers and enables them to coordinate books (particularly handbooks) with journals. This ties in with the proposal for an internet portal for journals (see the second SFM green paper, 'Journals and journal rankings').

As for management, most of the books published nowadays more and more resemble either recipe books, written by self-proclaimed gurus, or the memoirs of a war veteran. Neither of these try to contribute scientifically to the field but rather aim at a wider audience of managers and stakeholders or even readers from the general public looking for success recipes that are easy to put into practice rather than in-depth analyses of the methods, difficulties, context and/or long-term effects of management. There are fortunate exceptions, with some authoritative books written by scholars – Henry Mintzberg being one of them – which present practices and managerial innovations as well as critical analyses and landmarks for action with new models and new methods. In addition, even if handbooks can still be published, there is a lack of authors. Who is ready to commit the time needed to draft a book manuscript when this is no longer what pays off in an academic career? All in all, research books now struggle to find publishers unless the authors (or their universities) are ready to pay for it.

11.5   OBSERVATION 5: THERE ARE DIFFERENT KINDS OF MANAGEMENT BOOKS, AND THEIR QUALITY VARIES

The expression 'management book' is used to refer to many different kinds of works of varying quality, from accessible managerial literature to a research monograph minutely dissecting a case study and building a new theory.

Beyond handbooks, let us call upon Sophie Barluet's typology. She identified three other types of books (2004, p. 19): '"research readings" which offer without mediation … a hard-to-read text to those who already know'; '"pretext-books" dealing with fashionable issues, already demonstrated theses and already accomplished pieces of research around well-known issues'; and, finally, '"reason-books", whose necessity is rooted in a novel reflection, in a new questioning of the world, in a crossing of perspectives. … These books are essential. … They are the only ones to really have the power to bridge the gap between universities and societies. … Yet these books are the least profitable [for publishers].'

When transposed to the field of management sciences, this typology gives a means of distinguishing four types of works:

1.   Textbooks or manuals are very helpful to teaching. Listings of case studies may also be included in this first category. However, within handbooks, it is necessary to distinguish those which offer mere compilations without context or critical analyses from those which establish links and question the relevance of whatever practices, methods, theories or research is presented. One can see that the latter, more than the former, may claim to partake in the scientific production of our field.
2.   As for the 'research readings', they are very similar to published theses and mainly written for specialists. One might think these are the main competition to academic journals; however, they can be a logical and

    sometimes necessary addition. This category should also include specialised research works which compile chapter contributions around a narrow theme of investigation and allow the cross-discussion of methodological or theoretical approaches.

3. 'Reason-books' examine and compare in a more general manner the stakes, management processes, methods and effects, and offer alternatives. The small numbers and limited circulation of reason-books in management sciences offer one explanation for the unfortunate lack of management professors in public debate – whether to help understand the complex life of organisations or to analyse the role of private enterprise in the main issues faced by society.

4. 'Pretext-books' are doing well in management sciences. They offer simple solutions to complex problems. They do not need more attention from the academic community, other than merciless critical analyses.

The arguments of the status quo defenders are well known. They are quite happy with just articles and the evolution towards a quantitative evaluation, counting articles in higher- or lower-starred journals and using quotation indexes. They tend to consider textbooks as teaching media rather than knowledge productions; they believe 'research readings' are mostly made redundant by journals and coordinating works by special issues of journals (with the added advantage of the double-blind evaluation by reading committees). They hold 'reason-books' to be essays too difficult to evaluate and therefore to falsify, because of their blurry methodological base. Finally, they take 'pretext-books' to be unscientific, when they are not said to be cheap managerial novels.

One can see this is not all wrong, but it is just as clear that each of these arguments can be overturned. Why would a teachers' textbook be less important than a researcher's article? Why should the transmission of knowledge come second to its production and therefore be ignored in the evaluation of a researcher-teacher? Why would one not acknowledge the complementarity of research books and journals? How can one deny that an ambitious and visionary essay can open new perspectives? Why be stubbornly indiscriminate and disregard the production of any management book because some 'pretext-books' are conceptually poor – and indeed many are?

This discussion leads to one simple observation: there is more than one category of 'management books'. If one agrees with observation 3, according to which there is a need for the production and publication of management books, then there is a need for the evaluation of books.

11.6 OBSERVATION 6: THERE ARE MANY OPTIONS FOR THE EVALUATING PROCESS

Evaluating books may serve several aims: to help readers find their way in the abundance of productions; to choose among manuscripts to publish and support; to assist the production of manuscripts; to help with the recruiting and promoting of researchers; to guide institutions in their defining priorities and choosing whether or not to support some of the projects presented to them; and so on.

Categories of evaluation processes can thus be distinguished in the following way:

- Academic and/or commercial. Numerous publishers in management sciences ask of potential writers that they define the original contributions of their book-to-be and how it may benefit a reader. They nonetheless also expect that writers should undertake a market and competition analysis for their book. However formalised the procedure, this double expectation is present. In addition, even when the evaluation is academic, it can have, through its results, a significant impact on the author's access to funding.
- *Ex ante*, *ex post* and/or ongoing. Evaluating a book can happen when it is just a project, when it is a first draft to be completed or improved or when it is already published. The full writing of a book is such a high commitment and investment that it would seem difficult to decide on its publication based on the *ex post* evaluation of a finished manuscript. Yet certain university-related publishers do so. More often, a contract between the author and the publisher is signed outlining a detailed project, followed by a more or less active collaboration. Critical analyses and best book awards, on the other hand, pertain to a finished work.
- Ranking, selective and/or formative. Publishers, like reviewers, not only select manuscripts to be published, but also have the crucial role of supporting their authors. This is formative evaluation. More generally, research supervisors, research teams, academic societies and communities of peers – for example, during conferences, symposia and seminars – also contribute to the formative evaluation of authors by proofreading, arguing, disagreeing, suggesting clarifications, asking for elaboration, and so on. The many thanks and acknowledgements books present show they are often the work of a series of cooperations even though their authors alone take responsibility for them. As a result, limiting the evaluating process to its selective and ranking role would be a mistake that no company

would make in HR management today: the selective, just like the ranking, evaluation takes place only at the (important) point of attributing material or symbolic credit.

- Qualitative and/or quantitative. Just as some count the number of articles published in starred reviews, or calculate quotation indexes, a quantitative evaluation could, for example, take into account the number of books published within collections, themselves starred because of their evaluating and selecting processes. Such ways would make sense only with a reliable evaluation production chain: with clear policies from book series, and the scientific and academic criteria of publishers taken into account in an upfront way, as well as diversified, documented and debated accreditation (number of stars) of book series.[4] The issue of quotation indexes could be reasonably dealt with, since books are already taken into account – although not always very well, especially for books in other languages than English. It is clear that such a quantitative approach saves individuals and institutions from an in-depth reading of the books submitted to them. However, it is just as clear that numbers make little sense when dealing with books, and a qualitative evaluation remains highly preferable (by legitimate evaluators, chosen as such, on the basis of evaluating protocols which would be co-produced, debated, published and appropriate).

- Formalised and/or implicit. The increasing clarification of evaluating procedures and criteria is probably for the best, even though some elements will necessarily remain implied. However, should one intend to protect the diversity of the production of high-quality books, it would be detrimental to implement standardised evaluating processes and criteria, to be used by all evaluating bodies. There can be many criteria for qualitative appreciation, and their relevance depends on the aims one pursues: originality, precision, theoretical input, social or managerial usefulness, a practical or critical stance, and so on.

- Voluntary or imposed, one-off or generalised. Whilst a publisher chooses manuscripts for publication and some books are reviewed or receive awards, most books do not undergo an independent and communicable evaluation. Yet, for books to be taken into account in the evaluation of one's scientific production, many authors may want such a procedure to be in place. Similarly, institutions may wish their teaching and research staff's books to be evaluated, so as to give credit in their honours list, to improve their position in rankings which would take greater account of books, and/or to gain a certification.

- Undertaken by evaluators in various configurations. The process of evaluating books may bring together peers either on one occasion or as part of ongoing committees. These could establish procedures on how to assess book quality, but might also run the risk of developing a clan culture. In addition, evaluators could come solely from the academic community (in the field or, more widely, nationally or internationally) or they could include interested parties such as practitioners, analysts, union representatives, NGOs, political powers, librarians, bookstore owners, specialised journalists and so on.

These many dimensions of evaluation – even when narrowed to the specifics linked to the evaluation of books – show the need for more tangible proposals if one wants to move forward on this issue, whilst leaving things open and flexible.

11.7   OBSERVATION 7: VARIOUS OPTIONS FOR THE EVALUATION OF BOOKS ARE POSSIBLE, BUT ALL RELY ON COMPLEX AND EXPENSIVE PROCESSES

Let us go through the usual questions: What? When? How? Who?

The 'what' deals with management books (and chapters). This covers three of the four types of books discussed in observation 5 (excluding pretext-books).

The 'when' looks at relevant times for evaluation: *ex ante* (when it is still at the stage of a project), while the manuscript is being written, upon finishing the last draft, and finally *ex post* (after publication). It is generally agreed that *ex ante* evaluation is mostly the publishers' work, or that of institutions funding the research and/or the book. At the other end of the spectrum, evaluation *ex post* usually implies different means.

The 'how' links to possible models for such evaluations. Several models may guide the evaluation of books (or books-to-be):

- The thesis model, which brings together a jury for the evaluation of either a book or a group of chapters. The composition and functioning of such a jury rely on shared rules, such as inviting at least one colleague from a foreign university.
- The literary award model, which puts in competition, on a yearly basis, books published or to be published, independently from the

publisher. The composition of the jury varies depending on the style of the works and can be renewed, for example every year. The jury gives an award to one or more books, which thus gain a label and/or a financial reward.

- The model of journals, which have reading committees and call on reviewers from the scientific community. This model is nowadays informally adopted by some publishers, who ask peers for their opinion before signing an author. Such ways could be systematised and broadened to link publishers, academics and other stakeholders in order to maintain the labelling of books and offer financial support, where relevant, at the beginning of the writing process, on the basis of a project perceived as promising.
- The bibliometric model, which relies on a rigorous construction of indices, made possible by databases, but which is difficult to put into practice for books published in a language other than English. This raises once again, in the non-English-speaking countries, the issue of creating databases for texts published in the languages of those countries.
- The certification model, which consists in awarding stars to a book series, similarly to journal rankings. The stars then distinguish authors or the manuscript selection process just as much as the quality of the books already published in the book series.
- The model in which the selection of a book project relies on the quality and credibility of the team of authors undertaking it.

The 'who' deals with the individuals and bodies who need to be brought into such evaluating processes. Members of institutions requesting, identifying, facilitating and valuing research are bound to take part in the evaluating process for books or chapters. Yet plurality is necessary for the equity and the acceptability of evaluation results.

Evaluation requires competent, legitimate and involved evaluators, as well as time for reading and interaction. This work must be organised and acknowledged. It cannot remain just voluntary and invisible because of confidentiality. The evaluation process is costly, and this cost is greatly underestimated, yet it plays a part in the process of scientific production. It requires an investment, agreed by the individuals (and their institutions), in order to develop and disseminate knowledge. These efforts should be taken into account in the processes of evaluation of those undertaking them, though this is rarely the case today.

Informal networks of academics already exist to perform such evaluation tasks. It would be necessary to develop these networks further, especially with European scope, making them public without letting a small number of players take over the control of evaluation and whilst also making sure to bring independent people in.

11.8 OBSERVATION 8: THE WRITING OF A BOOK IS MORE NATURAL IN ONE'S OWN LANGUAGE, BUT THE BROAD DISTRIBUTION OF IDEAS REQUIRES ENGLISH, AND THEREFORE TRANSLATION IS NEEDED

The writing of a book is a complex, heavy and particularly delicate task, which is better done in one's own language. However, the dissemination and circulation of knowledge, when aiming at a wide audience, require English, which has become the lingua franca of management sciences.

This is a difficulty to be faced by article writers in journals, but it is all the more severe for books. For non-native English authors, it is quite reasonable to write a self-contained 15- to 20-page-long article in English; it is significantly more difficult for a 150- to 300-page piece.

There is a structural tension between fine writing and the wide circulation of books. Translation into English for books published in other languages is often the best compromise to deal with this problem, despite the many difficulties which come with translation. Let us point out that this can also suggest translations into other languages such as Spanish, Chinese, Portuguese or Russian.

It could therefore be interesting to put in place the means of distinguishing the best management books published in various languages, suggesting awards to fund, or at least encourage, the translations of the books that received the awards.

11.9 OBSERVATION 9: COORDINATED ACTION IS NEEDED TO PROMOTE THE EVALUATION OF MANAGEMENT BOOKS

The 'publish or perish' motto, the 'any article ASAP', and the rankings race led to an overwhelming dominance of quantitative forms of evaluation, frequent and systematised, whether they look at individual writers or institutions as a whole. This overlooked longer-term and qualitative evaluation. At the same time, a literature of 'pretext-books' of very little scientific value, if any, developed and acted as a foil to weaken the status of books as legitimate academic publications.

Interestingly enough, short-term attitudes were pointed out as one of the main triggers of the recent financial crisis, owing to too frequent and too superficial evaluation of the performance of companies by financial analysts. It would be paradoxical for us to extend this bias to our own sector of management research, where long-term investment is also needed.

It is left to us to reflect on and promote in-depth analyses of management books, for these are one of the types of academic production in our field.

This leads to nine recommendations.

11.10   RECOMMENDATION 1: PROMOTE THE PRODUCTION, DISTRIBUTION AND READING OF QUALITY BOOKS IN MANAGEMENT SCIENCES

Encourage all of the actors and research regulating institutions in management sciences to reinforce their contributions, be they financial or towards the production, distribution and recognition of high-quality books.

Stimulate students to read books; stimulate executive education teachers to highlight references in course outlines and include books in the teaching material.

Encourage national scientific associations, journals and specialised professional organisations – perhaps in association with the media – to set up awards for the best book in various categories (best research work, best teaching handbook, best essay), together with making quality labels for editors or book series as well known as possible.

Encourage journals to publish critical and in-depth accounts of book readings in order to develop scientific critique.

11.11   RECOMMENDATION 2: ENCOURAGE RESEARCHERS TO PUBLISH BOOKS THAT ANALYSE, DISCUSS, ENLIGHTEN AND IMPROVE MANAGEMENT PRACTICES IN CORPORATIONS

These books may be aimed at researchers, teachers and students, but also practitioners, decision makers and, more generally, all stakeholders interested in business and the life of corporations.

11.12 RECOMMENDATION 3: MAKE SURE THAT BOOKS ARE INCLUDED IN THE EVALUATION OF RESEARCHERS AND INSTITUTIONS

Ask institutions and evaluating authorities to explicitly include a 'book' category as a legitimate publication and acknowledged as such in the production of a researcher-teacher. In addition, ask them to agree on comparative bases between books and articles, whilst obviously taking into account the differences in the number of stars attached to a book as against an article.

Ask institutions and evaluating authorities to make public the principles and systems which they are using. This will allow comparisons to be made, as well as helping to identify and promote best practices on the matter.

11.13 RECOMMENDATION 4: BRING TOGETHER THE EUROPEAN PROTAGONISTS IN THE FIELD TO CREATE A MOVEMENT OF SUPPORT FOR THIS PRO-BOOK AND BOOK EVALUATION POLICY

Encourage European scientific associations (EURAM, EGOS and so on), journals, EIASM and EFMD, including in association with the media, to set up awards for the best book in various categories, taking into account the diversity of European languages. This should, in turn, promote the translation and distribution of rewarded books (best research book, best teaching handbook, best essay). Evaluate the putting in place of quality labels for book series, or even publishers, and make those public.

More globally, encourage the ranking of all books undergoing evaluation along similar lines to the journal ladder (A*, A, B, C, NC) in order to facilitate comparative systems, as mentioned earlier. Labels thus awarded to a book could then be publicised by the publisher.

11.14 RECOMMENDATION 5: FACILITATE THE SETTING UP OF A VARIETY OF EVALUATION NETWORKS

Accept that some of these networks choose to charge for their evaluation services, whether publishers, authors or institutions. The authors will then be able voluntarily to submit their pieces for evaluation; publishers will see their collections labelled.

Encourage scientific associations to play a major part in these networks, be it only by setting up best book awards alongside magazines, professional associations and so on.

Start retroactive experiments looking at books published in the field over the past five or ten years and reward the best research book, the best book aimed at practitioners and the best textbook.

Encourage different ways of setting up these networks (specialised fields, balance of practitioners and scholars, types of institutions they come from, nationalities and geographies, and so on) in order to match the objectives and different styles of books (various labels may be created for handbooks, essays, research books and so on). This would also guarantee the equity and accountability of the whole scheme. A diversity of apparatuses, in which all clearly state their respective criteria and means of evaluation, is greatly preferable to a unique, central and all-powerful committee.

11.15   RECOMMENDATION 6: ENCOURAGE THE CONSTRUCTION OF EVALUATING MEANS WHICH WOULD BE SHARED, EXPLICIT, CRITICISED AND MADE PUBLIC

Encourage institutions, evaluating authorities and evaluators to think about evaluating strategies they suggest using for books, discuss them, make them public and look at them critically regularly (such as every three years).

Promote clarification and transparency of the criteria they use for each category of book (handbook, case studies, research and so on) and book series.

11.16   RECOMMENDATION 7: AS MUCH AS POSSIBLE, COMBINE AND EVEN INTEGRATE THE SELECTION PROCESSES FOR RESEARCH PROJECTS, BOOK PROJECT EVALUATION, FUNDING MECHANISMS AND THE VALORISATION PROCESS, AS WELL AS *EX POST* EVALUATION OF PUBLISHED BOOKS

Make sure that the evaluation bodies and the research funding mechanisms (agencies, foundations, institutions and so on) encourage later publication not only of an article, but also, whenever appropriate, of a book. Whilst selecting among research projects, value projects which plan to publish results in the form of a book.

Encourage funding bodies to introduce financial help for writing, publishing and translating books as part of their scheme.

11.17   RECOMMENDATION 8: PROMOTE THE CREATION OF DATABASES FOR BOOKS IN MANAGEMENT PUBLISHED IN LANGUAGES OTHER THAN ENGLISH, AND USE OF DIGITISATION

Form a partnership with a new portal for journals (see the next green paper, 'Journals and journal rankings') so as to include a section listing books. This will facilitate the distribution and evaluation of books as well. It will also improve the relevance of quotation indices for such books.

11.18   RECOMMENDATION 9: ENCOURAGE EVALUATING AUTHORITIES TO TAKE INTO ACCOUNT THE WORK ACCOMPLISHED BY EVALUATORS AS PLAYING A PART IN THEIR SCIENTIFIC WORK

Encourage teacher-researchers to claim in their bibliographies the contributions they may have made to evaluation: thesis jury, evaluation of books or chapters (beyond the evaluation of articles, journals and number of journals evaluated). Request from evaluating authorities that they add an 'evaluation work' category and a 'books evaluation' sub-category.

NOTES

1. This green paper, like any SFM green paper, comes as the result of group work. It was written by Julienne Barbet and Thomas Durand with help from members of the SFM. Special thanks must go to Olivier Basso, Pierre-Jean Benghozi, Jean-Claude Thoenig, Alain Charles Martinet and Gérard Koenig.
2. One may even see university faculty members play the tricky game of getting in touch with private business school deans when they hear that they have had a paper accepted in a starred journal. They offer to swap a few months' contract as visiting lecturers, on top of the positions they already have at their universities, with the opportunity for the private business schools to appear among the affiliations of the authors when the paper comes out.

3. One may question the now common practice of handing over the evaluation of the production of teaching staff to a small number (two or three per article) of anonymous, and therefore unknown, reviewers. Evaluation is thereby left to the publisher of a journal, albeit a prestigious one. This type of evaluation by one's peers has, without a doubt, contributed to the improving of management sciences, but needs to be questioned when it is the beginning and end of evaluation.
4. On this matter, see the next SFM position paper presented, 'Journals and journal rankings'. The recognition of some book series from specific publishers may create difficulties for them commercially. However, this can be overcome, as shown by guidebooks for the catering and hotel industries.

REFERENCES

Barluet, Sophie (2004), *Édition de sciences humaines et sociales: Le Cœur en danger*, Paris: Presses Universitaires de France.
Déry, Richard (2007), 'Le management', École des HEC, Montréal.

12. Journals and journal rankings

Pierre-Jean Benghozi[1]

12.1 EIGHT PROPOSALS OF THE SFM[2]

- Proposal 1: Avoid a one-size-fits-all ranking list by promoting diverse journal rankings that are adapted to the scientific policies of each institution.
- Proposal 2: Contact all research institutions in order to collate and make public all journal ranking lists currently in use in France, and contact European partner associations for similar lists.
- Proposal 3: Include systematically online journals in journal rankings rather than restrict these to printed journals.
- Proposal 4: Encourage all institutions involved in producing journal rankings to publish them systematically with a guide for assessors – and authors – presenting the institution's scientific policy regarding rankings: range of criteria for activity evaluation, rules applying to publications other than journals (books, journals in other disciplines, and so on), concrete assessment methods, and incentive policies.
- Proposal 5: Draw up a scoring card for each journal with the editors involved, making public their characteristics, editorial lines and general organisation such as: circulation and readership rates, scope of the field, types of articles accepted, acceptance rates, publication delays, assessment grids, relevance of published articles for practitioners, and degree of internationalisation.
- Proposal 6: Promote the professionalisation of reviewers and characterise the tasks involved, competencies required, methods of distribution of articles submitted for review, and response delays. This entails the need for institutional recognition of the work of reviewers (on the local level as well as the national and European one) and the improvement of the qualitative and quantitative evaluation of such work.
- Proposal 7: Beyond the question of ranking, the referencing of journals appears just as important. The creation of an internet portal listing all the management publications in French seems critical.

- Proposal 8: Draw up a list of best practices concerning the publication of research works in management and initiate a labelling process for publishers and their series or books on the basis of a voluntary adherence to these best practices.

12.2   SFM POSITION PAPER ON 'JOURNALS AND JOURNAL RANKINGS'

12.2.1   Context and Expectations

In the past few years, the growing focus on questions pertaining to the assessment of research has been accompanied by increased instrumentation of evaluation practices. In some fields, the latter translated into the rising use of bibliometrics, while in management science indexes and ranking lists were developed to classify journals, institutions and programmes. Some of these rankings are restricted to publications and therefore apply to journals only. They can be produced by specific institutions, for local use only, and offer incentives for publication in the higher-ranked journals. These rankings, which are made public, can then be used elsewhere, as was the case for instance for the ranking list produced by the economics and management section of the French Comité national de la recherche scientifique (CNRS) for its mixed units.[3] Other journal rankings are produced by more cross-sectoral evaluation authorities: in France, this is the case for instance for the rankings produced by Section 06 of the Conseil National des Universités[4] or AERES;[5] other rankings, like that of the *Financial Times*, are of a different nature. They were designed by journalists to consecrate a new podium – that of business schools[6] and their programmes. (These rankings can make use of journal rankings and citation indicators in order to take into account the 'impact of knowledge produced' by professors working for the institutions or programmes under evaluation.) The present position paper addresses the issue of journal rankings in the context of publication evaluation, and does not include institution or programme rankings.

The following diagnosis and proposals, developed within the scope of the SFM, are not intended to lead to 'an SFM ranking of journal rankings' that would compare with the works of evaluation institutions and authorities (which would be neither relevant nor legitimate), but they aim rather to contribute to the drawing up of recommendations and to the identification of 'best practices' enabling a better structuring and identification of the field of evaluation of journal publications. These proposals are addressed to the heads of institutions and journals, as well as to assessors and authors.

12.2.2 Point 1: A Diversity of Journal Rankings

Experience in evaluation shows that appraisal of the design and nature of journal ranking lists should also take into account the process of evaluation of individuals, teams and organisations. The evaluation of scientific productions must be 'contextualised' in order to include the strategy of an institution, a team and also a researcher.

From this perspective, it seems particularly important not to focus on one ranking only. Such a focus would lead to a disregard of the fact that there are many management journal rankings or indexes produced by other institutions (schools, universities) and evaluation authorities. These diverse rankings are generally not mentioned, nor a fortiori discussed and taken into account.

Along the same lines of thought, our interest in management science publications leads us to focus on management journal rankings, but it is also essential to examine how one can take into account publications in journals belonging to fields other than management (medicine and health, economics, anthropology, sociology and so on).

It is therefore essential to devise, accept and even promote diverse rankings in different institutions, ensuring they are adapted to their audiences and objectives, rather than have one single large ranking. This work necessarily requires an agreement between assessors and authors on objectives and ranking methods.

12.2.3 Point 2: The Necessary Weight of Judgement

As highlighted by the works of T. Kuhn, the problem and risk of normal science is that it favours the 'normalisation' and standardisation of research. This trend is fostered by the instrumentation – of all kinds – of evaluation, namely through journal rankings or the creation of citation rates. In such a case, there is a risk that legitimate reactions against the automation of evaluation (restricted to counting or mere bibliometrics) could entail the rejection of evaluation as a whole.

It is therefore important, when ranking management journals, to avoid all types of automatic or mechanical evaluation. The part played by judgement must imperatively remain. Several reasons can justify this: the wish to adopt and foster a new paradigm, the proactive scientific positioning of an institution, and so on. This part must even be increased in many cases with regard to current practices. Evaluation must consequently be carried out in an extremely professional way, and be granted the necessary time and competencies.

For this objective not to remain mere wishful thinking, it is particularly important to design rankings that prevent any kind of automation, by breaking down classifications for instance, or limiting opportunities of intercomparisons, and so on.

12.2.4   Point 3: The Structural Variety of Journals

When practising, researchers are constantly faced with a great diversity of journals, differing by discipline, readership and also their degree of scientific openness, whether they refer to a narrow and standardised paradigm (normal science), as do some renowned international journals, support particularly specialised expertise, or have a wider scope that can be cross-disciplinary for instance.

The inter-ranking of journals with varying ambitions and statuses is unrealistic and leads one to compare very different material. It would be preferable for the community of management science researchers to draw up a typology of journals based on their publication policies, the scope of their thematic field, their openness and their subject.

12.2.5   Point 4: Support for Publication along with Support for Evaluation

The success of journal rankings and their usefulness stem from the fact that they play an essential part in information and support for publication, namely for younger researchers. (Besides, they can help foreign researchers find their bearings among publications in French or any other national language.)

It appears essential to develop judgement and an information tool offering an evaluation and a critical analysis of journal practices.

Such a tool could help, for instance, take into account the evolutions a journal may undergo in time (improvement in quality or loss in influence, shrinking or widening of its disciplinary scope, thematic refocusing). In this context, such information must be submitted, and the share of judgement of the journals themselves increased.

12.2.6   Point 5: The Limits of Peer Evaluation

Behind the apparently simple principle of the peer review process (PRP) adopted by all academic journals, there are actually complex and varied practices. Some can even put into question the exclusive character of the PRP principle, as revealed by the following points. Firstly, concerning the grounds for and trust in the judgement of journals on article projects: in the name of what, and following what tradition, is the evaluation carried out, how do reviewers make decisions, and what kind of polarisation is progressively constructed? Secondly, concerning the illusory anonymity of some authors: certain fields of specialisation are very limited, and the authors may have already presented their paper at a conference or seminar. If sought, Google and the internet can often reveal their identity in a matter of seconds. Lastly, the thoroughness of the revision process and allocation of reviewers is often not the same in special issues and regular ones. Besides, one can question the relevance of the choice of institutions that externalise the evaluation of their researchers' productions by entrusting them to third parties – journals – that resort to anonymous reviewers themselves.

From this perspective, it seems essential to encourage journals to make public their exchanges with reviewers and their concrete processes of editorial and evaluation work. One can in particular ponder the idea of encouraging journals to disclose the names of the reviewers who evaluated and accepted the articles they publish. One could also suggest journals advertise more explicitly the names of their most weighty reviewers in order to underline and valorise their contributions. Such recognition of the invisible work of reviewers (rereading, drafting of detailed commentaries, suggestions for arbitration, iterations) seems all the more important when the number of requests for reviews and the limits of effective anonymity of authors call for the even greater availability and thoroughness of reviewers.

12.2.7   Point 6: Online Journals and Online Access to Multiple Printed Journals

Traditional printed journals are no longer the only publishing outlet today. In management as in other fields, multiple ways of downloading one article at a time have appeared, along with baskets of journals sold to libraries and online journals.[7] In such a context, it is difficult to have a clear panorama of existing journals, nor a fortiori of their respective characteristics and positioning in the general field of printed or digital journals. The situation is particularly sensitive concerning online journals. Without greater clarification, it appears difficult to have a specific opinion on a given journal, or even for readers to choose the outlet best adapted to their publication projects.

It seems essential today to carry out a systematic survey of online journals by identifying their existence and position, and evaluating their value. This is a prerequisite to further considerations on the topic.

12.2.8   Point 7: The Absence of a Portal for French (resp. National) Journals

Already threatened by the growing weight of rankings, French journals are also jeopardised by a second phenomenon: the rising use of portals aggregating journals that are essentially written in English, such as EBSCO and mega-search engines (like Mercure+), which group several baskets and journal publishers (like Sage for instance).

Faced with this trend, the publishers of French management journals seem to react without a plan of action, each one having its own website or package. This translates into researchers not having the same degree of access to works published in French compared to those in English. Being more difficult to access, works in French have an even lower chance of being cited today than at the time when journals were consulted in libraries. Of course, the situation is exactly the same for other national and European languages.

12.2.9   Point 8: A Focus on Journals, to the Detriment of Books

Academic research productions are not restricted to publications in journals with editorial boards; they also include the publication of research books. The instrumentation of evaluation by journal articles tends to weaken the position of such research works when the activities of researchers or teams are examined. Thus an 'edited' research book, with contributions for each chapter hinging around a common theme, can often be likened to the special issue of a journal. However, all books cannot be compared, even among those which claim to be research works. There is therefore room and need for evaluation here too. But major differences in the writing and editing processes of articles and books prevent the development of a ranking tool that combines these two forms of scientific production.

The creation of rankings for publishers or series comes up against the very wide range of situations concerning the quality of works. The guarantee of scientific quality and a reliable production process can conflict in particular with the economic constraints publishers are confronted with. The very low circulation rates of management research books does not always give publishers – through lack of income – the means to ask the directors of series to spend a lot of time on editorial tasks such as follow-up and monitoring, nor to hire reviewers who can carry out evaluation and revision recommendations that are similar to the standards of journal articles.

Similarly to what is already done with journals, a labelling process could be envisaged in order to encourage scientific publishers by honouring those whose books or series are given special attention in terms of editorial work. This label could thus correspond to a series of collectively produced and accepted good practices, such as a real selection and reviewing process before publication, follow-up of the revision process through scientific editorial support down the line, and the obligation to submit the works to scientific bodies selected by the publisher (scientific associations, scientific committees of large conferences, editorial committees of journals that are unrelated to the publisher, and so on).

NOTES

1. The following paper has been edited by P.J. Benghozi, on the basis of contributions made by the members of the SFM. Members who have contributed are: F. Aggeri, J. Bathelemy, M. Berry, J. Brabet, J.-F. Chanlat, T. Durand, E. Fimbel, C. Jameux, M. Kalika, G. Koenig, P. Lorino, J.-P. Nioche, R. Pérez, Y. Pesqueux, F. Tannery and J.C. Thoenig. They cannot be held responsible for the statements made in this paper, but are here thanked for their work.
2. The SFM website can be found at http://www.sfmwebsite.org/. Contact sfmanag@ yahoo.fr.
3. http://sites.google.com/site/section37cnrs/Home/revues37.
4. http://www.fnege.fr/DOC2008/classementRFG.pdf.
5. http://www.aeres-evaluation.fr/Economie-Gestion.
6. For an international perspective on rankings in the field of management, one can refer to the work initiated a few years ago by Anne-Wil Harzing: http://www.harzing.com/.
7. The proliferation and diversity of access to downloading systems, and the growing bills they entail, are in fact becoming a financial concern for institutions.

Index